If you can keep your head when they're changing guard at Buckingham Palace

come live with me and be my love

off the golden daffodils

and the quality of mercy is not strained

Twas brillig

Dancing by the Light of the Moon

ABOUT THE AUTHOR

Gyles Brandreth is a writer, broadcaster, actor, former MP and Government Whip, now Chancellor of the University of Chester and the founder of the Poetry Together project that encourages young people and old people to learn poems by heart and share them over tea and cake. Probably best known these days as a reporter on BBC's *The One Show* and a regular on BBC Radio 4's *Just A Minute*, as a journalist he writes for the *Telegraph* and *Daily Mail* and is a columnist for the *Oldie*. On stage he has appeared in pantomime, in Shakespeare (most recently in *Hamlet* and *Twelfth Night*), in *The Importance of Being Earnest* (as Lady Bracknell) and in *Zipp!*, his own musical revue in London's West End. On TV he has featured in *Have I Got News For You, QI, Room 101, Countdown* and *This Is Your Life*, as well as too many programmes featuring the word 'Celebrity', including *Celebrity Mastermind, Celebrity Antiques Road Trip, Celebrity The Chase, Pointless Celebrities* and his personal favourite, *Celebrity Gogglebox*. The founder of the National Scrabble Championships, his books about words and language include the international bestseller *Have You Eaten Grandma?* His novels include seven Victorian murder mysteries featuring Oscar Wilde as his detective (he is President of the Oscar Wilde Society) and he has published two volumes of diaries, two royal biographies and *The 7 Secrets of Happiness*, based on lessons he learned from the psychiatrist Dr Anthony Clare. The Brandreth forebears include George R. Sims, who wrote the ballad *Christmas Day at the Workhouse*. As a schoolboy, Gyles won a number of 'poetry by heart' competitions and, aged eight, shook hands with T. S. Eliot. He has written a few poems himself and edited poetry anthologies with both Spike Milligan and Roger McGough. He is married to writer and publisher Michèle Brown and has three children, seven grandchildren, and lives in London with his wife, several rooms full of poetry anthologies, and Nala, the neighbour's cat.

www.gylesbrandreth.net
Twitter: @GylesB1

Dancing by the Light of the Moon

GYLES BRANDRETH

MICHAEL JOSEPH
an imprint of
PENGUIN BOOKS

MICHAEL JOSEPH

UK | USA | Canada | Ireland | Australia
India | New Zealand | South Africa

Michael Joseph is part of the Penguin Random House group of companies
whose addresses can be found at global.penguinrandomhouse.com.

First published 2019
001

Copyright © Gyles Brandreth, 2019

The moral right of the author has been asserted

Set in 13.5/16pt Garamond MT Std
Typeset by Jouve (UK), Milton Keynes
Printed and bound in Great Britain by Clays Ltd, Elcograf S.p.A.

A CIP catalogue record for this book is available from the British Library

HARDBACK ISBN: 978-0-241-39792-3

For Michèle
(see page 93)

Contents

Prologue

The Owl and the Pussy-cat
by Edward Lear

I

The Owl and the Pussy-cat went to sea
   In a beautiful pea-green boat,
They took some honey, and plenty of money,
   Wrapped up in a five-pound note.
The Owl looked up to the stars above,
   And sang to a small guitar,
'O lovely Pussy! O Pussy, my love,
   What a beautiful Pussy you are,
      You are,
      You are!
   What a beautiful Pussy you are!'

II

Pussy said to the Owl, 'You elegant fowl!
   How charmingly sweet you sing!
O let us be married! too long we have tarried:
   But what shall we do for a ring?'
They sailed away, for a year and a day,
   To the land where the Bong-tree grows

And there in a wood a Piggy-wig stood
  With a ring at the end of his nose,
     His nose,
     His nose,
  With a ring at the end of his nose.

III

'Dear Pig, are you willing to sell for one shilling
  Your ring?' Said the Piggy, 'I will.'
So they took it away, and were married next day
  By the Turkey who lives on the hill.
They dined on mince, and slices of quince,
  Which they ate with a runcible spoon;
And hand in hand, on the edge of the sand,
  They danced by the light of the moon,
     The moon,
     The moon,
  They danced by the light of the moon.

Chapter One

How I Got into This
And how this book can change your life

Welcome to *Dancing by the Light of the Moon* – a title inspired by my favourite poem, 'The Owl and the Pussy-cat' by Edward Lear, the first poem I remember learning by heart.

This is an anthology of poetry to read, to enjoy, and to learn by heart. It includes more than 250 poems, some of them the best-loved in the English language, others relatively unknown; some funny, some moving, many (I hope) surprising, all (by definition) memorable.

W. H. Auden said poetry is 'memorable speech'. Robert Frost said: 'Poetry is when an emotion has found its thought and the thought has found words.' Frank Sinatra said: 'doo-be-doo-be-doo'.

As a rule, Frank Sinatra didn't write the songs he sang, but 'doo-be-doo-be-doo' was all his own work and turned out to be one of his most memorable (and profitable) phrases. He earned millions of dollars from the song 'Strangers in the Night' and 'doo-be-doo-be-doo' is the only part of the song he actually wrote. For many, it's the bit they remember best. Why?

Whether it's song lyrics or nursery rhymes, Sinatra

('doo-be-doo-be-doo') or Shakespeare ('to-be-or-not-to-be'), why do we remember the words we remember? And what impact do those words have on our lives?

That's what this book is about: the power and importance of poetry. Read on and discover the extraordinary brain-boosting, heart-lifting, life-enhancing way in which learning poetry by heart can change your life.

- Speaking poetry to babies (even unborn ones), infants and young children can improve the speed at which they learn to speak and read – and even write.
- Learning poetry by heart as a child can improve your ability to succeed at school, in exams, in interviews, in life.
- Children who learn poetry by heart do better academically, concentrate more effectively, sleep better, and do better professionally in later life.
- Learning poetry by heart as an adult gives you a happier and more successful life (including a happier and more successful love-life: oh yes! See Chapter Twelve on page 242); improves your ability to communicate (and consequently the quality of your relationships); improves your memory; increases your brain capacity; and – glory be! – keeps dementia at bay.

These are bold claims, but I can back them up with the latest research from the Memory Laboratory at Cambridge University, from neuroscientists at Columbia University, and from recent studies undertaken by teachers and language experts across Asia, America and Europe.

Poetry can make you laugh and cry. Poetry can make you think and feel. Poetry can teach you, and sustain you, and

4

surprise you. Learning poetry by heart can – literally – transform you.

This chapter explains how I got into all this. In Chapter Two we delve into the science and examine the nature of memory. In Chapter Three we get down to the nitty-gritty of how to learn poetry by heart. And then we get on with the poetry proper, starting on the dolly slopes, in Chapter Four, warming up and working out with the short stuff: couplets, haikus, limericks and the like, including the three shortest poems ever penned.

Anyone can learn a two-line poem in a matter of minutes: learn seven of them and you have mastered the equivalent of a sonnet. You are ready then for lift-off, which begins with a selection of sonnets in Chapter Five, and culminates, in Chapter Sixteen, with an A to Z of poets who have created classic poems to learn by heart. From Auden to Zephaniah, at a fortnight a piece, you could learn them all inside a year and become a walking, talking anthology of versified wonder, wit and wisdom.

Let me begin by introducing myself and explaining how I presume to be your guide on this journey. My name is Gyles Brandreth (it's not an easy name to remember*); I am a husband, a father, a grandfather, an author and a broadcaster. I am British, born in a British Forces Hospital in Germany in

---

* It's too much of a mouthful. If I was starting over again, I'd make it something simpler, like 'Gyles Brown' or 'Ben Brandreth'. The Gyles with a *y* was my father's idea. (If I had been a girl I would have been called 'Mercedes'. A Mercedes is what he really wanted.) Gyles with a *y* is a bit fey, but it's different and I quite like that. Please think of me as 'Gyles'. It's only five letters and that's good. According to the poet and playwright, Oscar Wilde, to live in the public memory you need a name of just five letters – like Oscar or Wilde, or Jesus or Plato, or, as he pointed out when he was in New York and visiting the world's most famous elephant at P. T. Barnum's celebrated circus: Jumbo.

1948. My father was a lawyer (who had reams of poetry in his head); my mother was a teacher (who specialized in teaching children with reading difficulties). I have loved poetry for as long as I can remember and I have a weakness for name-dropping.*

That weakness for name-dropping leads me to say this: if ever we meet be sure to shake my hand. Over the years, I have been lucky enough to meet some poets of significance – T. S. Eliot, Seamus Heaney and Ted Hughes among them – so, when you shake my hand, at one remove you are shaking theirs. It may not be much, but it's something – and there's more: I went to school with the children of Robert Graves and Cecil Day-Lewis.

When I was at school (a co-educational boarding school in Hampshire called Bedales) I played Scrabble on Wednesday afternoons with the school's founder (John Badley, 1865–1967) and he had been friends with Oscar Wilde and Rabindranath Tagore – so I have shaken the hand that shook the hand of both the man who wrote 'The Ballad of Reading Gaol' in 1897 and the man who became the first Asian poet to win the Nobel Prize for Literature in 1913.†

---

* And for footnotes.

† At this point, my publisher reminds me that a gushing admirer once approached the great James Joyce in Zurich and asked, 'May I shake the hand that wrote *Ulysses*?' Joyce closed his eyes for a moment before replying, famously: 'No, it's done other things as well.'

> You can't cross the sea merely by standing and staring at the water.
>
> —
>
> Faith is the bird that feels the light when the dawn is still dark.
>
> —
>
> The butterfly counts not months but moments, and has time enough.
>
> Rabindranath Tagore (1861–1941)

In the 1980s, by chance, I became a friend of Christopher Robin, the son of A. A. Milne, so I have also shaken the hand that held the paw of Winnie-the-Pooh and inspired some of the most memorable children's verse in the two books his father wrote for him in the 1920s: *When We Were Very Young* and *Now We Are Six*. I am friend of the poet Pam Ayres (she and my wife were born on the same day; my wife was born in Swansea; my wife's mother went to the same school as Dylan Thomas . . . oh, there's no end to my poetic connections!) and of Roger McGough.

Roger is a neighbour and sometimes lets me see his work before it is published. Not long ago he dropped by with this:

New Poem
So far, so good

As well as being a poet, Roger is the presenter of the BBC's *Poetry Please*, the longest-running poetry programme broadcast anywhere in the world. My first BBC radio series, back in 1971, was a panel game all about poetry, called *A Rhyme in*

*Time.** Since then I have made hundreds of broadcasts about all sorts of subjects – some amusing, some serious – but only one of them has inspired a book: this book.

Last year, with an award-winning BBC producer, Tom Alban, I made a radio documentary called 'Gyles Brandreth's Poetry by Heart'. The programme was commissioned in the run-up to National Poetry Day in the UK to test my instinct that learning poetry by heart is 'a good thing' for one and all. It turned out that it is, of course, but much more fundamentally than even I could have imagined.

> The poems we learn when we're young stay with us for the rest of our lives. They become embedded in our thinking, and when we bring them to mind, or to our lips, they remind us who we are as people, and the things we believe in. They become personal and invaluable, and what's more they are free gifts – there for the taking. We call it learning by heart, and I think such learning can only make our hearts bigger and stronger.
>
> Simon Armitage (born 1962)

My head is full of snatches of poetry – as is yours, I'm sure. Mine is mostly verse I learnt as a child – and if you're of a similar generation (a post-war baby-boomer) it's likely to be similar stuff:

---

* The team captains were the comedian Cyril Fletcher, one of whose celebrated 'Odd Odes' appears on page 344, and the poet and eccentric, Caryl Brahms, who wrote a series of brilliant comic novels with S. J. Simon. (I reckon *No Bed for Bacon* is the one to start with.)

A. A. Milne ('They're changing guard at Buckingham Palace . . .'), Lewis Carroll (''Twas brillig, and the slithy toves did gyre and gimble in the wabe . . .'), John Masefield ('I must go down to the seas again . . .), Rupert Brooke ('If I should die, think only this of me . . .'), bits and pieces I learnt at home or at school, the first few lines of which have stayed with me across nearly seven decades. Rattling around inside my head I've got lyrics from Gilbert and Sullivan operas, from the songs of Flanders and Swann ('Mud, mud, glorious mud . . .'), from the popular music of my childhood ('doo-be-doo-be-doo'), snatches of Shakespeare and Milton, the opening of love poems (by John Keats and Christina Rossetti), bits of Edward Lear and John Betjeman – and I am not alone.

Making the radio programme, I met up with a number of my contemporaries and found that we had very similar stocks of stored memories. For example, Michael Rosen (poet and former Children's Laureate) and I were at university together, and, fifty years on, on the radio, unrehearsed, we found ourselves able to recite, in unison, Shelley's 'Ozymandias' – or at least the beginning of it:

> I met a traveller from an antique land
> Who said: Two vast and trunkless legs of stone
> Stand in the desert . . .

I began my research for the programme with HRH The Duchess of Cornwall, because she had just taken over from the Queen as Patron of the Royal Society of Literature and is actively involved in a number of charities that promote literacy and the importance of language and reading. She knew Ted Hughes (Britain's Poet Laureate from 1984 until his death in 1998) and he read some of his poetry to her children. One of her favourite poems is 'The Christmas Truce' by another Poet Laureate, Carol Ann Duffy. 'It moved me to tears,' the Duchess told me.

Was poetry part of her childhood? I asked. 'Very much so,' she said. 'My mother loved poetry. Her favourite was "Right Royal" by John Masefield.' It's a narrative poem that tells the story of a steeplechase, the winning horse, and the jockey's relationship with his beloved which is placed in jeopardy by the race – all rather apt, I suggested, given the Duchess's love of horses and her own royal story. She agreed. 'At school I had a Scottish teacher who got me into Burns. "My heart's in the Highlands, my heart is not here . . ." And a wonderful teacher who read to us from Chaucer's *Canterbury Tales*.' Her favourites from her schooldays include Christina Rossetti, Walter de la Mare and John Betjeman, but not Lord Byron. 'I never got to grips with "Child Harolde". But I love the poetry of Oscar Wilde. I still read Wilde.' (The Duchess of Cornwall has a curious connection with Oscar Wilde: her great-great-grandfather, Alec Shand, was secretly engaged to Constance Lloyd, who went on to marry Oscar Wilde.)

The poems that have stayed with the Duchess over the years are 'the poems with rhyme and rhythm'. Leaning towards my microphone, brow slightly furrowed, she launched into W. H. Auden's 'Night Mail':

> This is the Night Mail crossing the Border,
> Bringing the cheque and the postal order,
>
> Letters for the rich, letters for the poor,
> The shop at the corner, the girl next door . . .

Could she remember the first poem she learnt as a girl? 'Oh yes, definitely, "Matilda" ' – one of Hilaire Belloc's *Cautionary Tales* 'designed for the Admonition of Children between the ages of eight and fourteen'. '"Matilda told such Dreadful Lies, It made one Gasp and Stretch one's Eyes" . . . I think I was made to learn it because of some fib I'd told. I can still remember most of it.'

I put the Duchess to the test and she managed a good few lines. 'It's not so easy when you're under pressure,' she said. 'I knew it all last night. It's much easier for you, Gyles, because you're an actor.'

Only now and then – and then not much of one, if the critics are to be believed* – but I do know someone who, when it comes to acting, is indisputably the real deal; so, leaving the Duchess, I went on to see Dame Judi Dench.

It was September and I found Dame Judi in her country garden, enjoying the late summer sunshine, sitting with a friend called Pen (yes, a Pen friend!) who was helping her learn the lines for her next screen role.

What was the first poetry the great actress had learnt by heart? Was it A. A. Milne? Or Hilaire Belloc? Or Edward Lear? 'Oh, no. It was Shakespeare. Even when I was very little I knew lots and lots of Shakespeare. I don't know if I understood much of it, but I loved it. My older brother Jeffrey – he always wanted to be an actor, so even when he was a boy he was quoting Shakespeare. I don't remember reading it. I think I just picked it up from Jeff. I learnt lots of Shakespeare when I was a girl – the plays, the sonnets. I can give you lots of sonnets – and I can do all of *Twelfth Night* by heart and all of *Midsummer Night's Dream*, every word, I promise you.' I believe her. Her love of Shakespeare is palpable. 'My sight's going now. If we had to go on stage and read a sonnet, you'd have it written on just one page, but for me the

---

* They aren't. 'Has anybody ever seen a drama critic in the daytime? Of course not. They come out after dark, up to no good.' P. G. Wodehouse.

print would be so big I'd need fourteen pages.' She laughs, but she's not joking. 'Now I learn my lines with my friend, Pen. She reads me the lines and I repeat them. I can't drive any more and I find that difficult, but I manage. But I couldn't live without Shakespeare.'

Dame Judi has reams of poetry in her head and, like the Duchess, agrees that it's the stuff with rhythm and rhyme that's easiest to remember. 'Shakespeare's verse goes with the beat of your heart,' she says – and she's right.

Which brings us to the science – and Professor Goswami.

On that same sunny September afternoon, I left Dame Judi and her friend Pen learning lines in the garden and made my way to Cambridge and the Memory Laboratory at Cambridge University's Department for Neuroscience in Education. There I found my poetry-by-heart guru: Professor Usha Goswami, Fellow of the British Academy and multi-award-winning professor of Cognitive Developmental Neuroscience.

In a nutshell, the research undertaken by Professor Goswami and her team provides measurable proof of what my gut instinct has long told me: as you start out in life, having your parents recite poetry and sing songs to you will help you with your linguistic skills; as you grow older, learning poetry will keep dementia at bay.

You will find the detail in the professor's learned paper: 'A Neural Basis for Phonological Awareness? An Oscillatory Temporal-Sampling Perspective', published by the Association of Psychological Science. To cut to the chase, Professor Goswami has been studying and measuring what goes on inside the brains of babies and young children – measuring the neural oscillations (the brainwaves, as it were) that encode the signals through which we begin to learn and understand speech. The metrical structures and rhythmic patterns of nursery rhymes coincide with the brain's neural oscillations – starting with a trochaic rhythm (as in the beat of 'The cat sat on the mat') and quickly going on to the rhythm of the iambic pentameter (as in the 'da DUM da DUM da DUM da DUM da DUM' of Shakespearean verse) which explains why Dame Judi could indeed quite easily have been speaking Shakespeare from the age of three or four.

The professor and her team can measure the speech-sound awareness of babies, toddlers and young children and, on the basis of the data, accurately predict speech, reading and even spelling development.

Essentially, what the professor's studies of the 'rhythmic synchronization across modalities' establish is that the more you recite poetry to your children – before they are born as well as when they are babies and toddlers – the better they will be able to communicate, both when it comes to spoken and, later, even written language.

And why do we remember best the poems we learnt as children, I asked the professor. 'First in, last out, is the principle of it,' she explained, trying to put it in layman's terms for me. And why is the stuff we've learnt later more difficult to recall? 'It's all still in there,' she said, reassuringly. 'It's just sometimes difficult to retrieve because there is so much in there.'

The brain is a computer into which we are loading more and more stuff as the years go by. Those infamous 'senior moments' occur not because we have lost anything, but because it has been temporarily mislaid. It's a retrieval issue, not a memory one. Concentrate and focus and you should be able to bring it back.

'At whatever age you are,' according to Professor Goswami, 'you still have the capacity to learn new things if you put your mind to it. There's no shortage of brain cells as you grow older.'

Recent research from the Department of Neurobiology at Columbia University has established that new brain cells grow as quickly when you are in your seventies as when you are in your twenties. Remembering things, it seems, does not have to get more difficult as you grow older. According to the scientists at Columbia, gradual mental decline 'is not the inevitable process many of us think it is'. The researchers made their discovery after counting the number of new cells growing in the hippocampus, the part of the brain that processes memories and emotions.

The cerebrum is the largest part of the brain. It controls our personality, vision and hearing. It contains a range of brain structures including the hippocampus and the cerebral cortex. The cortex controls a number of advanced mental functions like language and planning. The hippocampus is where memories are stored and processed. The scientists at Columbia found that around seven hundred brain cells were created each day in the hippocampus, even in the oldest people they studied, and that there was no difference in the hippocampus in young and old brains.

Back at Cambridge University, Professor Goswami is unequivocal: learning poetry by heart is good for the brain. 'So it's true what they say,' I suggested to her. 'The brain is a muscle: if you don't use it, you lose it.' 'Exactly,' she said. 'You've got to keep the brain active. I have colleagues here at Cambridge in their seventies, eighties and nineties – none of them has dementia. The exercise and discipline of learning a poem by heart is certainly going to help keep dementia at bay.'

Did you hear that? There is no excuse. If you want to do it, you can.

When I was a boy, one of my heroines was the great English actress Dame Sybil Thorndike. When I lived with my parents in London, Dame Sybil lived near us and we used to see her sometimes waiting at the bus stop. She was a keen Christian Socialist and a natural enthusiast. 'Oh Lewis,' she said to her husband, Lewis Casson, when they were both in their eighties, 'if only we could be the first actors to play on the moon!' She lived into her nineties and famously made herself learn a new poem every day to keep her brain active.

Learning lines is good for you – and doable whatever your age. Dame Judi Dench, born in December 1934, is learning hers for her next film right now. As I write this, Dame Maggie Smith, also born in December 1934, is appearing in a new one-woman play in which she speaks, without pause, for one hour and three-quarters. Dame Eileen Atkins, their senior by six months, is currently appearing in a new play on Broadway. Glenda Jackson, eighty-three, is appearing in an old one – *King Lear*. They are all word perfect, of course. And my friend, Nicholas Parsons, born in October 1923, is not only as razor-sharp as ever on the BBC radio programme, *Just A Minute*, he is also touring the United Kingdom with his Lear – not a production of Shakespeare's great tragedy, but a one-man show about the poet and artist, Edward Lear, in which Nicholas, aged ninety-six, recites poem after poem after poem – and doesn't hesitate or deviate once.

The evidence is there. Learning poetry by heart will give you a happier, richer, longer, mentally active life. Go for it.

'How pleasant to know Mr Lear!'
by Edward Lear
(1812–88)

'How pleasant to know Mr. Lear!'
    Who has written such volumes of stuff!
Some think him ill-tempered and queer,
    But a few think him pleasant enough.

His mind is concrete and fastidious,
    His nose is remarkably big;
His visage is more or less hideous,
    His beard it resembles a wig.

He has ears, and two eyes, and ten fingers,
    Leastways if you reckon two thumbs;
Long ago he was one of the singers,
    But now he is one of the dumbs.

He sits in a beautiful parlour,
    With hundreds of books on the wall;
He drinks a great deal of Marsala,
    But never gets tipsy at all.

He has many friends, laymen and clerical,
    Old Foss is the name of his cat:
His body is perfectly spherical,
    He weareth a runcible hat.

When he walks in a waterproof white,
    The children run after him so!

Calling out, 'He's come out in his night-
    Gown, that crazy old Englishman, oh!'

He weeps by the side of the ocean,
    He weeps on the top of the hill;
He purchases pancakes and lotion,
    And chocolate shrimps from the mill.

He reads but he cannot speak Spanish,
    He cannot abide ginger-beer:
Ere the days of his pilgrimage vanish,
    How pleasant to know Mr. Lear!

Chapter Two

Thanks for the Memory
It's all in the mind

Everything you think and feel and do, everything you experience, everything you remember — it all starts in the brain, a pinkish-grey blob of matter that sits inside your skull and makes you who you are.

Your brain is the size of a cantaloupe melon and has the texture of mozzarella. The average brain weighs around 1.5 kilograms (that's 3lbs to older readers), with female brains coming in around 10 per cent lighter, so clearly it is a myth that the bigger your brain the brighter you are.

When Albert Einstein, the great Nobel Prize-winning physicist who gave the world the theory of relativity, died in Princeton Hospital in 1955, the pathologist on duty stole the great man's brain and took it to Philadelphia for an autopsy. It turned out that Einstein's brain was a touch smaller than the average. It seems, after all, that size doesn't matter: it's quality that counts.

Within your brain is a network of some 86 billion neurons, the nerve cells that are the building blocks of the brain and transmit information using electrical and chemical signals, enabling you to think, feel, taste, sense and remember. This neural network is made up of around 170,000 kilometres of nerve fibre – enough to get you around the earth four times, with 10,000 kilometres to spare. What Einstein appears to have had is a marginally smaller-than-average brain with very efficient neural networks, enabling his nifty neurons to communicate with one another at greater speed and in fewer steps than most other mortals. Einstein was 'quick-witted' – literally so.

Einstein was born, incidentally, on 14 March, so he shares a birthday with Lewis Carroll's Mad Hatter, as well as with my wife, Michèle, the poet Pam Ayres and the film actor, Sir Michael Caine. Not a lot of people know that.

---

14 March 1879
by Tom Stoppard
(born 1937)

Einstein born
Quite unprepared
For E to equal
MC squared

The human brain is amazing. Even for those of us not in the Einstein class, it is reckoned our brains can process a quadrillion computations per second. According to Professor Paul Reber, the memory man at Northwestern University in Illinois, if your average brain was a digital video recorder, its information-processing capacity would be sufficient to hold three million hours' worth of television programmes. You would need to leave it running continuously for more than three hundred years to use up all its storage.

The brain is the centre of the nervous system and controls all the other organ systems of the body, both the voluntary and the involuntary (like the beating of your heart). Almost all animals possess some type of brain, but they differ in size and complexity. Dolphins and chimps have relatively big brains. Cats and elephants have relatively small ones. Jelly-fish and starfish have no brains at all.

Our closest living relatives in the animal world are chimpanzees. They share 96 per cent of our DNA – but they do not speak. Language is what makes us human beings unique. Some parrots can mimic human speech, but they cannot speak of their own accord. Birds and beasts may inspire poetry (see Chapter Seven on page 124), but they can't create it. As another noted brainbox, the philosopher and mathematician Bertrand Russell, observed: 'No matter how eloquently a dog may bark, he cannot tell you that his parents were poor, but honest.' Only words can do that.

Language is power. You can communicate with a hug or an emoji, but you need words for the complex and the subtle stuff.

Poetry lifts the veil from the hidden beauty of the world, and makes familiar objects be as if they were not familiar.

Percy Bysshe Shelley (1792–1822)

Poetry is simply the most beautiful, impressive, and widely effective mode of saying things.

Matthew Arnold (1822–88)

Poetry is emotion put into measure. The emotion must come by nature, but the measure can be acquired by art.

Thomas Hardy (1840–1928)

Poetry is a search for syllables to shoot at the barriers of the unknown and the unknowable. Poetry is a phantom script telling how rainbows are made and why they go away.

Carl Sandburg (1878–1967)

Too many people in the modern world view poetry as a luxury, not a necessity like petrol. But to me it's the oil of life.

John Betjeman (1906–84)

Poetry is not an expression of the party line. It's that time of night, lying in bed, thinking what you really think, making the private world public, that's what the poet does.

Allen Ginsberg (1926–97)

You can find poetry in your everyday life, your memory, in what people say on the bus, in the news, or just what's in your heart.

Carol Ann Duffy (born 1955)

According to the scientists, 80 per cent of our mental experiences are verbal. You can feel the warmth of the sun on your back without words, but in your head you're probably saying to yourself, 'That's nice.' We articulate our thoughts with language and, intriguingly, language itself affects our perception. Saying the word 'sunshine' can make you feel warmer and sunnier. Words can trigger moods and memories and visual images. Given that I am British and of a certain vintage, saying the word 'sunshine' in my head as I typed it just now made me think at once of two of my favourite comedians, Eric Morecambe and Ernie Wise, kicking up their feet while singing their signature song, 'Bring Me Sunshine', originally written for the American singer and poet, Willie Nelson.

Bring me Sunshine, in your smile,
Bring me Laughter, all the while,
In this world where we live, there should be
more happiness,
So much joy you can give, to each brand new bright
tomorrow,
Make me happy, through the years,
Never bring me, any tears,
Let your arms be as warm as the sun from up above,
Bring me fun, bring me sunshine, bring me love.

Arthur Kent (1920–2009) and Sylvia Dee (1914–67)

Hugging your bump before your baby is born, in the Meghan Markle manner, is probably more comforting to you than it is to your unborn child. What makes the real difference to your future offspring is talking to it out loud throughout your pregnancy, but especially during months seven, eight and nine – the third trimester. Your baby will recognize your voice – and the language you use. (There is evidence that a new-born baby will suck more vigorously when hearing its mother's language than a foreign one.) From twenty-two to twenty-four weeks of gestation, an unborn baby's memory is beginning to form: it is becoming accustomed to experiences. From thirty weeks onwards, it is beginning to recognize and remember things, like its mother's voice and her smell.

Yes, you can be born with memories – of a voice, a smell, a piece of music – but, curiously, few adults can recall specific moments from before their third birthday. (My wife claims to remember sitting in her high chair aged two, being fed something orange from the end of a spoon – but my wife is exceptional in more ways than one.) Of course, we are remembering things from before we are born onwards: we are learning how to move and how to communicate, we are learning what we like and don't like, and remembering what we are learning. If we are learning so much so quickly – and remembering it – when we are so young, why can't we recall stuff that happened to us before we were about three? The research suggests that the number of neurons being created in the brain cells of infants (and the rapidity of their creation) may interfere with the storage of long-term memories.

You may recall little or nothing of what was happening to you as a baby, but you will certainly have vivid memories of what happened to you in your teens. Apparently, most of us have the keenest recollections of our adolescent years – when we first fell in love, when we left school and launched ourselves into the world, when we said goodbye to childhood. The people in the memory business call this period in our lives 'the reminiscence bump'.

The American comedian, Bob Hope, first sang 'Thanks for the memory' in 1938. When I saw him on stage, at the Royal Albert Hall in 1994, he was ninety-one and his memory wasn't what it used to be. His sensory memory was fine, but his semantic memory, short-term memory, working memory and long-term memory were fraying at the edges. As he said in his act, 'George Burns and I are now so old we get together on a Saturday night, have a few drinks and try to get in touch with the living.' Hope and Burns both lived to be a hundred, but Burns's synapses stayed peppier longer.

- A **synapse** is the junction between neurons. A **neuron** is the nerve cell that transmits information using chemical and electrical signals.
- We have five traditional senses: sight, hearing, taste, smell and touch. **Sensory memory** is a very brief memory that allows you to retain impressions of sensory information after the original stimulus has ceased.
- **Short-term memory** does what it says on the tin: keeps the memory in place briefly. Your short-term memory can hold a small amount of information (typically around seven items – a phone number or an address) in mind and ready to use in an active form for a short space of time (typically around fifteen seconds, sometimes up to a minute). For example, to understand a sentence as you hear it, the beginning of the sentence has to be kept in mind while the rest is spoken. The information then disappears unless you make a conscious effort to retain it and so transfer your short-term memory into a long-term memory.
- The term **working memory** is sometimes used interchangeably with 'short-term memory', but it

24

shouldn't be. Your working memory is what enables you to organize and manipulate the information that your short-term memory has received.

- Your **long-term memory** is essentially the storage facility where you keep everything you remember, from your date of birth and the nursery rhymes you learnt as a child to where you live and what you were doing at the moment of 9/11 or when you heard that Diana, Princess of Wales, had died.

- Your long-term memory will include **procedural memories**. These are the unconscious memories that ensure that you put on your underwear before your outerwear, tie your shoelaces without apparently thinking, and get on to your bike and ride it successfully – and on the correct side of the road.

- Your long-term memories will include **semantic memories**. These are the facts you recall: the date of the Battle of Hastings; the fact that Lewis Carroll's real name was Charles Dodgson; the name of the colour orange and the fact that there isn't a word that rhymes with 'orange'.*

- Your long-term memories will also include **autobiographical memories**. These are the personal memories of what has happened to you: being fed mashed-up carrot by your dad in your high chair; walking to school; the smell of the sea when you first

---

* There really isn't. Something does rhyme with 'purple', however, and that's 'hirple', an old English word meaning 'to walk with a limp'. How do I know that? My friend, the lexicographer, Susie Dent, told me. We do a podcast together and call it *Something Rhymes with Purple*. It was from Susie that I also learnt that the 'black box' flight recorder on aircraft is actually orange. Life is full of surprises.

went shrimping at Broadstairs; that first kiss; that last dance.

The Old Lover
by Jane McCulloch
(born 1941)

Was I?
Did I?
Seriously?
Was it so?
Were we?
Like that?
Really?
No!

Some memories will be more vivid than others – because they were unusual, or traumatic, or especially engaging. Some will be more blurred. Some will be inaccurate, because you have misremembered or modified the original memory with each recollection or retelling of it and now what you recall is your later version of what actually occurred.

All of these types of memory are jostling and jangling in the rattle-bag of your mind – and all these memory functions play their part when it comes to learning poetry by heart.

I Remember, I Remember
by *Thomas Hood*
(1799–1845)

I remember, I remember,
The house where I was born,
The little window where the sun
Came peeping in at morn;
He never came a wink too soon,
Nor brought too long a day,
But now, I often wish the night
Had borne my breath away!

I remember, I remember,
The roses, red and white,
The vi'lets, and the lily-cups,
Those flowers made of light!
The lilacs where the robin built,
And where my brother set
The laburnum on his birthday, –
The tree is living yet!

I remember, I remember,
Where I was used to swing,
And thought the air must rush as fresh
To swallows on the wing;
My spirit flew in feathers then,
That is so heavy now,
And summer pools could hardly cool
The fever on my brow!

I remember, I remember,
The fir trees dark and high;
I used to think their slender tops
Were close against the sky:
It was a childish ignorance,
But now 'tis little joy
To know I'm farther off from heav'n
Than when I was a boy.

Before you are born you can recognize your mother's voice and the language that she speaks. And tucked up in the womb you can recognize the sound of music and the rhythm of poetry, too.

Once you are out in the world, the learning never stops. You learn stuff naturally – simply by absorbing it as you go along – and deliberately, by focusing and application. What happens inside your brain when you are learning stuff is that, as the brain processes the information it receives, the synapses that connect the neurons grow and strengthen. The reason to go on learning new things is that the hippocampus grows new brain cells as it learns.

Children appear to be able to learn things faster than older people, but that's largely an illusion. There is less in the heads of the young to start with, so there is more to take in. And children, from birth onwards, are being actively taught stuff: from potty-training to cramming for A-levels, kids are in the learning business virtually full-time. If an older person gave the same time and attention to learning as a child at school or college does, they could learn as much as quickly – if not more so, because life may have taught them a few useful tricks to help their learning along the way.

With some 86 billion neurons and some 86 trillion synapses at your personal disposal, you can rest assured that your brain is not going to run out of storage capacity.

I was a friend of the actor, Alec McCowen, who, in the late 1970s when he was in his fifties, decided to learn the whole of St Mark's Gospel by heart. He did it over sixteen months, learning just three verses early each morning, while he was playing the lead in Peter Shaffer's *Equus* on Broadway and touring Britain in Shakespeare's *Antony and Cleopatra*. Once he had learnt the Gospel, he performed it, as a two-hour show, taking it around the world to huge acclaim, and went on doing so until he was in his seventies. He always took a copy of the Bible on to the stage with him, 'just in case', as he said. He never had recourse to it. From start to finish, he was word perfect.

More recently, a team at Wesleyan University in Connecticut studied the case of 'JB' who, at the age of fifty-eight, began to memorize John Milton's epic poem, *Paradise Lost*. Nine years and thousands of study hours later, he completed the process in 2001 and, over a three-day period, could recall from memory all twelve books of the 10,565-line poem. In 2008, the Wesleyan University team reported: 'Now 74, JB continues to recite this work. We tested his memory accuracy by cueing his recall with two lines from the beginning or middle of each book and asking JB to recall the next 10 lines. JB is an exceptional memorizer of Milton, both in our laboratory tests in which he did not know the specific tests or procedures in advance, and in our analysis of a videotaped, prepared performance. Consistent with *deliberate practice theory*, JB achieved this remarkable ability by deeply analysing the poem's structure and meaning over lengthy repetitions. Our findings suggest that exceptional memorizers such as JB are made, not born, and that cognitive expertise can be demonstrated even in later adulthood.'

What that's telling you is that, regardless of age or heritage, you, too, can learn reams of poetry – if you apply yourself. But don't be put off: 'deliberate practice theory' is not as alarming as it sounds. It just means concentrating on the business in hand. And 'analysing a poem's structure and meaning' is part of the fun of appreciating poetry: looking at how it's put together and getting to grips with what it's all about.

The opening of Book 1 of *Paradise Lost*
by John Milton
*(1608–74)**

Of man's first disobedience, and the fruit
Of that forbidden tree, whose mortal taste
Brought death into the world, and all our woe,
With loss of Eden, till one greater man
Restore us, and regain the blissful seat,
Sing heavenly Muse, that on the secret top
Of Oreb, or of Sinai, didst inspire
That shepherd, who first taught the chosen seed,
In the beginning how the heavens and Earth
Rose out of chaos; or if Sion hill

---

* I asked Google to give me Milton's dates just now, and up popped the dates for the forthcoming tour of my friend, Milton Jones – the comedian whose gems include my favourite line about his wife: 'It's difficult to say what she does . . . She sells seashells on the seashore.'

> Delight thee more, and Siloa's brook that flowed
> Fast by the Oracle of God, I thence
> Invoke thy aid to my advent'rous song,
> That with no middle flight intends to soar
> Above the Aonian mount, while it pursues
> Things unattempted yet in prose or rhyme.
> And chiefly thou O Spirit, that dost prefer
> Before all Temples the upright heart and pure,
> Instruct me, for Thou knowst; thou from the first
> Wast present, and with mighty wings outspread
> Dove-like satst brooding on the vast abyss
> And mad'st it pregnant: what in me is dark
> Illumine, what is low raise and support;
> That to the highth of this great argument
> I may assert eternal providence,
> And justify the ways of God to men.

There is no limit to how much you can learn. The one challenge as you get older is retrieving what you have learnt: as time goes by, there is so much in your brain that it can take longer than you might like to bring what you're after to the forefront of your mind. It's all in there: getting it out pronto can be the problem. The key is to keep at it.

When you learn something new, new connections are being made in the brain. Keep using those new connections and *myelination* takes place. What does that mean? A myelin sheath is a cover (a sheath) made out of fats and proteins that wraps around the end of a nerve cell, insulating your neurons so they can send electric signals faster and more efficiently.

Remember: whether you are seventeen or seventy, your

hippocampus grows new cells as it learns new things – and you can keep those new things in play by repetition and practice. The more you learn, the more you'll know. The more you use the circuits of your mind – the networks of synapses connecting the neurons made more efficient by the myelin sheaths – the sparkier and more efficient your mind will be.

Learning all 10,565 lines of *Paradise Lost* takes years of application, focus and practice. Learning Milton's sonnet 'When I consider how my light is spent' (page 88) calls for application, focus, and practice, too, but rather less of it. The poem only runs to fourteen lines. At two lines a day, you could learn it in a week. It would be brilliant exercise for your mind and it would give you a buzz. Literally.

Learning something new is stimulating in every sense. Inside the neural pathways of your mind are chemical receptors which sit on the surface of some of your brain cells and release pleasure-giving endorphins as you pick up new information and process it.

Learning something new and interesting for the first time gives you a high. With repetition, inevitably, the high doesn't quite hit the same height – which is why, when you reread a favourite book (or rewatch a much-loved movie) it is never quite as satisfying as it was first time around – unless, of course, you didn't 'get it' first time around. Small children like to hear the same story time and again, because, as a rule, it takes them longer to 'get it' than it takes adults, and because, as a child, there is something reassuring in the repetition of the familiar. It is part of what the psychologist, John Bowlby, the father of attachment theory, used to call 'the security of known relationships'.

'You are old, Father William'
by *Lewis Carroll*
(1832–98)

'You are old, Father William,' the young man said,
    'And your hair has become very white;
And yet you incessantly stand on your head –
    Do you think, at your age, it is right?'

'In my youth,' Father William replied to his son,
    'I feared it might injure the brain;
But, now that I'm perfectly sure I have none,
    Why, I do it again and again.'

'You are old,' said the youth, 'as I mentioned before,
    And have grown most uncommonly fat;
Yet you turned a back-somersault in at the door –
    Pray, what is the reason of that?'

'In my youth,' said the sage, as he shook his grey locks,
    'I kept all my limbs very supple
By the use of this ointment – one shilling the box –
    Allow me to sell you a couple.'

'You are old,' said the youth, 'and your jaws are too weak
    For anything tougher than suet;
Yet you finished the goose, with the bones and the beak –
    Pray, how did you manage to do it?'

'In my youth,' said his father, 'I took to the law,
    And argued each case with my wife;

And the muscular strength, which it gave to my jaw,
  Has lasted the rest of my life.'

'You are old,' said the youth; 'one would hardly suppose
  That your eye was as steady as ever;
Yet you balanced an eel on the end of your nose –
  What made you so awfully clever?'

'I have answered three questions, and that is enough,'
  Said his father; 'don't give yourself airs!
Do you think I can listen all day to such stuff?
  Be off, or I'll kick you down stairs!'

Lewis Carroll was not yet thirty-three when he wrote 'You are old, Father William', but he seems to have had an instinctive understanding of what it takes to stay sharp and in shape when you are old. Headstands, backward somersaults, maintaining your balance, and arguing your case with your spouse can all be of benefit to you as you grow older. Growing uncommonly fat, rather less so.

As you grow older, the bad news is that:

- the body does deteriorate (look in the mirror: it cannot be denied);
- the myelin sheaths around your neurons begin to erode, slowing down the signalling along your neural pathways;
- arteries narrow, diminishing blood supply to the brain;
- parts of the brain associated with memory and executive function (the skills that help you get things done) can shrink.

The good news is: all of that only slows you down a bit –
it doesn't affect your fundamental capacity. It may take you a
tad longer, but when it comes to mind-work an old guy can
do everything that a young guy can do.

Dementia is not inevitable. Dementia appears to be on the
increase, but it isn't. There are more people in the world than
ever and in the prosperous world they are living longer than
ever, so, yes, the number of people with dementia has grown,
but the proportion of people with dementia has dropped.
Why? Because, in the past seventy-five years since the end of
the Second World War, people on the whole have had a better
education and more years of it – and all the research suggests
that people with more education are more resilient to demen-
tia. Keeping your mind active throughout your life – learning
new skills; learning poetry by heart – will help equip it with
what it needs to keep dementia at bay.

However old you are, however young you are, I am telling
you: poetry should be part of your life.

> One, two,
> Buckle my shoe;
> Three, four,
> Knock at the door;
> Five, six,
> Pick up sticks;
> Seven, eight,
> Lay them straight;
> Nine, ten,
> A big fat hen.
> Eleven, twelve,
> Who will delve?

Thirteen, fourteen,
Maids a-courting;
Fifteen, sixteen,
Maids a-kissing;
Seventeen, eighteen,
Maids a-waiting;
Nineteen, twenty,
My stomach's empty.

When I visited the Centre for Neuroscience in Education at Cambridge University and looked in at their 'BabyLab' I found the researchers surrounded by babies. The babies, aged between two and eleven months, were wearing what looked like hairnets. The 'hairnets' turned out to be headcaps linked to electroencephalogy (EEG) equipment that was measuring the babies' brainwaves.

The BabyLab scientists know what they are about.* As they explain: 'Language lies at the heart of our experience as humans and disorders of language acquisition carry severe developmental costs.' Their research is bearing fruit: 'Recent results in auditory neuroscience show that speech processing depends on brainwave rhythms aligning to rhythms in speech, so the infant brain needs to learn to "copy" the rhythms produced when we talk. Consequently, successful language acquisition by infants must depend in part on successful rhythmic processing.'

At the BabyLab they are, as they put it, 'drilling down' into the relationship between brain rhythms, speech rhythms and

---

* If you and your baby want to help them with their research, you can find out more here: www.cnebabylab.psychol.cam.ac.uk.

language acquisition. And what they – and others at other universities in the UK and the US – are discovering can be summed up in four words:

Hear speech, learn language

The BabyLab is discovering how babies process sounds and build their vocabularies – and rhythm, it seems, is at the heart of it.

The rhythm of life
by Michael Rosen
(born 1946)

Hand on the bridge
feel the rhythm of the train.

Hand on the window
feel the rhythm of the rain.

Hand on your throat
feel the rhythm of your talk.

Hand on your leg
feel the rhythm of your walk.

Hand in the sea
feel the rhythm of the tide.

Hand on your heart
feel the rhythm inside.

Hand on the rhythm
feel the rhythm of the rhyme.

Hand on your life
feel the rhythm of time.
hand on your life
feel the rhythm of time
hand on your life
feel the rhythm of time.

'Babies got rhythm!' they chant at the BabyLab. 'Babies *need* rhythm,' they say, more seriously. Speak nursery rhymes and rhythmical poetry to your baby from three months before it is born and forever after, and you will be helping your baby not only to learn language but also to learn it sooner and better, and to be able to enjoy it more and use it more effectively.

You will be putting your baby – and yourself – in touch with the sound of beauty. Nearly two hundred years ago, the great Edgar Allan Poe defined poetry as 'The Rhythmical Creation of Beauty'. But never mind the beauty, just focus on the bottom line:

- Learning poetry by heart and speaking it to your child can give your child a better start in life.
- Learning poetry by heart can exercise your mind, boost your brainpower, and help keep dementia at bay.

Do you need more to convince you to pick a poem to learn right now – this moment, immediately?

You do? I'm surprised. But I'm ready.

A dozen other things a poem can do for you

1. A poem is a good companion. You'll never be alone if you've got a poem in your head. If you've got nothing to say to yourself, a poem will say something to you.
2. A poem can be a comforting link with the past. Many of the poems we remember best are the poems we learnt first. They have remained good companions all our lives.
3. A poem can be a challenge. What's it all about? It's good to stretch your mind.
4. A poem can stretch your vocabulary, too. When you are reading Milton, given his way with words and range of references, the googling never stops.
5. A poem can help you get to sleep. Reciting a poem about sheep is a more satisfying way to nod off than counting them. (I recommend Christina Rossetti's 'The Lambs of Grasmere', page 129.)
6. A poem can be an ice-breaker. 'Do you have a favourite poem? You don't? You must. I do. No, what's yours? You go first. "Ozymandias"? Really? You must be joking. Why?'
7. A poem can help you secure the partner of your dreams. (Oh yes it can: see Chapter Twelve on page 242.)
8. A poem can do stuff that prose can't. A poem can be elusive, elliptical, illogical, ambiguous, nonsensical, fantastical, phantasmagorical; it can create music and mood and magic and mystery as much as meaning. The American poet Wallace Stevens (1879–1955) said:

The poem must resist the intelligence
Almost successfully.

9. A poem can offer consolation – and catharsis.
10. A poem can make you laugh.
11. A poem can make you feel. According to T. S. Eliot (1888–1965), 'Genuine poetry can communicate before it is understood.'
12. A poem can make you think.

Whenever the question 'What does poetry do?' or 'What is it for?' is raised, I have no hesitation in replying that poetry is central to our culture, and that it is capable of being the most powerful and transformative of the arts.

There are poems that have, literally, changed my life, because they have changed the way I looked at and listened to the world; there are poems that, on repeated reading, have gradually revealed to me areas of my own experience that, for reasons both personal and societal, I had lost sight of; and there are poems that I have read over and over again, knowing they contained some secret knowledge that I had yet to discover, but refused to give up on. So, at the most basic level, poetry is important because it makes us think, it opens us up to wonder and the sometimes astonishing possibilities of language. It is, in its subtle yet powerful way, a discipline for re-engaging with a world we take too much for granted.

John Burnside (born 1955)

What is poetry? According to Plutarch (c. 46–120), 'Painting is silent poetry, and poetry is painting that speaks.' According to the great Romantic, William Wordsworth (1770–1850): 'Poetry is the spontaneous overflow of powerful feelings: it takes its origin from emotion recollected in tranquillity.' According to the great American poet, Carl Sandburg (1878–1967): 'Poetry is an echo, asking a shadow to dance.'

It's all that and more. And it comes in all shapes and sizes. It does not have to have either rhythm or rhyme, of course, but most of the poems that feature in my book have either or both, because poems with rhythm and rhyme are, as a rule, easier to learn by heart than those without.

Take 'Tarantella' by Hilaire Belloc. There can be few poems richer in rhythm and rhyme and consequently it's a favourite with old hands at the poetry-by-heart game. The tarantella is an up-tempo Italian folk dance for two people brought on by the intoxication induced by the sting of the tarantula, a sensation, apparently, similar to that induced by falling in love.

Tarantella
by Hilaire Belloc
(1870–1953)

Do you remember an Inn,
Miranda?
Do you remember an Inn?
And the tedding and the spreading
Of the straw for a bedding,
And the fleas that tease in the High Pyrenees,
And the wine that tasted of tar?
And the cheers and the jeers of the young muleteers
(Under the vine of the dark verandah)?
Do you remember an Inn, Miranda,

Do you remember an Inn?
And the cheers and the jeers of the young muleteers
Who hadn't got a penny,
And who weren't paying any,
And the hammer at the doors and the Din?
And the Hip! Hop! Hap!
Of the clap
Of the hands to the twirl and the swirl
Of the girl gone chancing,
Glancing,
Dancing,
Backing and advancing,
Snapping of a clapper to the spin
Out and in –
And the Ting, Tong, Tang of the Guitar.
Do you remember an Inn,
Miranda?
Do you remember an Inn?

    Never more;
    Miranda,
    Never more.
    Only the high peaks hoar:
    And Aragon a torrent at the door.
    No sound
    In the walls of the Halls where falls
    The tread
    Of the feet of the dead to the ground
    No sound:
    But the boom
    Of the far Waterfall like Doom.

You don't need to fully understand the poem to feel its power. Most people, I reckon, misunderstand the poem because they assume Miranda is a girl. It ain't necessarily so. In fact, no one knows for sure who is the Miranda in the poem. In 1929, Belloc gave an inscribed copy of his poem to Miranda Mackintosh, the daughter of a friend, but it was not her. She was only two in 1929 and the poem refers to the time Belloc visited an inn in the Pyrenean hamlet of Canfranc on the River Aragon twenty years before, in 1909. Many years later, Miranda Mackintosh suggested that the Miranda in the poem was probably not a girl at all, but the surname of one of Belloc's Spanish men friends – someone he went hunting with. Now you know that, read the poem again and you may find it tells you a slightly different story.

Whatever it is about, 'Tarantella' is undoubtedly a remarkable piece of poetry, hypnotic and evocative, and it's because of the relentless rhythm and the rush of rhymes that it has cast a special spell over so many for so long. It's a fun one to learn by heart.

Now take 'The Catch' by Simon Armitage, Britain's latest Poet Laureate. It is a short poem about a moment in a cricket match. There is no rhyme this time, and though there is a distinct shape to the poem there isn't an obvious rhythm in the dictionary sense of 'a strong, regular repeated pattern of movement or sound'.

Read it as it is written, noticing the punctuation when you get to it (the commas, the semi-colon, the full stop), noticing the punctuation when it isn't there, noticing the breaks that come after every three lines. Read the poem as it presented to you on the page, with the hint of pause at the end of each line, and a longer pause where the breaks fall. 'The Catch' is wonderfully evocative. It is a poem where the words and the very presentation of those words create the scene.

The Catch

by Simon Armitage
(born 1963)

Forget
the long, smouldering
afternoon. It is

this moment
when the ball scoots
off the edge

of the bat; upwards,
backwards, falling
seemingly

beyond him
yet he reaches
and picks it

out
of its loop
like

an apple
from a branch,
the first of the season.

Chapter Three

How Do You Learn a Poem by Heart?
Getting down to the nitty-gritty

First catch your hare

Famously, the recipe for hare soup in Mrs Glasse's *The Art of Cookery Made Plain and Easy* (1747) begins with the line, 'First catch your hare.'

Except it doesn't. The line doesn't appear in Mrs Glasse's celebrated book – or in Mrs Beeton's *Book of Household Management* (1861). Nobody seems to know the origins of the line (or its variants: 'First catch your carp', 'First catch your fish', 'First catch your dolphin'), but you get the point. Before you learn a poem, you need to choose a poem to learn.

There are hundreds of poems to choose from right here, so you could just close the book, open it again at random, and learn whatever poem your eye first hits upon: chance encounters can prove rewarding. But if you have not learnt a poem before – or not learnt one since your schooldays – my advice would be: start with something relatively short and relatively simple.

Begin by learning a poem that will give you a personal buzz – because it's funny and you like a chuckle; because it's profound and you are in a thoughtful frame of mind; because it does wonderful things with words and you are taken with its beauty or its ingenuity. Pick a poem whose company you think you might enjoy.

A poem you read to yourself and just the once is like a stranger briefly met and soon forgotten. A short poem you learn by heart is the stranger you begin to get to know because, having shared a cup of tea, you are now going on a train journey or a walk together. A long poem you learn by heart is a companion who is coming with you on holiday: you could be together for weeks and you will certainly be sharing the same bedroom – and standing in the shower together, too. (You will find the shower is an ace place for learning poetry by heart. Seriously.)

There are three elements to learning a poem by heart:

1. The understanding bit
2. The learning bit
3. The performing bit

It is possible to understand a poem and learn a poem by heart inside your head without uttering a word out loud. It is possible, but it isn't easy. Research shows that speaking the words out loud makes them easier to remember. When you say something out loud you 'commit' to it in a way that you don't when the same words are simply running through your head. And, once you have learnt the words to your poem, while you can repeat them to yourself silently in your head, there is a special satisfaction to be had from speaking them out loud.

Okay, let's get started.

The understanding bit

- Now you've chosen your poem, **read it**.
- **Reread it.**
- **Read it once more – out loud.**
- **Read it again out loud – but more slowly.** (My late friend, the actor Simon Cadell, was a wine buff and he used to say you should taste a poem like you taste wine: see it – swirl it – sniff it – sip it – savour it – fill your mouth with it and let it run all around your palate before you swallow.)
- **Understand your poem – understand the detail.** If there are specific words or references you're not sure of, look them up in the dictionary or online.
- **Understand your poem – decide what you think it's about.** At least for now.
- **Enjoy the journey.** Most worthwhile poems begin somewhere and end somewhere else. Look for the journey your poem takes. (In Hilaire Belloc's 'Tarantella', the mood changes dramatically on the words 'Never more'; in Simon Armitage's 'The Catch', you can follow the cricket ball's trajectory from line five onwards until the magical moment of the catch itself.)
- **Get in the mood.** What is the poem's mood? Sunny? Sober? Sweet? Sour? Mysterious? Menacing? Mournful? Elegiac? Gentle? Exhilarating? Playful? Romantic? As the man said, 'If you cannot be the poet, be the poem.'
- **Look at the words on the page.** Look at the way they sit there; look at the way they are punctuated; look at the way they are presented. And speak them as you find them.
- **Trust the poet.**

Of those ten steps, the last – *Trust the poet* – is probably the most important. Go with the flow. Accept the poem as it is, for what it is. Learn the words and say the words, simply, directly, as you find them written on the page.

At the funeral of Diana, Princess of Wales, in 1997, the then Prime Minister, Tony Blair, read from St Paul's First Letter to the Corinthians, one of the most poetic and beautiful passages from the Bible. He read it with clarity and conviction, but arguably with too much feeling. He put so much of himself and his own emphases into his speaking of the words that some people felt they ended up hearing more Blair than Bible.

Though I speak with the tongues of men and of angels, and have not love, I am become as sounding brass, or a tinkling cymbal.

And though I have the gift of prophecy, and understand all mysteries, and all knowledge; and though I have all faith, so that I could remove mountains, and have not love, I am nothing.

And though I bestow all my goods to feed the poor, and though I give my body to be burned, and have not love, it profiteth me nothing.

Love suffereth long, and is kind; love envieth not; love vaunteth not itself, is not puffed up,

Doth not behave itself unseemly, seeketh not her own, is not easily provoked, thinketh no evil;

Rejoiceth not in iniquity, but rejoiceth in the truth;

Beareth all things, believeth all things, hopeth all things, endureth all things.

Love never faileth: but whether there be prophecies, they shall fail; whether there be tongues, they shall cease; whether there be knowledge, it shall vanish away.

For we know in part, and we prophesy in part.

But when that which is perfect is come, then that which is in part shall be done away.

When I was a child, I spake as a child, I understood as a child, I thought as a child: but when I became a man, I put away childish things.

For now we see through a glass, darkly; but then face to face: now I know in part; but then shall I know even as also I am known.

And now abideth faith, hope, love, these three; but the greatest of these is love.

1 Corinthians 13*

In 1987, in the run-up to his eightieth birthday, the great actor Laurence Olivier recorded a television interview with the director, Patrick Garland. Towards the end of the recording, Garland handed Olivier a poem by Philip Larkin and asked him to read it on camera. Olivier did so. The reading was impeccable: affecting, arresting, moving. When he had finished, Olivier returned the poem to Garland, paused, and, after a moment, assuming he was now off camera, asked, 'What the fuck was that all about?'

---

* The thirteenth chapter of 1 Corinthians is all above love. In the original Greek, the word ἀγάπη (*agape*) is used throughout. This was translated into English as 'charity' in the 1604–11 King James Version, but the word 'love' is preferred by most other translations and the version here is the one that was read by Tony Blair and the one I would recommend to learn by heart.

Olivier had simply read what he had found on the page and what he had found on the page worked.

When he was a young actor, the playwright Alan Ayckbourn appeared in a production of Harold Pinter's play, *The Birthday Party*. Pinter came to see the play during rehearsals and Ayckbourn asked the author a series of questions about his character in the piece: 'Where does he come from? Where is he going to? What can you tell me about him that will give me more understanding?' Pinter replied: 'Mind your own fucking business. Concentrate on what's there.'

The learning bit

A touch of D-CAF, that's all you need. D-CAF is a mnemonic that will remind you of what is required to learn anything by heart:

Determination
Concentration
Application
Focus

If you want to learn a poem, keep at it and you will.

You recall 'JB', who at the age of 58 set out to memorize John Milton's epic poem, *Paradise Lost*? He learnt 10,565 lines using what the researchers at Wesleyan University in Connecticut call 'deliberate practice theory'. You can learn ten lines, or a hundred, or a thousand, in exactly the same way. 'Deliberate practice theory' simply means learning what you are learning intelligently (understanding it by analysing its structure and meaning), deliberately, carefully, methodically, line by line, with practice, practice, practice.

Anyone can learn a couple of lines of poetry a day, which

means anyone can learn a sonnet in a week, which means you could learn one of the world's most popular poems – William Wordsworth's twenty-four-liner about daffodils – in under a fortnight.

I wandered lonely as a Cloud
by *William Wordsworth*
(1770–1850)

I wandered lonely as a Cloud
That floats on high o'er Vales and Hills,
When all at once I saw a crowd,
A host of golden Daffodils;
Beside the Lake, beneath the trees,
Fluttering and dancing in the breeze.

Continuous as the stars that shine
And twinkle on the milky way,
They stretched in never-ending line
Along the margin of a bay:
Ten thousand saw I at a glance,
Tossing their heads in sprightly dance.

The waves beside them danced; but they
Out-did the sparkling waves in glee: –
A poet could not but be gay
In such a jocund company:
I gazed – and gazed – but little thought
What wealth the show to me had brought:

> For oft, when on my couch I lie
> In vacant or in pensive mood,
> They flash upon that inward eye
> Which is the bliss of solitude,
> And then my heart with pleasure fills,
> And dances with the Daffodils.

Some people find learning lines easier than others. The actor Sir Derek Jacobi is famous for his retentive memory: over the years he has managed to learn a great deal and quite quickly. Sometimes he is described in newspaper articles as having a 'photographic memory'. Not so. Indeed, there is no scientific proof that such a phenomenon as a 'photographic memory' exists. Some people can certainly recall individual words or phrases by picturing where they saw them on the page, but no one can look at a page of words, click something inside their mind and subsequently recall it in its entirety at will. The brain doesn't work that way. Sir Derek is just lucky that he absorbs the words he is trying to learn more quickly than many. He has had a lot of practice, of course. (He has appeared in more performances of *Hamlet* than anyone alive.) He is intelligent, too: he tries to analyse the structure and meaning of what he is learning. And he is conscientious: he keeps at it until it's in there.

The actor Simon Callow is intelligent and conscientious, too, but he claims to find learning lines more of a struggle. 'It's a matter of battling through,' he says. And in case when it comes to line-learning you think you may be more Callow than Jacobi, here is a battle plan for you: eleven specific strategies to help you master the poems you want to learn.

1. Repetition, repetition, repetition

Learn one line at a time and learn two lines in a day. Repeat tomorrow what you learnt today. Do as much of it as possible out loud.

2. Analyse and understand each line as you learn it

Look up words and references you don't know. Check pronunciations if you are uncertain about them. The clearer you are about what you are learning the easier it will be to learn it.

3. Find a friend

The actor Sir Simon Russell Beale learns his lines with the help of his friend Sir Susie. They sit facing one another. She checks the line as he learns it. She corrects him when he goes wrong. She prompts him when he hesitates. The actress Dame Judi Dench learns her lines the same way, with the help of her friend, Pen. Learning a poem with a friend is a good idea. Your friend can either simply listen to you and prompt you, or you can both learn the same poem and test each other as you progress.

4. Write it down

Copying out your poem is a good idea. The actor Sir Lenny Henry recommends writing out your lines at least ten times – not typing them out, *writing* them out. The act of putting the words on paper with pen or pencil helps embed them in the brain. The late, great Sir Ralph Richardson when appearing in a play used to write out all his speeches on separate scraps of paper and stick them up all over his dressing room.

5. Walk as you talk

Walk around your room – or your garden, if you have one – or a field – or a car park – or anywhere where there is space to move and you won't feel self-consciously conspicuous – and speak your lines out loud as you move, turning sharply in a different direction at the end of every line.

I wandered lonely as a Cloud	*Turn right*
That floats on high o'er Vales and Hills,	*Turn left*
When all at once I saw a crowd,	*Turn right*
A host of golden Daffodils;	*Turn left*
Beside the Lake, beneath the trees,	*Turn right*
Fluttering and dancing in the breeze.	*Turn left*

6. Visualize what you are saying

Picture what you are saying in your mind's eye and look in the appropriate direction as you speak.

I wandered lonely as a Cloud	*Look up into the sky*
That floats on high o'er Vales and Hills,	*Look ahead towards the hills*
When all at once I saw a crowd,	*Look somewhere closer to you*
A host of golden Daffodils;	*Look down*
Beside the Lake, beneath the trees,	*Picture the lake*
Fluttering and dancing in the breeze.	*Feel the breeze*

7. Rhyme and reason

If there are rhymes in your poem, use them. Note how they work:

I wandered lonely as a Cloud	*'a' rhyme*
That floats on high o'er Vales and Hills,	*'b' rhyme*
When all at once I saw a crowd,	*'a' rhyme*
A host of golden Daffodils;	*'b' rhyme*
Beside the Lake, beneath the trees,	*'c' rhyme*
Fluttering and dancing in the breeze.	*'c' rhyme*

'Cloud' will give you 'crowd'; 'Hills' will prompt 'Daffo-dils'; 'trees' will make it a 'breeze'.

8. Work on your trouble-spots

If there are words that keep tripping you up, or phrases where you always stall, stop and devise a way through the trouble-spot. For example, when I first tried to learn William Wordsworth's famous poem I always got stuck at 'o'er Vales and Hills'. I hesitated. Hesitation made me think of um-ing and er-ing, and the 'er' in 'er-ring' reminded me that the word I was looking for was 'o'er'. It sounds convoluted, but it worked. Similarly, in the fifth line I could never remember if it was the lake or the trees that came first. I know now it's the lake that comes first, because, alphabetically, 'l', the first letter of 'lake', comes before 't', the first letter of 'trees'. If you have a problem with a line or a word, find your own personal way to overcome it. Is it 'dancing and fluttering in the breeze' or the other way around? As you say the line, look first at your fingers and picture them fluttering, then look down at your feet and picture them dancing.

9. Mnemonics

In Greek mythology, Mnemosyne was the goddess of mem-ory, the daughter of Uranus (Heaven) and Gaea (Earth), and, if I remember right, the mother (by Zeus) of the nine Muses. A mnemonic is a device to help you remember things.

'Memory masters' – magicians and the like who perform feats of memory, recalling the names of scores of people hav-ing been introduced to them just once, for example – use the 'Memory Palace' as an elaborate mnemonic device. They cre-ate a virtual 'palace' in their mind's eye with a series of rooms and specific pieces of furniture within each room. They then attach the items they want to remember to the items in the rooms as they travel through the palace. It is less complicated than it sounds and if you want to explore its possibilities there are podcasts and websites galore out there to help you. I have a simplified version of the idea that I use to help me learn sonnets (see the beginning of Chapter Five on page 81), but, for learning a poem by heart – as opposed to a series of random names or words or numbers – I don't believe the Memory Palace is very useful.

When you are learning a poem you can devise your own mnemonics to help you overcome individual challenges. For example, if you have difficulty remembering that it's 'A host of golden Daffodils' at the beginning of the fourth line, make the smell of lightly burnt toast your mnemonic. You will get to the line, you will smell the toast, it's golden brown, and 'toast' rhymes with 'host', and immediately you're there, where you need to be, with 'A host of golden Daffodils'. Associating a word with a smell is a good form of mnemonic. Associating a word with a physical movement or with a specific standing position or with a physical touch works well, too. For example, if 'trees' is your stumbling block, touch wood when you get to it – or spread out the five fingers on your right hand. There are five letters in the word 'trees' and, holding up your hand, your five fingers remind you of five trees standing in a row.

You can use people as mnemonics, too:

I wandered lonely as a Cloud	*Think of yourself when you've been lonely – or another loner if you prefer*
That floats on high o'er Vales and Hills,	*Think of someone you know who is fat: 'floats' rhymes with 'bloats'*
When all at once I saw a crowd,	*Think of the last party you went to*

A host of golden Daffodils;	*Think of your host*
Beside the Lake, beneath the trees,	*Think of you being lonely*
	again, smoking a cigarette
	beside the lake, beneath the
	trees
Fluttering and dancing in the breeze.	*Think of the party crowd up at*
	the house, dancing on the lawn

The trick with a mnemonic is to make it personal. The closer it is to you, the quicker it will trigger the required memory.

10. Enjoy the journey

Almost every poem takes you on a journey of sorts – some, obviously, rather shorter than others. Whatever the journey, be aware of it. As you travel through your poem, look at each line or phrase or thought as a stepping stone – or as a stop on a country railway ride. If you are conscious of the journey you are taking, wherever you are it will help you know where you are going next.

11. Sleep on it

There is plenty of research to suggest that sleep helps boost learning – and not only a good night's sleep, but also a sixty- to ninety-minute post-learning nap. With an hour-long sleep, information absorbed into short-term storage in the hippocampus gets bedded into the prefrontal cortex where you will be needing it for executive action . . . the executive action in question being the speaking of the poem you have learnt by heart.

We will get to the fun of 'the performing bit' in due course. Let's start learning some poems now. It's time for the workout. Kindly turn the page and join me in the gym.

Take a Poem
by James Carter
(born 1959)

Why not take a poem
wherever you go?
Pop it in your pocket
nobody will know

Take it to your classroom
stick it on the wall
tell them about it
read it in the hall

Take it to the bathroom
tuck it up in bed
take the time to learn it
keep it in your head

Take it for a day trip
take it on a train
fold it as a hat
when it starts to rain

Take it to a river
fold it as a boat
pop it on the water
hope that it will float

Take it to a hilltop
fold it as a plane

throw it up skywards
time and time again

Take it to a mailbox
send it anywhere
out into the world
with
     tender
          loving
             care.

Chapter Four

There Was a Young Man from Peru
Whose limericks stopped at line two

Welcome to the poetry gym.

To get you going, to warm you up, here are some little poems by some big names.

For many years, the shortest poem in the English language was reckoned to be the nine-letter couplet by the American poet Strickland Gillilan (1869–1954). The poem's full title is 'Lines on the Antiquity of Microbes', but it is also known simply as 'Fleas':

> Adam
> Had 'em

A few years ago, I came up with a rhyming verse to rival Gillilan's masterpiece. When my children were small we kept a lot of pets. We had a sophisticated French poodle called Phydeaux and a lovely mongrel who thought his name was Down Boy. We kept hamsters, but they kept dying on us. (I wanted to put their remains through the blender and lay them to rest on the flowerbeds, having heard you get tulips from hamster jam, but my wife wouldn't have it.) We kept a goldfish, too, called Spot, but he died as well – eaten by Oscar, our cat, who was wild, though by no means as bad as his brothers, Thornton, Billy and Gene, who were wilder. (Thornton was a crafty cat, with a penchant for cheddar: he'd sit by the mouse-hole with baited bated breath.) Anyway, one day Oscar ate Spot, and at a family memorial gathering in the garden we remembered him, and I recited my poem in his memory. I believe it is the shortest rhyming poem in the language.

Ode to a Goldfish
by Gyles Brandreth
(born 1948)

Oh
Wet
Pet!

Another, more distinguished poet came up with a poem that may not have the powerful rhyme of mine, but has quite as much impact and is unquestionably shorter:

The Lover Writes a One-Word Poem
by Gavin Ewart
(1916–95)

You!

But we were both outclassed when the illustrator and poet, Colin McNaughton, came up with this:

Ode to the Invisible Man
by *Colin McNaughton*
(born 1951)

Among the easiest short poems to learn by heart are limericks, simply because we are familiar with the form and the *aabba* rhyming pattern. According to the dictionary on my desk, 'the five-line nonsense poem known as the Limerick originated with the eighteenth-century ale-house chorus, "Will you come up to Limerick?"' Not so. Limericks of a sort have been around for centuries. This one, for example, is more than five hundred years old:

> Ewe bleateth after lamb,
> Low'th after calf too.
> Bullock starteth
> Bucke farteth –
> Merry sing Cuckoo!

The great popularizer of the limerick was the Victorian artist and poet, Edward Lear (1812–88). These are five of his favourites:

There was an Old Person of Ischia,
Whose conduct grew friskier and friskier;
 He danced hornpipes and jigs,
 And ate thousands of figs,
That lively Old Person of Ischia.

There was an Old Man in a boat,
Who said, 'I'm afloat, I'm afloat!'
 When they said, 'No! you ain't!'
 He was ready to faint,
That unhappy Old Man in a boat.

There was an Old Person of Ewell,
Who chiefly subsisted on gruel;
 But to make it more nice,
 He inserted some mice,
Which refreshed that Old Person of Ewell.

There is a Young Lady whose nose
Continually prospers and grows;
 When it grew out of sight,
 She exclaimed in a fright,
'Oh! Farewell to the end of my nose!'

There was an Old Person of Dean,
Who dined on one pea and one bean;
 For he said, 'More than that
 Would make me too fat,'
That cautious Old Person of Dean.

Lear's limericks are underrated nowadays, largely because the fifth line often replays the first and we live in an age that craves novelty at every turn. That said:

> Although at the limericks of Lear
> We may be tempted to sneer
> We should never forget
> That we owe him a debt
> For his work as the first pioneer

Lear gave drawing lessons to Queen Victoria. He was a respectable fellow and his line in limericks reflects that. A sense of propriety (and the age of political correctness) prevents me from reproducing most of the limericks that I know by heart. That's the problem:

> The limerick is furtive and mean
> You must keep it in close quarantine
> Or it sneaks to the slums
> And quickly becomes
> Disorderly, drunk and obscene

Happily, that's not the case with this one, by Michael Palin (born 1943):

> A handsome young fellow called Frears
> Was attracted to girls by their ears
> He'd traverse the globe
> In search of a lobe,
> And the sight would reduce him to tears.

The first short poems I learnt by heart were some of the 'Ruthless Rhymes' of Harry Graham (1874–1936):

In the drinking-well
    (Which the plumber built her)
Aunt Eliza fell, –
    We must buy a filter.

Father heard his children scream,
So he threw them in the stream,
Saying, as he drowned the third,
'Children should be seen, *not* heard!'

Billy, in one of his nice new sashes,
Fell in the fire and was burnt to ashes;
Now, although the room grows chilly,
I haven't the heart to poke poor Billy.

Baby in the cauldron fell, –
    See the grief on Mother's brow;
Mother loved her darling well, –
    Darling's quite hard-boiled by now.

The Japanese haiku is an elegant short poetic form, presenting a thought (usually on a theme connected with nature) using exactly seventeen syllables in three contrasting phrases (with five, seven and five syllables in successive phrases). The haiku has been around for a thousand years. Matsuo Bashō (1644–94) is considered by many the master. Nature was his central theme:

An old silent pond . . .
A frog jumps into the pond,
splash! Silence again.

In the twilight rain
these brilliant-hued hibiscus –
A lovely sunset

Unfortunately with some of Bashō's most evocative haikus, the five/seven/five syllable pattern gets lost in translation:

> Bitten by fleas and lice
> I slept in a bed
> A horse urinating close by my pillow

Here are three created by Masaoka Shiki (1867–1902), credited with reviving the haiku in the nineteenth century and tolerating a looser approach to the form in which the 5/7/5 phrasing is not compulsory:

> After killing
> a spider, how lonely I feel
> in the cold of night!

> Night; and once again,
> the while I wait for you, cold wind
> turns into rain.

> A lightning flash:
> between the forest trees
> I have seen water.

When trying to get to sleep, I find reciting haikus – and, even, trying to compose them – quite helpful. This one, which fails the strict seventeen-syllable test, is by Richard Wright (1908–60):

> From across the lake,
> Past the black winter trees,
> Faint sounds of a flute.

This is by the contemporary performance poet, John Cooper Clarke (born 1949):

TO-CON-VEY ONE'S MOOD
IN SEV-EN-TEEN SYLL-ABLE-S
IS VE-RY DIF-FIC

This last one is my favourite. A number of people claim to have written it. I wish I had.

Haikus are easy
But sometimes they don't make sense
Refrigerator

The haiku is limited to three lines. The clerihew is limited to four. Edmund Clerihew Bentley (1875–1956) invented the form in 1905 as a whimsical slice of biography in verse. This was his first effort:

Sir Humphrey Davy
Abominated gravy.
He lived in the odium
Of having invented sodium.

These are four of his most famous:

Edward the Confessor
Slept under the dresser.
When that began to pall,
He slept in the hall.

Sir Christopher Wren
Said, 'I am going to dine with some men.

'If anyone calls
'Say I am designing St. Paul's.'

George the Third
Ought never to have occurred.
One can only wonder
At so grotesque a blunder.

John Stuart Mill,
By a mighty effort of will,
Overcame his natural bonhomie
And wrote 'Principles of Political Economy.'

The poet W. H. Auden (1907–83) loved clerihews and liked to compose them in bed when sleep eluded him. Here are three of my Auden favourites:

Lord Byron
Once succumbed to a Siren:
His flesh was weak,
Hers Greek.

Oscar Wilde
Was greatly beguiled,
When into the Café Royal walked Bosie
Wearing a tea-cosy.

Sir Henry Rider Haggard
Was completely staggered
When his bride-to-be
Announced, 'I am She!'

I like this one by Louis Phillips (born 1942):

> Robert de Niro
> Is a screen hero.
> Only a slob
> Would call him Bob.

And this, by Michael Shepherd, is pretty neat:

> Mick Jagger a-
> pparently doesn't need Viagra
>
> and might view as malice
> an Xmas gift of Cialis . . .

As a schoolboy, I listened to *The Goon Show* on the radio, but I did not find it very funny. That said, in 1963, for two shillings, I bought a book, *The Little Pot Boiler*, by the principal Goon, Spike Milligan (1918–2002), and committed a number of his short poems to memory:

> The Herring is a lucky fish,
> From all disease inured.
> Should he be ill when caught at sea;
> *Immediately* – he's cured!
>
> Things that go bump in the night
> Should not really give one a fright.
> It's the hole in each ear
> That lets in the fear,
> That, and the absence of light!

This was my Milligan favourite:

Return to Sorrento (3rd Class)

I must go down to the sea again,
To the lonely sea and sky,
I left my vest and socks there,
I wonder if they're dry?

In my book, the modern mistress of short, memorable poetry is Wendy Cope (born 1945):

Making Cocoa for Kingsley Amis

It was a dream I had last week
And some kind of record seemed vital.
I knew it wouldn't be much of a poem
But I love the title.

And the modern master is Roger McGough (born 1937):

Survivor

Everyday
I think about dying.
About disease, starvation,
violence, terrorism, war,
the end of the world.

It helps keep my mind off things.

In the late 1960s, the Professor of Poetry at Oxford University was Roy Fuller (1912–91). He was a serious poet, though he did not always write serious poems, nor take himself too seriously:

In the Bathroom

What is that blood-stained thing –
Hairy, as if it were frayed –
Stretching itself along
The slippery bath's steep side?

I approach it, ready to kill,
Or run away, aghast;
And find I have to deal
With a used elastoplast.

Harold Pinter (1930–2008) was also a serious poet – and actor, director, playwright and Nobel Laureate – and he did seem to take himself and his poetry quite seriously. Famously a cricket enthusiast, he was especially proud of this two-line effort:

I saw Len Hutton in his prime
Another time, another time

Having completed the poem, and rather pleased with it, Pinter sent it by fax and post to an assortment of his friends. A while later, not having had any response, he rang one of them, the playwright Simon Gray, to ask what he thought of it. Gray's reply? 'Sorry, Harold, I haven't finished it yet.'

Another actor and playwright is my friend Simon Williams (born 1946). This short verse is about the challenge facing the actor who is cast as a corpse.

Lying doggo

Actors have a dread
Of having to play dead.
If you are poisoned, stabbed or shot,
You'd better find a comfy spot.
What's really best to go for
Is a death behind the sofa,
Where you can blink,
Or breathe or think,
Hidden from the stalls,
At least until the curtain falls.

Here, arranged in chronological order, are fourteen short poems by serious poets. None is longer than a dozen lines. The first one isn't even a poem. It's a prose meditation, but so poetic and so memorable it's often presented as a piece of poetry. This is the work of a variety of British, American and Canadian poets, born across four centuries. I reckon the pieces are deeper than they look, but learning them should be easy. You can master the four-liners in a couple of days. At two lines a day, you could have the John Donne – some of the most powerful words in the English language – off by heart in under a week.

Meditation XVII
by John Donne
(1572–1631)

No man is an island,
Entire of itself;
Every man is a piece of the continent,
A part of the main;
If a clod be washed away by the sea,
Europe is the less,
As well as if a promontory were,
As well as if a manor of thy friend's,
Or of thine own were;
Any man's death diminishes me,
Because I am involved in mankind;
And therefore never send to know
For whom the bell tolls;
It tolls for thee.

Rondeau
by Leigh Hunt
(1784–1859)

Jenny kissed me when we met,
　Jumping from the chair she sat in;

Time, you thief, who love to get
    Sweets into your list, put that in:
Say I'm weary, say I'm sad,
    Say that health and wealth have missed me,
Say I'm growing old, but add,
    Jenny kissed me.

Pippa's Song from *Pippa Passes*
by Robert Browning
(1812–89)

The year's at the spring
And day's at the morn;
Morning's at seven;
The hill-side's dew-pearled;
The lark's on the wing;
The snail's on the thorn;
God's in his heaven –
All's right with the world!

I'm Nobody! Who Are You?
by Emily Dickinson
(1830–86)

I'm nobody! Who are you?
Are you nobody, too?
Then there's a pair of us – don't tell!
They'd banish us, you know.
How dreary to be somebody!
How public, like a frog
To tell your name the livelong day
To an admiring bog!

If I can stop one heart from breaking
by Emily Dickinson

If I can stop one heart from breaking,
I shall not live in vain;
If I can ease one life the aching,
Or cool one pain,
Or help one fainting robin
Unto his nest again,
I shall not live in vain

I stood upon a high place
by Stephen Crane
(1871–1900)

I stood upon a high place,
And saw, below, many devils
Running, leaping,
and carousing in sin.
One looked up, grinning,
And said, 'Comrade! Brother!'

This Is Just to Say
by William Carlos Williams
(1883–1963)

I have eaten
the plums
that were in
the icebox

and which
you were probably
saving
for breakfast

Forgive me
they were delicious
so sweet
and so cold

The Optimist
by D. H. Lawrence
(1885–1930)

The optimist builds himself safe inside a cell
and paints the inside walls sky-blue
and blocks up the door
and says he's in heaven.

And the days are not full enough
by Ezra Pound
(1885–1972)

And the days are not full enough
And the nights are not full enough
And life slips by like a field mouse
                    Not shaking the grass.

Trees

by (Alfred) Joyce Kilmer
(1886–1918)

I think that I shall never see
A poem lovely as a tree.

A tree whose hungry mouth is prest
Against the earth's sweet flowing breast;

A tree that looks at God all day,
And lifts her leafy arms to pray;

A tree that may in Summer wear
A nest of robins in her hair;

Upon whose bosom snow has lain;
Who intimately lives with rain.

Poems are made by fools like me,
But only God can make a tree.

First Fig
by Edna St Vincent Millay
(1892–1950)

My candle burns at both ends;
   It will not last the night;
But ah, my foes, and oh, my friends –
   It gives a lovely light!

J. P. Donleavy's Dublin
by Derek Mahon
(born 1941)

'When you stop to consider
the days spent dreaming of a future
and say then, that was my life' –

for the days are long:
from the first milk van
to the last shout in the night
an eternity. But the weeks go by
like birds; and the years, the years
fly past anticlockwise
like clock hands in a bar mirror.

Who's Who
by Benjamin Zephaniah
(born 1958)

I used to think nurses
Were women,
I used to think police
Were men,
I used to think poets
Were boring,
Until I became one of them.

And, finally, a little gem from the millennial phenomenon that is Rupi Kaur (born 1992), the Indian-born Canadian poet whose first collection, *Milk and Honey*, sold more than three million copies around the world and spent more than a year on the *New York Times* best-seller list:

loneliness is a sign you are in desperate need of yourself

Chapter Five

On Westminster Bridge
Seventeen sonnets

The Italian word *sonetto* means 'little song', as in:

> Just one *sonetto*,
> Give it to me:
> Delicious poetry
> From Italy!

The sonnet form was pioneered by the Italian scholar Petrarch (known locally as Francesco Petrarca, 1304–74) and fellow Italian Renaissance poets, and adopted and developed by the English from the 1500s onwards. William Shakespeare (1564–1616) is rightly regarded as the Elizabethan sonnet *maestro*.

The traditional sonnet:

- has 14 lines
- is written in iambic pentameters
- has a set rhyming scheme

To give you the jargon, an iambic 'foot' is an unstressed syllable followed by a stressed syllable:

da DUM

That 'da DUM' is the rhythm of the human heartbeat, which is why babies and toddlers respond well to Shakespeare and why Shakespearean verse is easy to learn at any age.

'Penta' means 'five' in Greek and 'meter' comes from the Greek for 'measure'. A standard line of iambic pentameter is five iambic feet in a row:

da DUM da DUM da DUM da DUM da DUM

You can hear the beat clearly in any number of Shakespeare's opening lines:

When I do count the clock that tells the time
Sonnet 12

In faith, I do not love thee with mine eyes
Sonnet 141

If music be the food of love, play on
Twelfth Night

Two households both alike in dignity
Romeo and Juliet

As Franco Zeffirelli (who directed the young Judi Dench in *Romeo and Juliet* in 1960) put it: 'Shakespeare's verse goes with the beat of your heart – no wonder he's captured the hearts of all mankind.'

With the Shakespearean sonnet the rhyming pattern is: *abab cdcd efef gg*. With the Petrarchan sonnet it is: *abba abba cdecde* or *abba abba cdcdcd*.

In the Petrarchan sonnet the sections are broken up into an *octave* (the first eight lines of the poem) and a *sestet* (the final six lines). In the Shakespearean sonnet there are three *quatrains* (three four-line stanzas) followed by a final *couplet*.

In both forms of sonnet there is something known as a *volta* that marks the transition to the final section of the poem. The original *volta* was an Italian dance that involved a sudden, quick twist or move. In a sonnet the *volta* is the turn of thought or argument that comes before the poem ends. In Petrarchan sonnets the *volta* comes between the octave and the sestet, and in Shakespearean sonnets it comes before the final couplet.

I don't think you need more of the poetic science than that, but that much should be helpful. For example, it should make it easier to memorize your Shakespeare sonnet if you do your learning bit by bit: first one quatrain, then the next, then the next, then the pay-off in the final couplet.

Given that sonnets always run to fourteen lines, a trick to help trigger each line in your memory is to attach each line to a room in your Memory Palace if you have one (see page 55–6), or do as I did when I was a romantic adolescent living in London and trying to learn Shakespearean sonnets by heart – connect each line of the sonnet with a particular place: it could be a stop on a bus route you know well or, as in my case, a London underground station.

As a teenager, I did the revision for my A-levels travelling round and round the Circle Line. I found the train juddering to a halt every two or three minutes kept me awake and every time the train reached Paddington I got off and allowed myself the treat of a cup of tea and a bun on the station concourse. When learning the sonnets, I travelled on the Bakerloo Line between Waterloo and Queen's Park. There are fourteen stations along that stretch of underground line and I would associate one line of the sonnet with each station in turn: when the train doors opened at the station, I would start the line and repeat it again and again until I reached the next station, when the doors opening would have me starting off on the next line. And so on.

It worked.

At least, it's how I learnt Shakespeare's Sonnet 116:

Let me not to the marriage of true minds	— *Waterloo*
Admit impediments; love is not love	— *Embankment*
Which alters when it alteration finds,	— *Charing Cross*
Or bends with the remover to remove.	— *Piccadilly*
O no, it is an ever-fixèd mark	— *Oxford Circus*
That looks on tempests and is never shaken;	— *Regent's Park*
It is the star to every wand'ring bark,	— *Baker Street*
Whose worth's unknown although his height	
be taken.	— *Marylebone*
Love's not time's fool, though rosy lips and cheeks	— *Edgware Road*
Within his bending sickle's compass come;	— *Paddington*
Love alters not with his brief hours and weeks,	— *Warwick Avenue*
But bears it out even to the edge of doom.	— *Maida Vale*
If this be error and upon me proved,	— *Kilburn Park*
I never writ, nor no man ever loved.	— *Queen's Park*

I created additional memory triggers for myself as well. For example, with line three, Charing Cross station was once known as 'Trafalgar Square', and the alteration in name reminds me instantly of the line 'which alters when it alteration finds'; and, in line seven of the sonnet, 'wand'ring bark' is almost a classic crossword puzzle clue for 'Baker Street' – the *b*, *a*, *r* and *k* 'wand'ring' off to form 'Baker', the apostrophe in 'wand'ring' indicating the *e* that will be missing from 'Baker' when it becomes 'bark'.

You may find it simpler simply to memorise the lines two-by-two or four-by-four, but over the years my Bakerloo Line mnemonic has reaped its rewards. Not long ago, I took part in an episode of the television programme, *Pointless Celebrities*, with Susan Calman as my partner. We won the trophy on the final question because I was able to name a station on the Bakerloo Line that nobody else had thought of: Queen's Park. As I murmured to Susan at the time: 'If this be error and upon me proved, I never writ, nor no man ever loved.'

The world is awash with glorious sonnets. You will find six hundred of the best in *The Penguin Book of the Sonnet: 500 Years of a Classic Tradition in English*, edited by Phillis Levin. I have chosen just seventeen – some Shakespearean in form, some Petrarchan, some more modern and a little looser. They deal with faith, hope, love and death – the usual stuff. The Milton and the Manley Hopkins are the two tough ones, I reckon, but on the bus, on the tube, in bed or in the shower, you should be able to master any one of them in a week. I learnt 'On Westminster Bridge' on Westminster Bridge. It was in the 1990s, when I was a Member of Parliament.* Late at night, I would slip out of the House of Commons between votes and cross and re-cross the River Thames trying to fix Wordsworth's lines in my head.

---

* A number of great poets have been MPs, among them four of my favourites: Geoffrey Chaucer (*c.*1343–1400), John Donne (1572–1631), George Herbert (1593–1633) and Andrew Marvell (1621–78). Chaucer does not feature in this book, simply because he is difficult to learn by heart without mastering the pronunciation of Middle English. There are some good readings of Chaucer readily available on YouTube to give you a flavour of how he sounds: keep listening, and quite quickly your ear adjusts and you get the gist of what he's saying.

Sonnet 18
by William Shakespeare
(1564–1616)

Shall I compare thee to a summer's day?
Thou art more lovely and more temperate.
Rough winds do shake the darling buds of May,
And summer's lease hath all too short a date.
Sometime too hot the eye of heaven shines,
And often is his gold complexion dimmed;
And every fair from fair sometime declines,
By chance or nature's changing course untrimmed.
But thy eternal summer shall not fade,
Nor lose possession of that fair thou ow'st,
Nor shall Death brag thou wand'rest in his shade,
When in eternal lines to time thou grow'st.
So long as men can breathe or eyes can see,
So long lives this, and this gives life to thee.

Shakespeare at School
by Wendy Cope
(born 1945)

Forty boys on benches with their quills
Six days a week through almost all the year,
Long hours of Latin with relentless drills
And repetition, all enforced by fear.
I picture Shakespeare sitting near the back,
Indulging in a risky bit of fun
By exercising his prodigious knack
Of thinking up an idiotic pun,
And whispering his gem to other boys,
Some of whom could not suppress their mirth –
Behaviour that unfailingly annoys
Any teacher anywhere on earth.
The fun was over when the master spoke:
Will Shakespeare, come up here and share the joke.

When I consider how my light is spent
by John Milton
(1608–74)*

When I consider how my light is spent,
   Ere half my days, in this dark world and wide,
   And that one talent which is death to hide
   Lodged with me useless, though my soul more bent
To serve therewith my maker, and present
   My true account, lest he returning chide,
   'Doth God exact day-labour, light denied?'
   I fondly ask; but patience to prevent
That murmur soon replies, 'God doth not need
   Either man's work or his own gifts; who best
   Bear his mild yoke, they serve him best, his state
Is kingly. Thousands at his bidding speed
   And post o'er land and ocean without rest:
   They also serve who only stand and wait.'

---

* This poem is also known as 'On His Blindness'. Milton's eyesight declined over several years, probably as the result of untreated glaucoma. By 1652, he was completely blind. His first published poem was 'On Shakespeare' (1630); his most famous, *Paradise Lost* (1667). A Puritan and a passionate Christian, the 'one talent which is death to hide' in this Petrarchan sonnet refers to the parable of the talents in St Matthew's Gospel.

Composed upon Westminster Bridge, September 3, 1802
by William Wordsworth
(1770–1850)

Earth has not anything to show more fair:
Dull would he be of soul who could pass by
A sight so touching in its majesty:
This City now doth, like a garment, wear
The beauty of the morning; silent, bare,
Ships, towers, domes, theatres, and temples lie
Open unto the fields, and to the sky;
All bright and glittering in the smokeless air.
Never did sun more beautifully steep
In his first splendour, valley, rock, or hill;
Ne'er saw I, never felt, a calm so deep!
The river glideth at his own sweet will:
Dear God! the very houses seem asleep;
And all that mighty heart is lying still!

Toussaint L'Ouverture Acknowledges Wordsworth's Sonnet 'To Toussaint L'Ouverture'

by John Agard
(born 1949)*

I have never walked on Westminster Bridge
or had a close-up view of daffodils.
My childhood's roots are the Haitian hills
where runaway slaves made a freedom pledge
and scarlet poincianas flaunt their scent.
I have never walked on Westminster Bridge
or speak, like you, with Cumbrian accent.
My tongue bridges Europe to Dahomey.
Yet how sweet is the smell of liberty
when human beings share a common garment.
So thanks, brother, for your sonnet's tribute.
May it resound when the Thames' text stays mute.
And what better ground than a city's bridge
for my unchained ghost to trumpet love's decree.

---

* François Dominique Toussaint L'Ouverture (1743–1803) was a Haitian revolutionary who was imprisoned by the French and whose plight caught the imagination of radical Romantics like the Cumbrian poet, William Wordsworth, who wrote a sonnet in L'Ouverture's praise not long before he died in French captivity in 1803. Two hundred years later, John Agard, poet and playwright of Afro-Guyanese heritage, wrote this sonnet in praise of Wordsworth.

Ozymandias
by Percy Bysshe Shelley
(1792–1822)*

I met a traveller from an antique land
Who said: Two vast and trunkless legs of stone
Stand in the desert. Near them, on the sand,
Half sunk a shattered visage lies, whose frown,
And wrinkled lip, and sneer of cold command,
Tell that its sculptor well those passions read
Which yet survive, stamped on these lifeless things,
The hand that mocked them, and the heart that fed;
And on the pedestal, these words appear:
'My name is Ozymandias, king of kings:
Look on my works, ye Mighty, and despair!'
Nothing beside remains. Round the decay
Of that colossal wreck, boundless and bare
The lone and level sands stretch far away.

---

* Ozymandias was a Greek name for the Egyptian pharaoh, Rameses II.
Shelley began writing this sonnet in 1817, soon after the announcement of
the British Museum's acquisition of a large fragment of a statue of Rameses
II from the thirteenth century BC.

Bright star, would I were stedfast as thou art
by John Keats
*(1795–1821)**

Bright star, would I were stedfast as thou art –
　　Not in lone splendour hung aloft the night,
And watching, with eternal lids apart,
　　Like nature's patient, sleepless Eremite,
The moving waters at their priestlike task
　　Of pure ablution round earth's human shores,
Or gazing on the new soft-fallen masque
　　Of snow upon the mountains and the moors.
No – yet still stedfast, still unchangeable,
　　Pillow'd upon my fair love's ripening breast,
To feel for ever its soft swell and fall,
　　Awake for ever in a sweet unrest,
Still, still to hear her tender-taken breath,
And so live ever – or else swoon to death.

---

* Keats wrote this sonnet in 1819, revising it in 1820, possibly on his final trip to Italy, where he hoped to find a cure for his tuberculosis. Aware that he was dying, the poem contrasts the transience of human life with the steadfast eternity of the bright star in the heavens. Some critics interpret the poem as a love sonnet addressed to Keats's fiancée, Fanny Brawne. An 'eremite' was a hermit or recluse; 'pure ablution' was ritual cleansing.

From *Sonnets from the Portuguese*
(Sonnet XLII)
by Elizabeth Barrett Browning
*(1806–61)**

How do I love thee? Let me count the ways.
I love thee to the depth and breadth and height
My soul can reach, when feeling out of sight
For the ends of Being and Ideal Grace.
I love thee to the level of everyday's
Most quiet need, by sun and candlelight.
I love thee freely, as men strive for Right;
I love thee purely, as they turn from Praise;
I love thee with the passion put to use
In my old griefs, and with my childhood's faith;
I love thee with a love I seemed to lose
With my lost saints, – I love thee with the breath,
Smiles, tears, of all my life! – and, if God choose,
I shall but love thee better after death.

---

* The relationship between Elizabeth Barrett and Robert Browning is one of
the great love stories of literary history. In the 1840s, Elizabeth Barrett, already
known as a poet, lived as an invalid in London with her father, who supported
her writing but did not want her to marry. Robert Browning, five years her
junior and less successful, admired her poetry, as she admired his. 'I love your
verse with all my heart, dear Miss Barrett,' he wrote in January 1845, 'and I love
you too.' In September 1846 they eloped to Italy, where they lived until her
death in 1861. Over the twenty months of their secret courtship, Elizabeth and
Robert wrote some six hundred letters to one another. Elizabeth also began a
series of sonnets under the title *Sonnets from the Portuguese* – so called to give the
impression they were merely translations. In fact, they were original, though
loosely inspired by the love sonnets of a Portuguese poet, Luís de Camões.

Remember
by Christina Rossetti
*(1830–94)**

Remember me when I am gone away,
   Gone far away into the silent land;
   When you can no more hold me by the hand,
Nor I half turn to go yet turning stay.
Remember me when no more day by day
   You tell me of our future that you planned:
   Only remember me; you understand
It will be late to counsel then or pray.
Yet if you should forget me for a while
   And afterwards remember, do not grieve:
   For if the darkness and corruption leave
   A vestige of the thoughts that once I had,
Better by far you should forget and smile
   Than that you should remember and be sad.

---

* Intriguingly, this celebrated sonnet of remembrance was written when Christina Rossetti was still a teenager. Her claims to fame include being the model for the Virgin Mary in the first completed oil painting by her brother, Dante Gabriel Rossetti, *The Girlhood of Mary Virgin*, the first work to be inscribed with the initials 'PRB', standing for the 'Pre-Raphaelite Brotherhood'. She also wrote the poem 'In the bleak mid-winter', which, more than once, has been voted 'the world's best-loved Christmas carol'.

The Windhover

by Gerard Manley Hopkins
(1844–89)*
To Christ Our Lord

I caught this morning morning's minion, king-
    dom of daylight's dauphin, dapple-dawn-drawn Falcon, in
      his riding
    Of the rolling level underneath him steady air, and
      striding
High there, how he rung upon the rein of a wimpling wing
In his ecstasy! then off, off forth on swing,
    As a skate's heel sweeps smooth on a bow-bend: the hurl
      and gliding
    Rebuffed the big wind. My heart in hiding
Stirred for a bird, – the achieve of, the mastery of the thing!

Brute beauty and valour and act, oh, air, pride, plume, here
    Buckle! AND the fire that breaks from thee then, a billion
Times told lovelier, more dangerous, O my chevalier!

---

* This is a tough one to learn and to perform – but do both and you will feel
good. Hopkins was a Jesuit priest (hence the poem's dedication) and a lover
of nature: 'windhover' is another name for a kestrel and the last six lines of
the sonnet liken the bird's majesty to Christ's. Hopkins was a Victorian, but
his way with the sonnet broke the mould and his genius was only fully rec-
ognized posthumously. This is a Petrarchan sonnet, with (if you look for it)
a definite *abba abba cdcdcd* rhyming scheme, but to achieve the effect of the
swooping windhover Hopkins does amazing things with his vocabulary and
the length of his lines.

No wonder of it: shéer plód makes plough down sillion
Shine, and blue-bleak embers, ah my dear,
    Fall, gall themselves, and gash gold-vermilion.

Desespoir
by Oscar Wilde
(1854–1900)*

The seasons mend their ruin as they go,
    For in the spring the narciss shows its head
    Nor withers till the rose has flamed to red,
And in the autumn purple violets blow,
And the slim crocus stirs the winter snow;
    Wherefore yon leafless trees will bloom again
    And this grey land grow green with summer rain
And send up cowslips for some boy to mow.
But what of Life whose bitter hungry sea
    Flows at our heels, and gloom of sunless night
    Covers the days which never more return?
Ambition, love and all the thoughts that burn
    We lose too soon, and only find delight
    In withered husks of some dead memory.

---

* *Désespoir* is French for 'despair'. Two other fine Wilde sonnets to learn by heart are 'Hélas' and 'On the Sale by Auction of Keats' Love Letters'. 'A great poet, a really great poet,' wrote Wilde, 'is the most unpoetical of creatures. But inferior poets are absolutely fascinating. The worse their rhymes are, the more picturesque they look. The mere fact of having published a book of second-rate sonnets make a man quite irresistible. He lives the poetry that he cannot write. The others write the poetry that they dare not realize.'

What lips my lips have kissed, and where, and why

by *Edna St Vincent Millay*
*(1892–1950)**

What lips my lips have kissed, and where, and why,
I have forgotten, and what arms have lain
Under my head till morning; but the rain
Is full of ghosts tonight, that tap and sigh
Upon the glass and listen for reply,
And in my heart there stirs a quiet pain
For unremembered lads that not again
Will turn to me at midnight with a cry.
Thus in the winter stands the lonely tree,
Nor knows what birds have vanished one by one,
Yet knows its boughs more silent than before:
I cannot say what loves have come and gone,
I only know that summer sang in me
A little while, that in me sings no more.

---

* The American poet, playwright and feminist, Edna St Vincent Millay, is
reckoned by some the greatest sonneteer of the twentieth century. The English novelist Thomas Hardy said that America had two great attractions: 'the
skyscraper and the poetry of Edna St Vincent Millay'.

Yet Do I Marvel
by Countee Cullen
*(1903–46)**

I doubt not God is good, well-meaning, kind,
And did He stoop to quibble could tell why
The little buried mole continues blind,
Why flesh that mirrors Him must some day die,
Make plain the reason tortured Tantalus
Is baited by the fickle fruit, declare
If merely brute caprice dooms Sisyphus
To struggle up a never-ending stair.
Inscrutable His ways are, and immune
To catechism by a mind too strewn
With petty cares to slightly understand
What awful brain compels His awful hand.
Yet do I marvel at this curious thing:
To make a poet black, and bid him sing!

* Countee LeRoy Porter's first years are shrouded in mystery. What we do
know is that he was brought to Harlem, New York, by his grandmother, who
cared for him until her death in 1917. He was then adopted by the Reverend
Frederick Cullen, pastor of the Salem Methodist Episcopal Church, who later
became president of the Harlem chapter of the National Association for the
Advancement of Colored People. Countee, who was gay, published his first
collection of poems, *Color*, in 1925. 'Yet Do I Marvel' is a traditional sonnet
(with classical references to Tantalus and Sisyphus) in which Cullen questions
the challenges God presents to a black poet. *Color* became a key publication
in what is known as the Harlem Renaissance.

High Flight
by John Gillespie Magee, Jr.
*(1922–41)**

Oh! I have slipped the surly bonds of Earth
And danced the skies on laughter-silvered wings;
Sunward I've climbed, and joined the tumbling mirth
Of sun-split clouds, – and done a hundred things
You have not dreamed of – wheeled and soared and swung
High in the sunlit silence. Hov'ring there,
I've chased the shouting wind along, and flung
My eager craft through footless halls of air . . .
Up, up the long, delirious burning blue
I've topped the wind-swept heights with easy grace
Where never lark, or ever eagle flew –
And, while with silent, lifting mind I've trod
The high untrespassed sanctity of space,
Put out my hand, and touched the face of God.

---

* Magee was an Anglo-American Royal Canadian Air Force fighter pilot and poet, who was killed in an accidental mid-air collision over England in 1941.

Anne Hathaway
by Carol Ann Duffy
(born 1955)
'Item I gyve unto my wief my second best bed . . .'
(from Shakespeare's will)

The bed we loved in was a spinning world
of forests, castles, torchlight, clifftops, seas
where he would dive for pearls. My lover's words
were shooting stars which fell to earth as kisses
on these lips; my body now a softer rhyme
to his, now echo, assonance; his touch
a verb dancing in the centre of a noun.
Some nights I dreamed he'd written me, the bed
a page beneath his writer's hands. Romance
and drama played by touch, by scent, by taste.
In the other bed, the best, our guests dozed on,
dribbling their prose. My living laughing love –
I hold him in the casket of my widow's head
as he held me upon that next best bed.

Waking with Russell
by Don Paterson
(born 1963)

Whatever the difference is, it all began
the day we woke up face-to-face like lovers
and his four-day-old smile dawned on him again,
possessed him, till it would not fall or waver;
and I pitched back not my old hard-pressed grin
but his own smile, or one I'd rediscovered.
Dear son, I was *mezzo del cammin*
and the true path was as lost to me as ever
when you cut in front and lit it as you ran.
See how the true gift never leaves the giver:
returned and redelivered, it rolled on
until the smile poured through us like a river.
How fine, I thought, this waking amongst men!
I kissed your mouth and pledged myself forever.

Wedding

by Alice Oswald

(born 1966)

From time to time our love is like a sail
and when the sail begins to alternate
from tack to tack, it's like a swallowtail
and when the swallow flies it's like a coat;
and if the coat is yours, it has a tear
like a wide mouth and when the mouth begins
to draw the wind, it's like a trumpeter
and when the trumpet blows, it blows like millions . . .
and this, my love, when millions come and go
beyond the need of us, is like a trick;
and when the trick begins, it's like a toe
tip-toeing on a rope, which is like luck;
and when the luck begins, it's like a wedding,
which is like love, which is like everything.

Chapter Six

A Lot of Nonsense
From Edward Lear to Monty Python

> A little nonsense now and then
> is relished by the wisest men.
>
> Roald Dahl (1916–90)

'Don't talk to me about a man's being able to talk sense,' said William Pitt (1759–1806), at twenty-four Britain's youngest serving Prime Minister and, with almost nineteen years in office, the second longest serving. 'Everyone can talk sense. Can he talk nonsense?'

It's a rare gift. 'Nonsense and beauty have close connections,' said the novelist E. M. Forster (1879–1970). 'Nonsense wakes up the brain cells,' according to Dr Seuss (1904–91).*

---

* My mother met Dr Seuss (aka Theodor Seuss Geisel) once in a bookshop in La Jolla, California. She found him delightful. I met Roald Dahl on a number of occasions. Once we travelled together on a train from London to Cornwall. I found him as dark as some of his stories.

'And it helps develop a sense of humour, which is awfully important in this day and age.'

Dr Seuss is the American modern master of versified nonsense. The acknowledged European masters of nonsense are the two Victorian pioneers of the genre: Edward Lear and Lewis Carroll.

Lear was an artist, illustrator, musician and composer, as well as a poet and author. One of twenty-one children, as a child he suffered from seizures, as an adult he suffered from bouts of depression: he called them 'the Morbids'. He had difficulty forming relationships, but no difficulty creating nonsense. He invented all manner of creatures – Pobbles, Quangle-Wangles and Jumblies, among them – and a variety of original words – 'runcible' being the most famous. His poems feature a 'runcible wall', a 'runcible hat', a 'runcible cat' and 'a runcible goose', as well as a 'runcible spoon'. Happily, to this day nobody quite knows what 'runcible' means.

Lewis Carroll invented words, too. As Charles Lutwidge Dodgson he was a clergyman, mathematician, teacher and portrait photographer. As Lewis Carroll, he was a poet and author. One of eleven children, he suffered from chronic shyness and a severe stammer, except in the company of little girls – for three of whom, the Liddell sisters (daughters of the Dean of Christ Church, Oxford, where he lived and worked for many years), he created the story of *Alice's Adventures in Wonderland*.

Dodgson had many girl-friends: children and young women who were special friends, with whom he corresponded at length, took tea, and occasionally even took with him on holiday. In 1893 his sister, Mary, wrote to him about the gossip that was attached to these relationships. He replied to her: 'You need not be shocked at my being spoken against. *Any*body who is spoken about at all, is *sure* to be spoken against by *somebody*: and any action, however innocent in itself, is liable, and not at all unlikely, to be blamed by *somebody*. If you limit your actions in life to things that *nobody* can possibly find fault with, you will not do much!'

Lewis Carroll did a great deal, including creating some of the most remarkable characters in all fiction. He invented his own pen-name, 'Lewis Carroll' (based on a Latin inversion of his first two names), and much besides. He pioneered 'portmanteau words' that combine two existing words to create a third new one – like 'brunch' (1895), 'Brexit' (2016), and 'chortle', a Carroll original. 'Chortle' is a combination of 'chuckle' and 'snort' and Carroll conjured it up for *Through the Looking-Glass* (1871), his second book about the adventures of Alice.

You don't need to make sense of any of this chapter. Some critics claim the Louis MacNeice bagpipe ballad is a coded critique of the literary scene of his day, but I think it's just a bit of fun. Whether it's MacNeice or Milligan, Lear or Carroll, just let it roll around in your head and enjoy.

Two Dead Boys
by Anon.

One fine day in the middle of the night,
Two dead boys got up to fight,
Back to back they faced each other,
Drew their swords and shot each other.

One was blind and the other couldn't see
So they chose a dummy for a referee.
A blind man went to see fair play,
A dumb man went to shout 'hooray!'

A paralysed donkey passing by,
Kicked the blind man in the eye,
Knocked him through a nine inch wall,
Into a dry ditch and drowned them all.

A deaf policeman heard the noise,
And came to arrest the two dead boys,
If you don't believe this story's true,
Ask the blind man he saw it too!

The Pobble who has no toes
by Edward Lear
(1812–88)

I

The Pobble who has no toes
    Had once as many as we;
When they said, 'Some day you may lose them all;' –
    He replied, – 'Fish fiddle de-dee!'
And his Aunt Jobiska made him drink,
Lavender water tinged with pink,
For she said, 'The World in general knows
'There's nothing so good for a Pobble's toes!'

II

The Pobble who has no toes,
    Swam across the Bristol Channel;
But before he set out he wrapped his nose,
    In a piece of scarlet flannel.
For his Aunt Jobiska said, 'No harm
'Can come to his toes if his nose is warm;
'And it's perfectly known that a Pobble's toes
'Are safe, – provided he minds his nose.'

III

The Pobble swam fast and well
    And when boats or ships came near him
He tinkedly-binkledy-winkled a bell
    So that all the world could hear him.
And all the Sailors and Admirals cried,
When they saw him nearing the further side, –
'He has gone to fish, for his Aunt Jobiska's
'Runcible Cat with crimson whiskers!'

IV

But before he touched the shore,
    The shore of the Bristol Channel,
A sea-green Porpoise carried away
    His wrapper of scarlet flannel.
And when he came to observe his feet
Formerly garnished with toes so neat
His face at once became forlorn
On perceiving that all his toes were gone!

V

And nobody ever knew
    From that dark day to the present,
Whoso had taken the Pobble's toes,
    In a manner so far from pleasant.
Whether the shrimps or crawfish gray,
Or crafty Mermaids stole them away –
Nobody knew; and nobody knows
How the Pobble was robbed of his twice five toes!

VI

The Pobble who has no toes
    Was placed in a friendly Bark,
And they rowed him back, and carried him up,
    To his Aunt Jobiska's Park.
And she made him a feast at his earnest wish
Of eggs and buttercups fried with fish; –
And she said, – 'It's a fact the whole world knows,
'That Pobbles are happier without their toes.'

Jabberwocky
by Lewis Carroll
(1832–98)

'Twas brillig, and the slithy toves
    Did gyre and gimble in the wabe;
All mimsy were the borogoves,
    And the mome raths outgrabe.

'Beware the Jabberwock, my son!
    The jaws that bite, the claws that catch!
Beware the Jubjub bird, and shun
    The frumious Bandersnatch!'

He took his vorpal sword in hand:
    Long time the manxome foe he sought –
So rested he by the Tumtum tree,
    And stood awhile in thought.

And, as in uffish thought he stood,
    The Jabberwock, with eyes of flame,
Came whiffling through the tulgey wood,
    And burbled as it came!

One, two! One, two! And through and through
    The vorpal blade went snicker-snack!
He left it dead, and with its head
    He went galumphing back.

'And hast thou slain the Jabberwock?
    Come to my arms, my beamish boy!
O frabjous day! Callooh! Callay!'
    He chortled in his joy.

'Twas brillig, and the slithy toves
    Did gyre and gimble in the wabe;
All mimsy were the borogoves,
    And the mome raths outgrabe.

A dozen of Lewis Carroll's ingenious linguistic creations make their first appearance in the poem 'Jabberwocky' in Chapter 1 of *Through the Looking-Glass*. These definitions (sometimes contradictory) are the ones supplied by Carroll, Humpty Dumpty and Alice:

Jabberwock is the name of the fabulous monster in the poem and is formed on the verb 'to jabber'.

Brillig, according to Humpty Dumpty in Chapter 6, means 'four o'clock in the afternoon – the time you begin broiling things for dinner'.

Slithy, Humpty Dumpty says, 'means "lithe and slimy." "Lithe" is the same as "active." You see it's like a portmanteau – there are two meanings packed up into one word.'

Toves are 'something like badgers – they are something like lizards – and they are something like corkscrews'.

Gyre, according to Humpty Dumpty, means 'to go round and round like a gyroscope'. According to Carroll it means, 'to scratch like a dog'. Since Carroll invented Humpty Dumpty, which of them was right?

Gimble is to make holes like a gimlet.

Wabe, as Alice rightly guesses, is the grass plot around a sundial frequented by *toves*.

Mimsy is another portmanteau: 'flimsy and miserable'.

Borogrove is 'a thin shabby-looking bird with its feathers sticking out all round – something like a live mop'.

Mome, lost, missing home or solemn.

Raths, a sort of green pig; a species of turtle.

Outgrabe, according to Carroll, 'the past tense of the verb "outgribe", meaning to shriek or creak.'

Wynken, Blynken, and Nod
by Eugene Field
(1850–95)*

Wynken, Blynken, and Nod one night
   Sailed off in a wooden shoe, –
Sailed on a river of misty light
   Into a sea of dew.
'Where are you going, and what do you wish?'
   The old moon asked the three.
'We have come to fish for the herring-fish
   That live in this beautiful sea;
   Nets of silver and gold have we,'
        Said Wynken,
        Blynken,
        And Nod.

The old moon laughed and sung a song,
   As they rocked in the wooden shoe;
And the wind that sped them all night long
   Ruffled the waves of dew;
The little stars were the herring-fish
   That lived in that beautiful sea.

---

* In nineteenth-century America, Field was known as 'the poet of child-hood'. There is a statue of Wynken, Blynken and Nod in Washington Park, near Field's home in Denver, Colorado. Posthumously, he gained notoriety for a bit of nonsense of a different sort: a story he had written called 'Only a Boy', a vivid account of a twelve-year-old schoolboy being seduced by a woman in her thirties. Issued anonymously in his lifetime, it was published by the Grove Press in 1968 under Field's own name.

'Now cast your nets wherever you wish,
    But never afeard are we!'
So cried the stars to the fishermen three,
        Wynken,
        Blynken,
        And Nod.

All night long their nets they threw
    For the fish in the twinkling foam,
Then down from the sky came the wooden shoe,
    Bringing the fishermen home;
'T was all so pretty a sail, it seemed
    As if it could not be;
And some folks thought 't was a dream they'd dreamed
    Of sailing that beautiful sea;
    But I shall name you the fishermen three:
        Wynken,
        Blynken,
        And Nod.

Wynken and Blynken are two little eyes,
    And Nod is a little head,
And the wooden shoe that sailed the skies
    Is a wee one's trundle-bed;
So shut your eyes while Mother sings
    Of wonderful sights that be,
And you shall see the beautiful things
    As you rock in the misty sea,
    Where the old shoe rocked the fishermen three, –
        Wynken,
        Blynken,
        And Nod.

Bagpipe Music
by Louis MacNeice
(1907–63)

It's no go the merrygoround, it's no go the rickshaw,
All we want is a limousine and a ticket for the peepshow.
Their knickers are made of crêpe-de-chine, their shoes are
    made of python,
Their halls are lined with tiger rugs and their walls with
heads of bison.

John MacDonald found a corpse, put it under the sofa,
Waited till it came to life and hit it with a poker,
Sold its eyes for souvenirs, sold its blood for whisky,
Kept its bones for dumb-bells to use when he was fifty.

It's no go the Yogi-Man, it's no go Blavatsky,
All we want is a bank balance and a bit of skirt in a taxi.

Annie MacDougall went to milk, caught her foot in the
    heather,
Woke to hear a dance record playing of Old Vienna.
It's no go your maidenheads, it's no go your culture,
All we want is a Dunlop tyre and the devil mend the
    puncture.

The Laird o' Phelps spent Hogmanay declaring he was sober,
Counted his feet to prove the fact and found he had one
    foot over.

Mrs Carmichael had her fifth, looked at the job with
    repulsion,
Said to the midwife 'Take it away; I'm through with
    over-production'.

It's no go the gossip column, it's no go the Ceilidh,
All we want is a mother's help and a sugar-stick for the baby.

Willie Murray cut his thumb, couldn't count the damage,
Took the hide of an Ayrshire cow and used it for a bandage.
His brother caught three hundred cran when the seas were
    lavish,
Threw the bleeders back in the sea and went upon the
    parish.

It's no go the Herring Board, it's no go the Bible,
All we want is a packet of fags when our hands are idle.

It's no go the picture palace, it's no go the stadium,
It's no go the country cot with a pot of pink geraniums,
It's no go the Government grants, it's no go the elections,
Sit on your arse for fifty years and hang your hat on a
    pension.

It's no go my honey love, it's no go my poppet;
Work your hands from day to day, the winds will blow the
    profit.
The glass is falling hour by hour, the glass will fall for ever,
But if you break the bloody glass you won't hold up the
    weather.

The Cow Who Jumped over the Moon
by *Celia Johnson*
*(1908–82)**

The cow who jumped over the moon remarked,
Gazing up at the sky,
I think I shall try those Olympics,
There's no one as clever as I.
If I went in for the high jump
I'd be sure of a medal you see –
Or is it grammatically better to say,
There's no one as clever as me?

The head of the herd, called Daisy,
Methodically chewing the cud,
Said: 'You haven't jumped over the moon my dear,
Since eons before the flood –
And though it was simply delightful
I must proffer a slight demur,
What I am trying to say is –
You are not so young as you were.'

'As far as I can remember
That dog was rather a flop,
I am all for some laughter and jollity

---

* This piece of nonsense was written by the distinguished British actress, Dame Celia Johnson (best remembered for the 1945 film, *Brief Encounter*) and performed by her at a house party given by Queen Elizabeth the Queen Mother in March 1982, only a few weeks before Dame Celia died. According to Sir Roy Strong, who was there, the 'wonderfully silly readings' stole the show.

But he never knew when to stop –
And the spoon with that dish were disgraceful
They caused the most fearful to do.
There hasn't been quite such a rumpus
Since the woman who lived in that shoe.'

The cow who jumped over the moon replied
Giving a tentative hop:
'There may be something in what you say
It's a long way over the top.
I think I shall have to forgo the fame
And the dais with me in the middle
And the honour and glory, the flags and the cheers
And the band playing "Hey diddle-diddle".'

The head of the herd (called Daisy)
Said with a satisfied glance:
'Your nobleness does you credit
One must give the heifers a chance,
And thanks to your shining example
Some of them aren't too dud,'
And after this selfless decision
They returned to chewing the cud.

Of pygmies, palms and pirates
by Mervyn Peake
(1911–68)

Of pygmies, palms and pirates,
Of islands and lagoons,
Of blood-bespattered frigates,
Of crags and Octoroons,
Of whales and broken bottles,
Of quicksands cold and grey,
Of ullages and dottles,
I have no more to say.

Of barley, corn and furrows,
Of farms and turf that heaves
Above such ghostly burrows
As twitch on summer eves
Of fallow-land and pasture,
Of skies both pink and grey,
I made my statement last year
And have no more to say.

Hot and Cold
by Roald Dahl
(1916–90)

A woman who my mother knows
Came in and took off all her clothes.

Said I, not being very old,
'By golly gosh, you must be cold!'

'No, no!' she cried. 'Indeed I'm not!
I'm feeling devilishly hot!'

In the Land of the Bumbley Boo
by Spike Milligan
(1918–2002)

In the Land of the Bumbley Boo
The People are red white and blue,
They never blow noses,
Or ever wear closes,
What a sensible thing to do!

In the Land of the Bumbley Boo
You can buy Lemon pie at the zoo;

They give away foxes
In little Pink Boxes
And Bottles of Dandylion Stew.

In the Land of the Bumbley Boo
You never see a Gnu,
But thousands of cats
Wearing trousers and hats
Made of Pumpkins and Pelican Glue!

Chorus
Oh, the Bumbley Boo! the Bumbley Boo!
That's the place for me and you!
So hurry! Let's run!
The train leaves at one!
For the Land of the Bumbley Boo!
The wonderful Bumbley Boo-Boo-Boo!
The Wonderful Bumbley BOO!!!

The Midnight Skaters
by Roger McGough
(born 1937)

It is midnight in the ice-rink
And all is cool and still.
Darkness seems to hold its breath
Nothing moves, until

Out of the kitchen, one by one,
    The cutlery comes creeping,
Quiet as mice to the brink of the ice
    While all the world is sleeping.

Then suddenly, a serving-spoon
    Switches on the light,
And the silver swoops upon the ice
    Screaming with delight.

The knives are high-speed skaters
    Round and round they race,
Blades hissing, sissing,
    Whizzing at a dizzy pace.

Forks twirl like dancers
    Pirouetting on the spot.
Teaspoons (who take no chances)
    Hold hands and giggle a lot.

All night long the fun goes on
    Until the sun, their friend,
Gives the warning signal
    That all good things must end.

So they slink back to the darkness
    Of the kitchen cutlery-drawer
And steel themselves to wait
    Until it's time to skate once more.

At eight the canteen ladies
   Breeze in as good as gold
To lay the tables and wonder
   Why the cutlery is so cold.

Teabag
by Peter Dixon
(born 1937)

I'd like to be a teabag,
and stay at home all day
and talk to other teabags
in a teabag sort of way.

I'd love to be a teabag,
and lie in a little box
and never have to wash my face
or change my dirty socks.

I'd like to be a Tetley bag,
an Earl Grey one perhaps,
and doze all day and lie around
with Earl Grey kind of chaps.

I wouldn't have to do a thing,
no homework, jobs or chores –
just lie inside a comfy box
of teabags and their snores.

I wouldn't have to do exams,
I needn't tidy rooms,
or sweep the floor or feed the cat
or wash up all the spoons.

I wouldn't have to do a thing –
a life of bliss, you see . . .
except that once in all my life

I'd make a cup of tea!

Horace
by Monty Python
(1971)*

Much to his Mum and Dad's dismay,
Horace ate himself one day.
He didn't stop to say his grace,
He just sat down and ate his face.
'We can't have this!' His Dad declared,

* John Cleese, Terry Gilliam, Eric Idle, Terry Jones, Michael Palin and Gra-
ham Chapman created *Monty Python's Flying Circus* for BBC television in 1969.
Forty-five episodes were made over four series. 'Horace' appeared in *Monty
Python's Big Red Book*, published by Methuen in 1971. To sell the book the
publishers took the Pythons on a promotional bus tour around the UK. Jilly
Cooper, Leslie Thomas and I went, too, because we also had books published
by Methuen that year. I remember Michael Palin telling us that the title they
had thought of for the series was *A Horse, a Spoon and a Bucket*, but the BBC
suggested *John Cleese's Flying Circus*. The team agreed to the *Flying Circus* bit,
but wanted a made-up name to go with it. As a group they came up with 'Mr
Python'; Eric Idle came up with 'Monty'.

'If that lad's ate, he should be shared.'
But even as they spoke they saw,
Horace eating more and more:
First his legs and then his thighs,
His arms, his nose, his hair, his eyes . . .
'Stop him someone!' Mother cried,
'Those eyeballs would be better fried!'
But all too late, for they were gone,
And he had started on his dong . . .
'Oh! foolish child!' the father mourns,
'You could have deep fried that with prawns,
Some parsely and some tartar sauce . . .'
But H. was on his second course:
His liver and his lights and lung,
His ears, his neck, his chin, his tongue;
'To think I raised him from the cot,
And now he's going to scoff the lot!'
His Mother cried: 'What shall we do?
What's left won't even make a stew . . .'
And as she wept her son was seen,
To eat his head, his heart, his spleen.
And there he lay, a boy no more,
Just a stomach, on the floor . . .
None the less, since it was his,
They ate it – that's what haggis is.*

---

* No it isn't. Haggis is a kind of stuffed black pudding eaten by the Scots and
considered by them to be not only a delicacy but fit for human consumption.
The minced heart, liver and lungs of a sheep, calf or other animal's inner
organs are mixed with oatmeal, sealed and boiled in maw in the sheep's intes-
tinal stomach-bag and . . . Excuse me a minute. (Ed.)

Chapter Seven

Animal Magic
Welcome to the menagerie

Meow means 'woof' in cat.

George Carlin (1937–2008)

I'm with Anatole France: 'Until one has loved an animal, a part of one's soul remains unawakened.'

I could have created a complete anthology of animal poems to learn by heart, but I have forced myself to settle on sixteen:

Four poems about cats
– by Thomas Gray, Eleanor Farjeon, T. S. Eliot
and Brian Patten

Three favourites, so well loved they could almost
be described as poetic national treasures
– by William Blake, Christina Rossetti and
G. K. Chesterton

Three verses to make you smile
– by Ogden Nash (American), Theodore
Roethke (American), and Flanders and
Swann (English, very)

Four great nature poems
– by one American poet, Denise Levertov, and
two English ones, Thom Gunn and Ted Hughes

Plus a poem by the contemporary performance
poet, Hollie McNish, about the possibility
of becoming a butterfly, 'Cocoon' – and,
as a playful bonus, a verse that's definitely
not for vegetarians: 'Any Part of Piggy'
by Noël Coward

Tuck in.

'Ode on the Death of a Favourite Cat
Drowned in a Tub of Goldfishes'
by Thomas Gray
*(1716-71)**

'Twas on a lofty vase's side,
Where China's gayest art had dyed
The azure flowers that blow;
Demurest of the tabby kind,
The pensive Selima, reclined,
Gazed on the lake below.

Her conscious tail her joy declared;
The fair round face, the snowy beard,
The velvet of her paws,
Her coat, that with the tortoise vies,
Her ears of jet, and emerald eyes,
She saw; and purred applause.

---

* Gray was a classical scholar, a don at Cambridge, and a popular poet, although he only published thirteen poems during his lifetime and declined the invitation to become Poet Laureate in 1857. (William Whitehead got the gig instead. Indeed, who he?) This playful elegy (telling the reverse of the story that led to my own brief ode featured on page 61) commemorates the passing of Selima, the cat of Horace Walpole, the writer best remembered for saying, 'The world is a tragedy to those who feel, but a comedy to those who think.' Walpole later displayed the fatal china vase on a pedestal at his house, Strawberry Hill, in Twickenham.

Still had she gazed; but 'midst the tide
Two angel forms were seen to glide,
The genii of the stream;
Their scaly armour's Tyrian hue
Through richest purple to the view
Betrayed a golden gleam.

The hapless nymph with wonder saw;
A whisker first and then a claw,
With many an ardent wish,
She stretched in vain to reach the prize.
What female heart can gold despise?
What cat's averse to fish?

Presumptuous maid! with looks intent
Again she stretch'd, again she bent,
Nor knew the gulf between.
(Malignant Fate sat by, and smiled)
The slippery verge her feet beguiled,
She tumbled headlong in.
Eight times emerging from the flood
She mewed to every watery god,
Some speedy aid to send.
No dolphin came, no Nereid stirred;
Nor cruel Tom, nor Susan heard;
A Favourite has no friend!

From hence, ye beauties, undeceived,
Know, one false step is ne'er retrieved,
And be with caution bold.
Not all that tempts your wandering eyes
And heedless hearts, is lawful prize;
Nor all that glisters, gold.

The Tyger*
by *William Blake*
(1757–1827)

Tyger Tyger, burning bright,
In the forests of the night;
What immortal hand or eye,
Could frame thy fearful symmetry?

In what distant deeps or skies,
Burnt the fire of thine eyes?
On what wings dare he aspire?
What the hand, dare seize the fire?

And what shoulder, & what art,
Could twist the sinews of thy heart?
And when thy heart began to beat,
What dread hand? & what dread feet?

---

* Why did Blake spell his 'Tyger' with a *y*? It was a less archaic spelling of the word then than it is now, but it was still an old-style spelling even in 1794 when the poem was first published. Perhaps Blake wanted to give his Tyger a measure of mystery and felt the *y* helped with that. Perhaps he liked the *y* in 'Tyger' because it chimed with the double *y* in 'symmetry'. Today, with Shakespeare and Milton, for example, editors usually modernize the spelling and punctuation. Not so with Blake in this instance, not only because the *y* feels integral to the poem, but also because Blake was an artist and engraver and published many of his poems, including this one, as visual compositions. The *y* in 'Tyger' is there in Blake's original artwork and, consequently, for ever.

What the hammer? what the chain,
In what furnace was thy brain?
What the anvil? what dread grasp,
Dare its deadly terrors clasp!

When the stars threw down their spears
And water'd heaven with their tears:
Did he smile his work to see?
Did he who made the Lamb make thee?

Tyger Tyger burning bright,
In the forests of the night:
What immortal hand or eye,
Dare frame thy fearful symmetry?

The Lambs of Grasmere
by *Christina Rossetti*
(1830–94)

The upland flocks grew starved and thinned;
   Their shepherds scarce could feed the lambs
Whose milkless mothers butted them,
   Or who were orphaned of their dams.
The lambs athirst for mother's milk
   Filled all the place with piteous sounds:
Their mothers' bones made white for miles
   The pastureless wet pasture grounds.

Day after day, night after night,
    From lamb to lamb the shepherds went,
With teapots for the bleating mouths
    Instead of nature's nourishment.
The little shivering gaping things
    Soon knew the step that brought them aid,
And fondled the protecting hand,
    And rubbed it with a woolly head.

Then, as the days waxed on to weeks,
    It was a pretty sight to see
These lambs with frisky heads and tails
    Skipping and leaping on the lea,
Bleating in tender, trustful tones,
    Resting on rocky crag or mound,
And following the beloved feet
    That once had sought for them and found.

These very shepherds of their flocks,
    These loving lambs so meek to please,
Are worthy of recording words
    And honour in their due degrees:
So I might live a hundred years,
    And roam from strand to foreign strand,
Yet not forget this flooded spring
    And scarce-saved lambs of Westmoreland.

The Donkey
by G. K. Chesterton
(1874–1936)

When fishes flew and forests walked
  And figs grew upon thorn,
Some moment when the moon was blood
  Then surely I was born.

With monstrous head and sickening cry
  And ears like errant wings,
The devil's walking parody
  On all four-footed things.

The tattered outlaw of the earth,
  Of ancient crooked will;
Starve, scourge, deride me: I am dumb,
  I keep my secret still.

Fools! For I also had my hour;
  One far fierce hour and sweet:
There was a shout about my ears,
  And palms before my feet.

Cats sleep, anywhere

by Eleanor Farjeon

(1881–1965)

Cats sleep, anywhere,
Any table, any chair
Top of piano, window-ledge,
In the middle, on the edge,
Open drawer, empty shoe,
Anybody's lap will do,
Fitted in a cardboard box,
In the cupboard, with your frocks –
Anywhere! They don't care!
Cats sleep anywhere.

Macavity: the Mystery Cat
by T. S. Eliot
*(1888–1965)**

Macavity's a Mystery Cat: he's called the Hidden Paw –
For he's the master criminal who can defy the Law.
He's the bafflement of Scotland Yard, the Flying Squad's
    despair:
For when they reach the scene of crime – *Macavity's not there*!

Macavity, Macavity, there's no one like Macavity,
He's broken every human law, he breaks the law of gravity.
His powers of levitation would make a fakir stare,
And when you reach the scene of crime – *Macavity's not there*!
You may seek him in the basement, you may look up in
    the air –
But I tell you once and once again, *Macavity's not there*!

---

* Like so many of the greatest poets – Edward Lear, Edgar Allan Poe, W. B. Yeats, William Carlos Williams, Allen Ginsberg, Sylvia Plath – and so many of the giants of literature – Samuel Johnson, Charles Dickens, Mark Twain, Ernest Hemingway, William Burroughs, Patricia Highsmith – Thomas Stearns Eliot loved cats. In the 1930s, as 'Old Possum', he wrote a series of amusing poems about cats and sent them to his godchildren. They were collected and published in 1939, with Eliot's own cover illustrations, and then republished in 1940, illustrated in full by Nicolas Bentley, son of Eric Bentley, the man who invented the clerihew. In the 1950s, as a small boy, I was a server at St Stephen's, a High Anglican church, in London's Gloucester Road, which is where I met Eliot, who worshipped at the church and had been a churchwarden there. One Christmas, I was chosen to given a reading at the St Stephen's carol service. Mr Eliot generously congratulated me afterwards and inspired me to learn 'Macavity' by heart and perform it for him.

Macavity's a ginger cat, he's very tall and thin;
You would know him if you saw him, for his eyes are sunken in.
His brow is deeply lined with thought, his head is highly
   domed;
His coat is dusty from neglect, his whiskers are uncombed.
He sways his head from side to side, with movements like a
   snake;
And when you think he's half asleep, he's always wide awake.

Macavity, Macavity, there's no one like Macavity,
For he's a fiend in feline shape, a monster of depravity.
You may meet him in a by-street, you may see him in the
   square —
But when a crime's discovered, then *Macavity's not there*!

He's outwardly respectable. (They say he cheats at cards.)
And his footprints are not found in any file of Scotland Yard's.
And when the larder's looted, or the jewel-case is rifled,
Or when the milk is missing, or another Peke's been stifled,
Or the greenhouse glass is broken, and the trellis past repair —
Ay, there's the wonder of the thing! *Macavity's not there*!

And when the Foreign Office find a Treaty's gone astray,
Or the Admiralty lose some plans and drawings by the way,
There may be a scrap of paper in the hall or on the stair —
But it's useless to investigate — *Macavity's not there*!
And when the loss has been disclosed, the Secret Service say:
'It *must* have been Macavity!' – but he's a mile away.
You'll be sure to find him resting, or a-licking of his thumbs,
Or engaged in doing complicated long division sums.

Macavity, Macavity, there's no one like Macavity,
There never was a Cat of such deceitfulness and suavity.

He always has an alibi, and one or two to spare:
At whatever time the deed took place – MACAVITY WASN'T
  THERE!
And they say that all the Cats whose wicked deeds are widely
  known
(I might mention Mungojerrie, I might mention
  Griddlebone)
Are nothing more than agents for the Cat who all the time
Just controls their operations: the Napoleon of Crime!

Any Part of Piggy
by Noël Coward
(1899–1973)

Any part of piggy
Is quite all right with me
Ham from Westphalia, ham from Parma
Ham as lean as the Dalai Lama
Ham from Virginia, ham from York,
Trotters, sausages, hot roast pork.
Crackling crisp for my teeth to grind on
Bacon with or without the rind on
Though humanitarian
I'm not a vegetarian.
I'm neither crank nor prude nor prig
And though it may sound infra dig
Any part of darling pig
Is perfectly fine with me.

The Turkey
by Ogden Nash
(1902–71)*

There is nothing more perky
Than a masculine turkey
When he struts he struts
With no ifs or buts.
When his face is apoplectic
His harem grows hectic,
And when he gobbles
Their universe wobbles.

The Sloth
by Theodore Roethke
(1908–63)

In moving-slow he has no Peer.
You ask him something in his Ear,
He thinks about it for a Year;

---

* The American poet Frederic Ogden Nash wrote scores of terse verses cele-
brating the animal kingdom and even produced a little book called *Ogden
Nash's Zoo*. In my view, someone needs to do for Nash's *Zoo* what Andrew
Lloyd Webber did for T. S. Eliot's *Cats*.

And, then, before he says a Word
There, upside down (unlike a Bird),
He will assume that you have Heard –

A most Ex-as-per-at-ing Lug.
But should you call his manner Smug,
He'll sigh and give his Branch a Hug;

Then off again to Sleep he goes,
Still swaying gently by his Toes,
And you just *know* he knows he knows.

To the Snake
by Denise Levertov
(1923–97)

Green Snake, when I hung you round my neck
and stroked your cold, pulsing throat
                as you hissed to me, glinting
arrowy gold scales, and I felt
                the weight of you on my shoulders,
and the whispering silver of your dryness
                sounded close at my ears –

Green Snake – I swore to my companions that certainly
                you were harmless! But truly
I had no certainty, and no hope, only desiring
                to hold you, for that joy,
                                which left

a long wake of pleasure, as the leaves moved
and you faded into the pattern
of grass and shadows, and I returned
smiling and haunted, to a dark morning.

The Hippopotamus Song
*by Michael Flanders (1922–75) and
Donald Swann (1923–94)**

A bold hippopotamus was standing one day
On the banks of the cool Shalimar
He gazed at the bottom as he peacefully lay
By the light of the evening star
Away on the hilltop sat combing her hair
His fair hippopotami maid
The hippopotamus was no ignoramus
And sang her this sweet serenade

Chorus:
Mud, mud, glorious mud

---

* Flanders and Swann were a British musical double-act. They went to the
same school (Westminster) and university college (Christ Church, Oxford),
and wrote more than a hundred comic songs together. In 1956 they performed
At the Drop of a Hat, the first of their two long-running shows. The Suez Crisis
that same year, sparked by President Nasser of Egypt's decision to national-
ize the Anglo-French Suez Canal Company to pay for the construction of the
Aswan High Dam, prompted the addition of the extra verse to this, probably
their most popular song.

Nothing quite like it for cooling the blood
So follow me follow, down to the hollow
And there let me wallow in glorious mud

The fair hippopotama he aimed to entice
From her seat on that hilltop above
As she hadn't got a ma to give her advice
Came tiptoeing down to her love
Like thunder the forest re-echoed the sound
Of the song that they sang when they met
His inamorata adjusted her garter
And lifted her voice in duet

Chorus

Now more hippopotami began to convene
On the banks of that river so wide
I wonder now what am I to say of the scene
That ensued by the Shalimar side
They dived all at once with an ear-splitting sposh
Then rose to the surface again
A regular army of hippopotami
All singing this haunting refrain

Chorus

(*Extra verse:*)
The amorous hippopotamus whose love song we know
Is now married and father of ten,
He murmurs, 'God rot 'em!' as he watches them grow,
And he longs to be single again!
He'll gambol no more on the banks of the Nile,
Which Nasser is flooding next spring,

With hippopotamas in silken pyjamas
No more will he teach them to sing . . .

Chorus

Considering the Snail
by Thom Gunn
(1929–2004)

The snail pushes through a green
night, for the grass is heavy
with water and meets over
the bright path he makes, where rain
has darkened the earth's dark. He
moves in a wood of desire,

pale antlers barely stirring
as he hunts. I cannot tell
what power is at work, drenched there
with purpose, knowing nothing.
What is a snail's fury? All
I think is that if later

I parted the blades above
the tunnel and saw the thin
trail of broken white across
litter, I would never have
imagined the slow passion
to that deliberate progress.

Hawk Roosting

by Ted Hughes
(1930–98)

I sit in the top of the wood, my eyes closed.
Inaction, no falsifying dream
Between my hooked head and hooked feet:
Or in sleep rehearse perfect kills and eat.

The convenience of the high trees!
The air's buoyancy and the sun's ray
Are of advantage to me;
And the earth's face upward for my inspection.

My feet are locked upon the rough bark.
It took the whole of Creation
To produce my foot, my each feather:
Now I hold Creation in my foot

Or fly up, and revolve it all slowly –
I kill where I please because it is all mine.
There is no sophistry in my body:
My manners are tearing off heads –

The allotment of death.
For the one path of my flight is direct
Through the bones of the living.
No arguments assert my right:

The sun is behind me.
Nothing has changed since I began.
My eye has permitted no change.
I am going to keep things like this.

Inessential Things
by Brian Patten
(born 1946)

What do cats remember of days?

They remember the ways in from the cold,
The warmest spot, the place of food.
They remember the places of pain, their enemies,
the irritation of birds, the warm fumes of the soil,
the usefulness of dust.
They remember the creak of a bed, the sound
of their owner's footsteps,
the taste of fish, the loveliness of cream.
Cats remember what is essential of days.
Letting all other memories go as of no worth
they sleep sounder than we,
whose hearts break remembering so many
inessential things.

Cocoon
by Hollie McNish
(born 1984)

I really love cycling. If I could get a job cycling and doing poetry, that would be ace. Anyhow, wrote this when I got to work . . .

This is as close as I'll ever be to a butterfly
rain coat zipped up to my chin
for the half hour bike ride
to work

Hair bunned
at the back
to fit in the hood
helmet clipped tightly
– I am waterproof

Now pace reaches peak
the streets are attacked
Cold frosts the trees
but the sweat coats my back

until one minute left
I let myself go
cycling slow
as I unbutton clothes
jacket unzipped
helmet unclipped
from beneath
hood stripped from my forehead
hairband released

143

Hair ruffled with hands
to be free in the wind
body to elements
cool down my skin

At that moment
I open
and peel myself free

I feel as close to
a new butterfly
as I'll ever be

Chapter Eight

The Upstart Crow
'Speak the speech, I pray you'

As you will know if you have seen Ben Elton's brilliant television sitcom about William Shakespeare, it was Shakespeare's contemporary, the playwright Robert Greene, who first called Shakespeare the 'upstart crow'. Greene was jealous of Shakespeare's genius. Ben Jonson, another poet-playwright of the era, was more generous. He dubbed Shakespeare 'the Swan of Avon' and recognized 'He was not of an age, but for all time!'

The poet Robert Graves (1895–1985) said: 'The remarkable thing about Shakespeare is that he is really very good – in spite of all the people who say he is very good.' The critic William Hazlitt (1778–1830) was on the money, too: 'If we wish to know the force of human genius we should read Shakespeare. If we wish to see the insignificance of human learning we may study his commentators.'

So much guff has been written about Shakespeare, I am not going to add to it here. I am simply offering you ten great Shakespeare speeches to learn by heart. If you enjoy them, you will be pleased to know there are many more where they came from.

And you will be pleased to know, too, that if you can learn

and speak 'The Owl and the Pussy-cat', you can learn and speak the poetry of Shakespeare. As ever, 'trust the author' is the basic rule.

Speak the speech, I pray you, as I pronounced it to you, trippingly on the tongue. But if you mouth it as many of your players do, I had as lief the town-crier spoke my lines. Nor do not saw the air too much with your hand, thus, but use all gently. For in the very torrent, tempest, and as I may say, the whirlwind of your passion, you must acquire and beget a temperance that may give it smoothness. O, it offends me to the soul to hear a robustious periwig-pated fellow tear a passion to tatters, to very rags, to split the ears of the groundlings, who for the most part are capable of nothing but inexplicable dumb shows and noise . . . Be not too tame neither, but let your own discretion be your tutor. Suit the action to the word, the word to the action, with this special observance: that you o'erstep not the modesty of nature. For anything so o'erdone is from the purpose of playing, whose end, both at the first and now, was and is, to hold, as 'twere, the mirror up to nature; to show virtue her own feature, scorn her own image, and the very age and body of the time his form and pressure.

Hamlet's Advice to the Players
Hamlet, Act 3, Scene 2

There are other rules, of course, and, if you want to dig deeper, I reckon the best two books on the subject are *Speaking the Speech* by Giles Block, sometime 'Master of the Word' at Shakespeare's Globe in London, and *Shakespeare's Advice to the Players* by Sir Peter Hall, the founder of the Royal Shake-speare Company. For both of them, it's all there on the page. For Peter Hall, 'the sanctity of the line is paramount'. Hall claimed that any actor could learn to speak Shakespeare in 'a few weeks', although greatness might take a little longer: 'Laurence Olivier took nearly twenty years before he began to ride on the lines like an expert skier.'

In case you don't have twenty years to spare, here are the Brandreth Rules for Speaking Shakespeare:

1. Read the speech right through.
2. Understand it. Translate it into modern English, phrase by phrase, to make sure you know exactly what Shakespeare is saying. Look up any words or references that seem unfamiliar.
3. Learn it line by line, one line at a time. Understand each sentence or thought sequence, but don't learn it by sentence, punctuation or thought: learn it line by line. Remember: 'the sanctity of the line is paramount'.
4. Find the beat, feel the rhythm. It's the basic da DUM da DUM da DUM da DUM da DUM that makes much of Shakespeare surprisingly easy to learn. (Judi Dench was doing it at three, FFS!)
5. Use your own voice. Just because it's Shakespeare, you don't have to put on a specially sonorous actory voice or speak in a strange accent that isn't your own. Be yourself. Sound as you sound.
6. Trust the words and tell the story. You don't need to add any extra 'feeling'. Shakespeare has done it all for you.

On 27 February 1995, when they were about to make a film together of Shakespeare's Richard III, *the actor Sir Ian McKellen wrote to the director, Richard Loncraine, on the subject of Shakespeare's blank verse.*

I'm glad at last we're going to do this film.
Three years has been a long, long time to wait.
But now I thought I should sit down and try
to clarify what blank verse means to me;
and thereby reassure your doubting heart.
If, incidentally, you read these lines out loud,
I'm sure you'll find them tripping off the tongue.
And yet, of course, they're written in blank verse!

I'll stop that game and go back to the start. (And that's another blank verse line, dear heart!) Before Christopher Marlowe (who was born in the same year as Shakespeare – 1564) came down from Cambridge and wrote his first play, the only English drama had been written in rather doggerelly verse and told simple allegorical stories about good and evil, mostly culled from the Bible. Marlowe was also concerned with morality but introduced to the London stage fictional stories about famous people (*Tamburlaine the Great* and *Dr. Faustus* for example). He needed a more pliant sort of speech than the old drama. It didn't occur to him that the prose of everyday speech would be appropriate – after all his characters were often bigger than life and he wanted them to sound especially grand. And so he lighted upon a formal rhythm which linked all the possibilities of poetry with the informality of the audience's normal speech.

Blank verse means verse that doesn't rhyme. Its meter is called pentameter because there are five (the Greek 'penta') feet to each line. Each foot contains two beats, in the rhythm of the heart – 'de-dum' – with the stress on the second beat. And that's all there is to it. I like the heartbeat point – just as it's nice that we have ten fingers and the blank verse line has ten beats. I imagine Marlowe counting out the beat with his digits. Not that he'd really have needed to, because (cf. my opening paragraph) the general rhythm of English speech – and modern English – often coincides with the sound of blank verse. Shakespeare took blank verse and ran with it. By the end of his career – in *Coriolanus*, say, and *Antony & Cleopatra* – he scarcely wrote a regular blank verse line being more fascinated by complicated counterpoint and jazzy rhythms. But *Richard III* is an early play – the first really good one he wrote . . .

I hope you'll want you and me to go through it all line by line but here are a few general notes that I would expect the cast to take into account, as they indicate that the verse is designed to help and not hinder:

1. Read the line out loud and stress the 'de-dums' . . .

2. Appreciate that the last word of the line is invariably the most important for the sense and for the sound and it is a sort of teaser, leading on to the beginning of the line that follows. That's the energy of blank verse – it is always moving onwards, often urgently . . .

3. In regular blank verse, each line generally contains one thought, so that the speeches are made up of a series of logical links. It disturbs this forward movement if the actor does too many 'naturalistic' pauses in the middle of the lines. Shakespeare's characters love talking (rather like the Irish) and speak simultaneously with thinking. The

time for the actors to think what they will say next is whilst someone else is speaking. During their own speeches, the natural place to pause (but then only when really necessary for effect) is usually at the end of the blank verse line – even if the end of a sentence occurs in the middle of the line . . .

4. There is never a need for the verse to be obvious to the audience. The 'voice beautiful' is a relic not of Shakespeare's style but of Victorian theatres, which were so huge that actors needed to sing out the lines in order to be heard at the back of the distant gallery. I would expect our dialogue to sound swiftly conversational most of the time; as Hamlet advised the actors at Elsinore:

'Speak the speech, I pray you, as I pronounced it to you, trippingly on the tongue. But if you "mouth" it, as many of your players do, I had as lief the town-crier spoke my lines.'

And that, for now, is all I've got to say. – Ian McKellen

From *Richard III*
first performed around
1592–3

Richard, Duke of Gloucester, begins the play with this speech addressed to himself and to the audience. After a lengthy civil war, Richard's older brother, Edward IV, now sits on the throne as the first Yorkist King of England, but Richard, born deformed, sees himself as sovereign and plans to set his brother the king against his other brother, the Duke of Clarence.

Now is the winter of our discontent
Made glorious summer by this son of York,
And all the clouds that loured upon our house
In the deep bosom of the ocean buried.
Now are our brows bound with victorious wreaths,
Our bruisèd arms hung up for monuments,
Our stern alarums changed to merry meetings,
Our dreadful marches to delightful measures.
Grim-visaged war hath smoothed his wrinkled front,
And now, instead of mounting barbèd steeds
To fright the souls of fearful adversaries,
He capers nimbly in a lady's chamber
To the lascivious pleasing of a lute.
But I, that am not shaped for sportive tricks,
Nor made to court an amorous looking-glass;
I, that am rudely stamped, and want love's majesty
To strut before a wanton ambling nymph;
I, that am curtailed of this fair proportion,
Cheated of feature by dissembling nature,
Deformed, unfinished, sent before my time
Into this breathing world scarce half made up,
And that so lamely and unfashionable
That dogs bark at me as I halt by them –
Why, I in this weak piping time of peace
Have no delight to pass away the time,
Unless to spy my shadow in the sun
And descant on mine own deformity.
And therefore, since I cannot prove a lover,
To entertain these fair well-spoken days,
I am determinèd to prove a villain,
And hate the idle pleasures of these days.
Plots have I laid, inductions dangerous,
By drunken prophecies, libels, and dreams

To set my brother Clarence and the King
In deadly hate the one against the other.
And if King Edward be as true and just
As I am subtle, false, and treacherous,
This day should Clarence closely be mewed up
About a prophecy, which says that 'G'
Of Edward's heirs the murderer shall be.
Dive thoughts down to my soul; here
Clarence comes.

From *Romeo and Juliet*
first performed around
1594–5

Juliet appears at her balcony and Romeo, in the garden below, sees her and is smitten.

But soft, what light through yonder window breaks?
It is the east, and Juliet is the sun.
Arise, fair sun, and kill the envious moon,
Who is already sick and pale with grief
That thou, her maid, art far more fair than she.
Be not her maid, since she is envious.
Her vestal livery is but sick and green,
And none but fools do wear it; cast it off.
It is my lady, O, it is my love.
O that she knew she were!
She speaks, yet she says nothing. What of that?

Her eye discourses; I will answer it.
I am too bold; 'tis not to me she speaks.
Two of the fairest stars in all the heaven,
Having some business, do entreat her eyes
To twinkle in their spheres till they return.
What if her eyes were there, they in her head?
The brightness of her cheek would shame those stars
As daylight doth a lamp; her eyes in heaven
Would through the airy region stream so bright
That birds would sing and think it were not night.
See how she leans her cheek upon her hand.
O, that I were a glove upon that hand,
That I might touch that cheek.

From *Richard II*
first performed around
1595–6

John of Gaunt, Duke of Lancaster, is dying. Critical of the king, Richard II, he awaits his arrival at Ely House in London, and talks with his brother, the Duke of York, reflecting on the nature of England and the country's future prospects.

Methinks I am a prophet new inspired
And thus expiring do foretell of him.
His rash, fierce blaze of riot cannot last,
For violent fires soon burn out themselves;
Small showers last long, but sudden storms are short.

He tires betimes that spurs too fast betimes.
With eager feeding food doth choke the feeder.
Light vanity, insatiate cormorant,
Consuming means, soon preys upon itself.
This royal throne of kings, this sceptred isle,
This earth of majesty, this seat of Mars,
This other Eden, demi-paradise,
This fortress built by nature for herself
Against infection and the hand of war,
This happy breed of men, this little world,
This precious stone set in the silver sea,
Which serves it in the office of a wall,
Or as a moat defensive to a house
Against the envy of less happier lands;
This blessèd plot, this earth, this realm, this England,
This nurse, this teeming womb of royal kings,
Feared by their breed and famous by their birth,
Renownèd for their deeds as far from home
For Christian service and true chivalry
As is the sepulchre in stubborn Jewry,
Of the world's ransom, blessèd Mary's son;
This land of such dear souls, this dear, dear land,
Dear for her reputation through the world,
Is now leased out – I die pronouncing it –
Like to a tenement or pelting farm.
England, bound in with the triumphant sea,
Whose rocky shore beats back the envious siege
Of wat'ry Neptune, is now bound in with shame,
With inky blots and rotten parchment bonds.
That England that was wont to conquer others
Hath made a shameful conquest of itself.
Ah, would the scandal vanish with my life,
How happy then were my ensuing death!

From *The Merchant of Venice*
first performed around
1596–7

*In court, Portia, disguised as the young lawyer Balthazar, pleads with
Shylock, the Jew, to show mercy in his suit against Antonio, the merchant
of Venice, who owes him a considerable sum of money.*

The quality of mercy is not strained.
It droppeth as the gentle rain from heaven
Upon the place beneath. It is twice blest:
It blesseth him that gives, and him that takes.
'Tis mightiest in the mightiest; it becomes
The thronèd monarch better than his crown.
His sceptre shows the force of temporal power,
The attribute to awe and majesty,
Wherein doth sit the dread and fear of kings;
But mercy is above this sceptred sway.
It is enthronèd in the hearts of kings;
It is an attribute to God himself;
And earthly power doth then show likest God's
When mercy seasons justice. Therefore, Jew,
Though justice be thy plea, consider this:
That in the course of justice none of us
Should see salvation. We do pray for mercy,
And that same prayer doth teach us all to render
The deeds of mercy. I have spoke thus much
To mitigate the justice of thy plea,
Which, if thou follow, this strict court of Venice
Must needs give sentence 'gainst the merchant there.

From *Henry V*
first performed around
1598–9

Only having space for one speech from Henry V, *I have chosen this rather than the equally famous 'Once more unto the breach, dear friends' because, to me, though less rousing, it is more moving. St Crispin's Day falls on 25 October and is the feast day of the Christian saints Crispin and Crispinian (also known as Crispinus and Crispianus), twins who were martyred around the year 286. The Battle of Agincourt took place on St Crispin's Day in 1415, when the English achieved a famous victory although their forces were greatly outnumbered by the French. Another notable battle to take place on St Crispin's Day was the Battle of Balaclava during the Crimean War in 1584 (see Tennyson's poem, 'The Charge of the Light Brigade', on page 194).*

This day is called the feast of Crispian.
He that outlives this day and comes safe home
Will stand a-tiptoe when the day is named,
And rouse him at the name of Crispian.
He that shall live this day, and see old age
Will yearly on the vigil feast his neighbours,
And say, 'Tomorrow is Saint Crispian.'
Then will he strip his sleeve and show his scars,
And say, 'These wounds I had on Crispin's day.'
Old men forget; yea, all shall be forgot,
But he'll remember, with advantages,
What feats he did that day. Then shall our names,
Familiar in his mouth as household words –
Harry the King, Bedford and Exeter,

Warwick and Talbot, Salisbury and Gloucester –
Be in their flowing cups freshly remembered.
This story shall the good man teach his son,
And Crispin Crispian shall ne'er go by
From this day to the ending of the world
But we in it shall be rememberèd,
We few, we happy few, we band of brothers.
For he today that sheds his blood with me
Shall be my brother; be he ne'er so vile,
This day shall gentle his condition.
And gentlemen in England now abed
Shall think themselves accursed they were not here,
And hold their manhoods cheap whiles any speaks
That fought with us upon Saint Crispin's day.

From *As You Like It*
first performed around
1599–1600

*The 'Melancholy Jaques', a courtier to the exiled Duke Senior, speaks
this famous speech in Act 2 Scene 7 of* As You Like It.

      All the world's a stage,
And all the men and women merely players.
They have their exits and their entrances,
And one man in his time plays many parts,
His acts being seven ages. At first the infant,
Mewling and puking in the nurse's arms.

Then the whining schoolboy with his satchel
And shining morning face, creeping like snail
Unwillingly to school. And then the lover,
Sighing like furnace, with a woeful ballad
Made to his mistress' eyebrow. Then a soldier,
Full of strange oaths, and bearded like the pard,
Jealous in honour, sudden and quick in quarrel,
Seeking the bubble reputation
Even in the cannon's mouth. And then the justice,
In fair round belly, with good capon lined,
With eyes severe and beard of formal cut,
Full of wise saws and modern instances;
And so he plays his part. The sixth age shifts
Into the lean and slippered pantaloon,
With spectacles on nose and pouch on side,
His youthful hose well saved, a world too wide
For his shrunk shank, and his big manly voice,
Turning again toward childish treble, pipes
And whistles in his sound. Last scene of all,
That ends this strange eventful history,
Is second childishness, and mere oblivion,
Sans teeth, sans eyes, sans taste, sans everything.

From *Hamlet*
First performed around
1600–1601

This is probably the most famous speech in the English language: give it a go! When I first played Hamlet, many years ago, it was not a success. The audience threw eggs at me. I went on as Hamlet – and came off as omelette. Just a little joke: I have never played Hamlet, Prince of Denmark. I have played Hamlet, however – Hamlet Senior, King of Denmark, the Ghost who appears to his son on the ramparts at the beginning of the play. It was in a production at the Park Theatre in London in 2017 in which my son, Benet Brandreth, played Hamlet, and my daughter-in-law, Kosha Engler, played Ophelia, Gertrude and Laertes. I played Claudius and Polonius, as well as the Ghost. The idea was to have three members of one family explore Hamlet *as a family drama – and, for family bonding and for shared fun, I can report that there is nothing quite like learning and performing Shakespeare with your son and daughter-in-law. The great Sir Derek Jacobi came to see the production and told us afterwards that when he played Hamlet he did not regard 'To be, or not to be' as a soliloquy, but as a speech directed towards Ophelia. 'She does not arrive on "Soft you now: The fair Ophelia",' he said. 'She's been there all along.'*

To be, or not to be, that is the question:
Whether 'tis nobler in the mind to suffer
The slings and arrows of outrageous fortune
Or to take arms against a sea of troubles
And, by opposing, end them. To die, to sleep:
No more; and, by a sleep, to say we end
The heartache and the thousand natural shocks

That flesh is heir to: 'tis a consummation
Devoutly to be wished, to die, to sleep –
To sleep, perchance to dream, ay, there's the rub.
For in that sleep of death what dreams may come
When we have shuffled off this mortal coil
Must give us pause. There's the respect
That makes calamity of so long life.
For who would bear the whips and scorns of time,
Th'oppressor's wrong, the proud man's contumely,
The pangs of dèspised love, the law's delay,
The insolence of office, and the spurns
That patient merit of th'unworthy takes,
When he himself might his quietus make
With a bare bodkin? Who would fardels bear,
To grunt and sweat under a weary life,
But that the dread of something after death,
The undiscovered country, from whose bourn
No traveller returns, puzzles the will,
And makes us rather bear those ills we have
Than fly to others that we know not of.
Thus conscience does make cowards of us all,
And thus the native hue of resolution
Is sicklied o'er with the pale cast of thought,
And enterprises of great pitch and moment
With this regard their currents turn awry,
And lose the name of action. Soft you now:
The fair Ophelia! – Nymph, in thy orisons
Be all my sins remembered.

From *Othello*

First performed around
1604–5

Othello, a much-respected general, the Moor of Venice, explains to the
Senate how he wooed and won Desdemona, the daughter of Brabantio
who has accused him of using witchcraft to beguile her.

Her father loved me, oft invited me,
Still questioned me the story of my life
From year to year, the battles, sieges, fortunes
That I have passed.
I ran it through, even from my boyish days
To th' very moment that he bade me tell it,
Wherein I spoke of most disastrous chances,
Of moving accidents by flood and field,
Of hair-breadth scapes i' th' imminent deadly breach,
Of being taken by the insolent foe
And sold to slavery, of my redemption thence
And portance in my traveller's history,
Wherein of antres vast and deserts idle,
Rough quarries, rocks, hills whose heads touch heaven,
It was my hint to speak. Such was my process,
And of the Cannibals that each other eat,
The Anthropophagi, and men whose heads
Grew beneath their shoulders. These things to hear
Would Desdemona seriously incline,
But still the house affairs would draw her thence,
Which ever as she could with haste dispatch
She'd come again, and with a greedy ear

Devour up my discourse; which I observing,
Took once a pliant hour, and found good means
To draw from her a prayer of earnest heart
That I would all my pilgrimage dilate,
Whereof by parcels she had something heard,
But not intentively. I did consent,
And often did beguile her of her tears
When I did speak of some distressful stroke
That my youth suffered. My story being done,
She gave me for my pains a world of kisses.
She swore, in faith, 'twas strange, 'twas passing strange,
'Twas pitiful, 'twas wondrous pitiful.
She wished she had not heard it, yet she wished
That heaven had made her such a man. She thanked me,
And bade me, if I had a friend that loved her,
I should but teach him how to tell my story,
And that would woo her. Upon this hint I spoke.
She loved me for the dangers I had passed,
And I loved her that she did pity them.
This only is the witchcraft I have used.

From *King Lear*
first performed around
1605–6

The ageing King Lear, having lost his kingdom and been betrayed by two of his daughters, is on the heath during a storm, cursing the elements and his daughters, and lamenting his own frailty.

Blow, wind, and crack your cheeks! Rage, blow,
You cataracts and hurricanos, spout
Till you have drenched the steeples, drowned the cocks!
You sulphurous and thought-executing fires,
Vaunt-couriers to oak-cleaving thunderbolts,
Singe my white head! And thou, all-shaking thunder,
Smite flat the thick rotundity of the world!
Crack nature's mould, all germens spill at once
That make ingrateful man!
Rumble thy bellyful; spit fire! spout rain!
Nor rain, wind, thunder, fire, are my daughters.
I tax not you, you elements, with unkindness.
I never gave you kingdom, called you children.
You owe me no subscription. Why then, let fall
Your horrible pleasure. Here I stand your slave,
A poor, infirm, weak, and despised old man.
But yet I call you servile ministers,
That have with two pernicious daughters joined
Your high-engendered battles 'gainst a head
So old and white as this. O, 'tis foul!

From *The Tempest*
first performed around
1611—12

Prospero interrupts the celebrations of his daughter Miranda's wedding to
speak these now-celebrated lines, often interpreted as Shakespeare's own fare-
well to the stage, given that they come towards the end of his last great play.

Our revels now are ended. These our actors,
As I foretold you, were all spirits, and
Are melted into air, into thin air;
And, like the baseless fabric of this vision,
The cloud-capped towers, the gorgeous palaces,
The solemn temples, the great globe itself,
Yea, all which it inherit, shall dissolve,
And, like this insubstantial pageant faded,
Leave not a rack behind. We are such stuff
As dreams are made on, and our little life
Is rounded with a sleep.

The actor's primary responsibility is to make the text understandable at first hearing. That's quite a big thing, and quite difficult, especially if it's a fairly complicated text. Know the rules about verse-speaking. After that, I don't care whether you break those rules – just make me understand what you're saying, the first time you say it.

Simon Russell Beale

Chapter Nine

The Seven Ages
A life in poems

Using Jaques's famous speech from *As You Like It* as a spring-board, we are now going to go on the journey of a lifetime, taking each of his 'seven ages' in turn and finding appropriate poems for them.

1. 'First the infant'

Morning Song
by Sylvia Plath
(1932–63)

Love set you going like a fat gold watch.
The midwife slapped your footsoles, and your bald cry
Took its place among the elements.

Our voices echo, magnifying your arrival. New statue.
In a drafty museum, your nakedness
Shadows our safety. We stand round blankly as walls.

I'm no more your mother
Than the cloud that distills a mirror to reflect its own slow
Effacement at the wind's hand.

All night your moth-breath
Flickers among the flat pink roses. I wake to listen:
A far sea moves in my ear.

One cry, and I stumble from bed, cow-heavy and floral
In my Victorian nightgown.
Your mouth opens clean as a cat's. The window square

Whitens and swallows its dull stars. And now you try
Your handful of notes;
The clear vowels rise like balloons.

These days, children sleep under *duvets*. When my parents and grandparents were children, they slept between sheets, with the top sheet covered by a blanket (or two) and the blanket covered by a counterpane – a coverlet thrown over the bed. When my parents were little children, during and after the First World War, this was among their favourite poems:

The Land of Counterpane
by Robert Louis Stevenson
(1850–94)

When I was sick and lay a-bed,
I had two pillows at my head,
And all my toys beside me lay
To keep me happy all the day.

And sometimes for an hour or so
I watched my leaden soldiers go,
With different uniforms and drills,
Among the bed-clothes, through the hills;

And sometimes sent my ships in fleets
All up and down among the sheets;
Or brought my trees and houses out,
And planted cities all about.

I was the giant great and still
That sits upon the pillow-hill,
And sees before him, dale and plain,
The pleasant land of counterpane.

For baby-boomers of my generation, born after the Second
World War, our nursery poetry was written by A. A. Milne,
playwright, humorist, polemicist, and father of Christopher
Robin, who wasn't just a child in a story-book, but a real, liv-
ing, breathing human being.

When I first met him, in the early 1980s, Christopher Robin

had just turned sixty. He seemed older. He was tall, slight, a little bent, with owlish glasses and a mischievous twinkle in his eye. (He looked a little like my father.) I had been warned that I would find him painfully shy, diffident about his parents and certainly reluctant to talk about Winnie-the-Pooh. In fact, he was charming, courteous, gentle but forthcoming. He said at once, 'Of course, we must talk about Pooh. It's been something of a love–hate relationship down the years, but it's all right now. Believe it or not, I can look at those four books without flinching. I'm quite fond of them really.'

'Those four books' dominated his life. The first, *When We Were Very Young*, was published in November 1924, dedicated to 'Christopher Robin Milne', just turned four; the last, *The House at Pooh Corner*, in October 1928. Within eight weeks, the first collection of nursery verses had sold more than 50,000 copies; by the time the last book appeared, each title in the series was selling several hundred thousand worldwide.

Christopher told me that, until he was eight or nine, he 'quite liked being famous'. He corresponded with his fans, made public appearances, even made a record. 'It was exciting and made me feel grand and important.' He felt differently when he went away to boarding school where he was teased and bullied. He learnt to box to defend himself. He came to despise the boy in the books called 'Christopher Robin'. He had a particular loathing of the child depicted in 'Vespers', the poem that begins:

> Little Boy kneels at the foot of the bed,
> Droops on the little hands little gold head.

'I vividly recall how intensely painful it was to sit in my study at Stowe while my neighbours played the famous – now cursed – gramophone record remorselessly over and over again. Eventually I took the record and broke it into a hundred fragments and scattered them over a distant field.'

That's why I'm not suggesting you learn 'Vespers'. I am hoping you might learn these two instead. The rhythm and the rhymes make them easy to learn and perfect to perform to little ones, however small.

Sneezles
by A. A. Milne
(1882–1956)

Christopher Robin
Had wheezles
And sneezles,
They bundled him
Into
His bed.
They gave him what goes
With a cold in the nose,
And some more for a cold
In the head.
They wondered
If wheezles
Could turn
Into measles,
If sneezles
Would turn
Into mumps;

They examined his chest
For a rash,
And the rest
Of his body for swellings and lumps.
They sent for some doctors
In sneezles
And wheezles
To tell them what ought
To be done.
All sorts and conditions
Of famous physicians
Came hurrying round
At a run.
They all made a note
Of the state of his throat,
They asked if he suffered from thirst;
They asked if the sneezles
Came *after* the wheezles,
Or if the first sneezle
Came first.
They said, 'If you teazle
A sneezle
Or wheezle,
A measle
May easily grow.
But humour or pleazle
The wheezle
Or sneezle,
The measle
Will certainly go.'
They expounded the reazles
For sneezles
And wheezles,

The manner of measles
When new.
They said 'If he freezles
In draughts and in breezles,
Then PHTHEEZLES
May even ensue.'

Christopher Robin
Got up in the morning,
The sneezles had vanished away.
And the look in his eye
Seemed to say to the sky,
'Now, how to amuse them to-day?'

The King's Breakfast
by A. A. Milne

The King asked
The Queen, and
The Queen asked
The Dairymaid:
'Could we have some butter for
The Royal slice of bread?'
The Queen asked the Dairymaid,
The Dairymaid
Said, 'Certainly,
I'll go and tell
The cow

Now
Before she goes to bed.'

The Dairymaid
She curtsied,
And went and told
The Alderney:
'Don't forget the butter for
The Royal slice of bread.'
The Alderney
Said sleepily:
'You'd better tell
His Majesty
That many people nowadays
Like marmalade
Instead.'

The Dairymaid
Said, 'Fancy!'
And went to
Her Majesty.
She curtsied to the Queen, and
She turned a little red:
'Excuse me,
Your Majesty,
For taking of
The liberty,
But marmalade is tasty, if
It's very
Thickly
Spread.'

The Queen said
'Oh!'
And went to
His Majesty:
'Talking of the butter for
The Royal slice of bread,
Many people
Think that
Marmalade
Is nicer.
Would you like to try a little
Marmalade
Instead?'

The King said,
'Bother!'
And then he said,
'Oh, deary me!'
The King sobbed, 'Oh, deary me!'
And went back to bed.
'Nobody,'
He whimpered,
'Could call me
A fussy man;
I *only* want
A little bit
Of butter for
My bread!'

The Queen said,
'There, there!'
And went to
The Dairymaid.

The Dairymaid
Said, 'There, there!'
And went to the shed.
The cow said,
'There, there!
I didn't really
Mean it;
Here's milk for his porringer,
And butter for his bread.'

The Queen took
The butter
And brought it to
His Majesty;
The King said,
'Butter, eh?'
And bounced out of bed.
'Nobody,' he said,
As he kissed her
Tenderly,
'Nobody,' he said,
As he slid down the banisters,
'Nobody,
My darling,
Could call me
A fussy man —
BUT
I do like a little bit of butter to my bread!'

2. 'Then the whining schoolboy'

Here are two of my children's favourites by two of America's
most popular children's poets:

Please Mrs Butler
by Allan Ahlberg
(born 1938)

Please Mrs Butler
This boy Derek Drew
Keeps copying my work, Miss.
What shall I do?

Go and sit in the hall, dear.
Go and sit in the sink.
Take your books on the roof, my lamb.
Do whatever you think.

Please Mrs Butler
This boy Derek Drew
Keeps taking my rubber, Miss.
What shall I do?

Keep it in your hand, dear.
Hide it up your vest.
Swallow it if you like, love.
Do what you think best.

Please Mrs Butler
This boy Derek Drew
Keeps calling me rude names, Miss.
What shall I do?

Lock yourself in the cupboard, dear.
Run away to sea.
Do whatever you can, my flower.
But don't ask me!

Today Is Very Boring
by Jack Prelutsky
(born 1940)

Today is very boring,
it's a very boring day,
there is nothing much to look at,
there is nothing much to say,
there's a peacock on my sneakers,
there's a penguin on my head,
there's a dormouse on my doorstep,
I am going back to bed.

Today is very boring,
it is boring through and through,
there is absolutely nothing
that I think I want to do,
I see giants riding rhinos,
and an ogre with a sword,
there's a dragon blowing smoke rings,
I am positively bored.

Today is very boring,
I can hardly help but yawn,
there's a flying saucer landing
in the middle of my lawn,
a volcano just erupted
less than half a mile away,
and I think I felt an earthquake,
it's a very boring day.

Next up are two very different poems reflecting different aspects of childhood.

The first is by Eleanor Farjeon, an English girl from a literary family who was educated at home and was so painfully shy that she spent much of her childhood hidden up in the attic, reading and (from the age of five) writing. She had three brothers.

I quarreled with my brother
by Eleanor Farjeon
(1881–1965)

I quarreled with my brother,
I don't know what about,
One thing led to another
And somehow we fell out.
The start of it was slight,
The end of it was strong,
He said he was right,

I knew he was wrong!
We hated one another.
The afternoon turned black.
Then suddenly my brother
Thumped me on the back,
And said, 'Oh, come on!
We can't go on all night –
I was in the wrong.'
So he was in the right.

James Mercer Langston Hughes was a twentieth-century American poet, playwright, novelist and activist, who moved to New York City from Joplin, Missouri, when he was young. He was a pioneer of what came to be known as 'jazz poetry' and was part of the Harlem Renaissance when, as he put it, 'the negro was in vogue'.

Merry-Go-Round
Colored child
at carnival
by Langston Hughes
(1901–67)

Where is the Jim Crow section
On this merry-go-round,
Mister, cause I want to ride?
Down South where I come from
White and colored

Can't sit side by side.
Down South on the train
There's a Jim Crow car.
On the bus we're put in the back –
But there ain't no back
To a merry-go-round!
Where's the horse
For a kid that's black?

And here are two poems about sons and their fathers. The first is by Theodore Roethke, a twentieth-century American poet (and revered teacher of poetry) from Michigan, whose father was a German immigrant.

My Papa's Waltz
by Theodore Roethke
(1908–63)

The whiskey on your breath
Could make a small boy dizzy;
But I hung on like death:
Such waltzing was not easy.

We romped until the pans
Slid from the kitchen shelf;
My mother's countenance
Could not unfrown itself.

The hand that held my wrist
Was battered on one knuckle;
At every step you missed
My right ear scraped a buckle.

You beat time on my head
With a palm caked hard by dirt,
Then waltzed me off to bed
Still clinging to your shirt.

There is a touching passage in A. A. Milne's autobiography (entitled, tellingly, *It's Too Late Now*) where Milne reflects on his own relationship with his father and anatomizes the 'life-long process of saying goodbye'. He pictures himself as a schoolboy approaching his teens, bidding his father farewell: 'From now on we shall begin to grow out of each other. I shall be impatient, but you will be patient with me; unloving, but you will not cease to love me. "Well," you will tell your-self, "it lasted until he was twelve; they grow up and resent our care for them, they form their own ideas, and think ours old-fashioned. It is natural."'

Cecil Day-Lewis is best known for being Britain's Poet Laureate (from 1968 to 1972, between John Masefield and John Betjeman), for writing detective stories under the name Nicholas Blake, and for being the father of Oscar-winning actor Daniel Day-Lewis. This poem is about Sean, Day-Lewis's son from his first marriage. Sean was born in 1931 and the poem was written in 1956.

Walking Away
by Cecil Day-Lewis
(1904–72)

It is eighteen years ago, almost to the day –
A sunny day with leaves just turning,
The touch-lines new-ruled – since I watched you play
Your first game of football, then, like a satellite
Wrenched from its orbit, go drifting away

Behind a scatter of boys. I can see
You walking away from me towards the school
With the pathos of a half-fledged thing set free
Into a wilderness, the gait of one
Who finds no path where the path should be.

That hesitant figure, eddying away
Like a winged seed loosened from its parent stem,
Has something I never quite grasp to convey
About nature's give-and-take – the small, the scorching
Ordeals which fire one's irresolute clay.

I have had worse partings, but none that so
Gnaws at my mind still. Perhaps it is roughly
Saying what God alone could perfectly show –
How selfhood begins with a walking away,
And love is proved in the letting go.

3. 'Then the lover'

These aren't poems to learn and perform to your beloved: you will find those in Chapter Twelve on page 242. These are nine poems, presented in chronological order, that explore the bitter-sweet nature of love and the not-always-easy reality of the lover's lot.

The Sun Rising
by *John Donne*
(1572–1631)

Busy old fool, unruly sun,
    Why dost thou thus,
Through windows, and through curtains call on us?
Must to thy motions lovers' seasons run?
    Saucy pedantic wretch, go chide
    Late school boys and sour prentices,
  Go tell court huntsmen that the King will ride,
  Call country ants to harvest offices,
Love, all alike, no season knows, nor clime,
Nor hours, days, months, which are the rags of time.

Thy beams, so reverend and strong
    Why shouldst thou think?
I could eclipse and cloud them with a wink,
But that I would not lose her sight so long:
    If her eyes have not blinded thine,

Look, and tomorrow late, tell me,
　Whether both th' Indias of spice and mine
　Be where thou left'st them, or lie here with me.
Ask for those kings whom thou saw'st yesterday,
And thou shalt hear, All here in one bed lay.

　　She's all states, and all princes, I,
　　Nothing else is.
Princes do but play us; compared to this,
All honour's mimic; all wealth alchemy.
　　Thou, sun, art half as happy as we,
　　In that the world's contracted thus;
　Thine age asks ease, and since thy duties be
　To warm the world, that's done in warming us.
Shine here to us, and thou art everywhere;
This bed thy centre is, these walls, thy sphere.

When We Two Parted
by George Gordon, Lord Byron
(1788–1824)

When we two parted
　In silence and tears,
Half broken-hearted
　To sever for years,
Pale grew thy cheek and cold,
　Colder thy kiss;
Truly that hour foretold
　Sorrow to this.

The dew of the morning
   Sunk chill on my brow –
It felt like the warning
   Of what I feel now.
Thy vows are all broken,
   And light is thy fame;
I hear thy name spoken,
   And share in its shame.

They name thee before me,
   A knell to mine ear;
A shudder comes o'er me –
   Why wert thou so dear?
They know not I knew thee,
   Who knew thee too well: –
Long, long shall I rue thee,
   Too deeply to tell.

In secret we met –
   In silence I grieve,
That thy heart could forget,
   Thy spirit deceive.
If I should meet thee
   After long years,
How should I greet thee! –
   With silence and tears.

Unfortunate Coincidence
by Dorothy Parker
(1893–1967)

By the time you swear you're his,
   Shivering and sighing,
And he vows his passion is
   Infinite, undying –
Lady, make a note of this:
   One of you is lying.

Social Note
by Dorothy Parker

Lady, lady, should you meet
One whose ways are all discreet,
One who murmurs that his wife
Is the lodestar of his life,
One who keeps assuring you
That he never was untrue,
Never loved another one . . .
Lady, lady, better run!

A Subaltern's Love-song
by John Betjeman
(1906–84)

Miss J. Hunter Dunn, Miss J. Hunter Dunn,
Furnish'd and burnish'd by Aldershot sun,
What strenuous singles we played after tea,
We in the tournament – you against me!

Love-thirty, love-forty, oh! weakness of joy,
The speed of a swallow, the grace of a boy,
With carefullest carelessness, gaily you won,
I am weak from your loveliness, Joan Hunter Dunn.

Miss Joan Hunter Dunn, Miss Joan Hunter Dunn,
How mad I am, sad I am, glad that you won,
The warm-handled racket is back in its press,
But my shock-headed victor, she loves me no less.

Her father's euonymus shines as we walk,
And swing past the summer-house, buried in talk,
And cool the verandah that welcomes us in
To the six-o'clock news and a lime-juice and gin.

The scent of the conifers, sound of the bath,
The view from my bedroom of moss-dappled path,
As I struggle with double-end evening tie,
For we dance at the Golf Club, my victor and I.

On the floor of her bedroom lie blazer and shorts
And the cream-coloured walls are be-trophied with sports,
And westering, questioning settles the sun,
On your low-leaded window, Miss Joan Hunter Dunn.

The Hillman is waiting, the light's in the hall,
The pictures of Egypt are bright on the wall,
My sweet, I am standing beside the oak stair
And there on the landing's the light on your hair.

By roads 'not adopted', by woodlanded ways,
She drove to the club in the late summer haze,
Into nine-o'clock Camberley, heavy with bells
And mushroomy, pine-woody, evergreen smells.

Miss Joan Hunter Dunn, Miss Joan Hunter Dunn,
I can hear from the car park the dance has begun,
Oh! full Surrey twilight! importunate band!
Oh! strongly adorable tennis-girl's hand!

Around us are Rovers and Austins afar,
Above us the intimate roof of the car,
And here on my right is the girl of my choice,
With the tilt of her nose and the chime of her voice.

And the scent of her wrap, and the words never said,
And the ominous, ominous dancing ahead.
We sat in the car park till twenty to one
And now I'm engaged to Miss Joan Hunter Dunn.

Growing Pain

by Vernon Scannell

(1922–2007)

The boy was barely five years old.
We sent him to the little school
And left him there to learn the names
Of flowers in jam jars on the sill
And learn to do as he was told.
He seemed quite happy there until
Three weeks afterwards, at night,
The darkness whimpered in his room.
I went upstairs, switched on his light,
And found him wide awake, distraught,
Sheets mangled and his eiderdown
Untidy carpet on the floor.
I said, 'Why can't you sleep? A pain?'
He snuffled, gave a little moan,
And then he spoke a single word:
'Jessica.' The sound was blurred.
'Jessica? What do you mean?'
'A girl at school called Jessica.
She hurts –' He touched himself between
The heart and stomach '– she has been
Aching here and I can see her.'
Nothing I had read or heard
Instructed me in what to do.
I covered him and stroked his head.
'The pain will go, in time,' I said.

In the palm of his hand
by Connie Bensley
(born 1929)

I'm in love, I'm in love!
I know – I've cried Wolf before
but this time it's true.
I'm in for the full agony:
the contrived encounters:
the heart-shock of the doorbell,
the new meaning to life; the new lingerie.

How do I know it will get that far?
Because of his meaningful look
When he weighs my mange-tout, my pink fir apples.
Because he slips an extra nectarine into my basket.
Because on Tuesday he offered to deliver
to me personally, and he wrote my address
in the palm of his hand.

I Long to Hold Some Lady
by Leonard Cohen
(1934–2016)

I long to hold some lady
For my love is far away,
And will not come tomorrow
And was not here today.
There is no flesh so perfect
As on my lady's bone,
And yet it seems so distant
When I am all alone:
As though she were a masterpiece
In some castled town,
That pilgrims come to visit
And priests to copy down.
Alas, I cannot travel
To a love I have so deep
Or sleep too close beside
A love I want to keep.
But I long to hold some lady,
For flesh is warm and sweet.
Cold skeletons go marching
Each night beside my feet.

Dusting the Phone
by Jackie Kay
(born 1961)

I am spending my time imagining the worst that could
    happen.
I know this is not a good idea, and that being in love, I
    could be
spending my time going over the best that has been
    happening.
The phone rings heralding some disaster. Sirens.
Or it doesn't ring which also means disaster. Sirens.
In which case, who would ring me to tell? Nobody knows.
The future is a long gloved hand. An empty cup.
A marriage. A full house. One night per week
in stranger's white sheets. Forget tomorrow,
You say, don't mention love. I try. It doesn't work.
I assault the postman for a letter. I look for flowers.
I go over and over our times together, re-read them.
This very second I am waiting on the phone.
Silver service. I polish it. I dress for it.
I'll give it extra in return for your call.
Infuriatingly, it sends me hoaxes, wrong numbers;
or worse, calls from boring people. Your voice
disappears into my lonely cotton sheets.
I am trapped in it. I can't move. I want you.
All the time. This is awful – only a photo.
Come on, damn you, ring me. Or else. What?
I don't know what.

4. 'Then a soldier'

The most famous anthology of poetry compiled by a soldier is probably *Other Men's Flowers*, a collection of poems brought together and published by Field Marshal Archibald Percival Wavell, 1st Earl Wavell, in 1944. Wavell (1883–1950) served in the Second Boer War, the First World War (during which he was wounded in the Second Battle of Ypres) and in the Second World War, when he was initially Commander-in-Chief Middle East and, later, Commander-in-Chief India. Both my father and maternal grandfather served under him and admired him, although he was a controversial figure and, as a general, knew failure as well as success. The great love – and solace – of his life was poetry. In every battle, from the Boer War onwards, he had a book of poetry at his side. He had a prodigious memory and scores of the poems he included in *Other Men's Flowers* were ones that he knew by heart. He believed in the power of poetry to keep men sane and steady. Somewhat gruff and awkward in manner, and not especially articulate himself, he expressed himself through speaking poetry out loud. In 1961, eleven years after Wavell's death, T. S. Eliot wrote: 'I do not pretend to be a judge of Wavell as a soldier . . . What I do know from personal acquaintance with the man, is that he was a great man. This is not a term I use easily.'

I trust Wavell would have approved of the six poems I have chosen here – war poems to learn by heart and to speak out loud. 'The Charge of the Light Brigade' was written by the Poet Laureate, Alfred, Lord Tennyson, in 1854, after the British army's Light Cavalry Brigade suffered great casualties at the Battle of Balaclava during the Crimean War. Field Marshal Lord Wavell knew the poem by heart. Alfred, Lord Tennyson, recorded it on a wax cylinder in 1890, and on YouTube and in the archives of the British Library you can hear his powerful and passionate rendering of the poem. The other five poems all relate to the First World War – in which Wavell won the Military Cross and was mentioned in dispatches. They are contrasting poems, inspired by war 'and the pity of war' (in Wilfred Owen's famous phrase), but quite different in tone and approach. They are by A. E. Housman, Siegfried Sassoon, May Wedderburn Cannan, Owen (who was killed in combat on 4 November 1918 – a week before the Armistice) and Rupert Brooke (who died in Greece in 1915, having developed blood poisoning following an insect bite). The four men are famous: May Wedderburn Cannan less so. In 1911, aged eighteen, she joined the Voluntary Aid Detachment, training as a nurse and eventually reaching the rank of quartermaster. During the war, she went to Rouen in the spring of 1915, helping to run the canteen at the railhead there. Philip Larkin loved her poem 'Rouen', saying it 'had all the warmth and idealism of the VADs in the First World War. I find it enchanting.'

For a contemporary poem about the reality of soldiering I recommend 'Ballad of a Hero', a beautiful poem by the performance poet, Kate Tempest (born 1985). It begins:

> Your Daddy is a soldier son,
> Your Daddy's gone to War,
> His steady hands they hold his gun,
> His aim is keen and sure.

It's too long to include here, but it is one of the poems featured in my list of longer poems to learn by heart on page 421–2.

The Charge of the Light Brigade
by Alfred, Lord Tennyson
(1809–92)

I

Half a league, half a league,
  Half a league onward,
All in the valley of Death
  Rode the six hundred.
'Forward, the Light Brigade!
Charge for the guns!' he said:
Into the valley of Death
  Rode the six hundred.

II

'Forward, the Light Brigade!'
Was there a man dismay'd?
Not tho' the soldier knew
  Some one had blunder'd.
Their's not to make reply,
Their's not to reason why,
Their's but to do and die:
Into the valley of Death
  Rode the six hundred.

III

Cannon to right of them,
Cannon to left of them,
Cannon in front of them
  Volley'd and thunder'd;

Storm'd at with shot and shell,
Boldly they rode and well,
Into the jaws of Death,
Into the mouth of Hell
　　Rode the six hundred.

　　　　IV
Flash'd all their sabres bare,
Flash'd as they turn'd in air
Sabring the gunners there,
Charging an army, while
　　All the world wonder'd.
Plunged in the battery-smoke
Right thro' the line they broke;
Cossack and Russian
Reel'd from the sabre-stroke
　　Shatter'd and sunder'd.
Then they rode back, but not
　　Not the six hundred.

　　　　V
Cannon to right of them,
Cannon to left of them,
Cannon behind them
　　Volley'd and thunder'd;
Storm'd at with shot and shell,
While horse and hero fell,
They that had fought so well
Came thro' the jaws of Death,
Back from the mouth of Hell,
All that was left of them,
　　Left of six hundred.

VI

When can their glory fade?
O the wild charge they made!
   All the world wonder'd.
Honour the charge they made!
Honour the Light Brigade,
   Noble six hundred!

Here Dead We Lie
by A. E. Housman
(1859–1936)

Here dead lie we because we did not choose
   To live and shame the land from which we sprung.
Life, to be sure, is nothing much to lose,
   But young men think it is, and we were young.

Everyone Sang
by Siegfried Sassoon
(1886–1967)

Everyone suddenly burst out singing;
And I was filled with such delight
As prisoned birds must find in freedom,
Winging wildly across the white
Orchards and dark-green fields; on – on – and out of sight.

Everyone's voice was suddenly lifted;
And beauty came like the setting sun:
My heart was shaken with tears; and horror
Drifted away . . . O, but Everyone
Was a bird; and the song was wordless; the singing will never
   be done.

Rouen

April 26–May 25, 1915
by May Wedderburn Cannan
*(1893–1973)**

Early morning over Rouen, hopeful, high, courageous
    morning,
And the laughter of adventure and the steepness of the stair,
And the dawn across the river, and the wind across the bridges,
And the empty littered station and the tired people there.

Can you recall those mornings and the hurry of awakening,
And the long-forgotten wonder if we should miss the way,
And the unfamiliar faces, and the coming of provisions,
And the freshness and the glory of the labour of the day?

Hot noontide over Rouen, and the sun upon the city,
Sun and dust unceasing, and the glare of cloudless skies,
And the voices of the Indians and the endless stream of
    soldiers,
And the clicking of the tatties, and the buzzing of the flies.

Can you recall those noontides and the reek of steam and
    coffee,
Heavy-laden noontides with the evening's peace to win,

---

* What May was doing in Rouen: May spent a month in 1915 working – as a
volunteer – in a canteen known as The Coffee Shop, which had been set up
in a large shed at Rouen railway station, providing coffee and sandwiches for
soldiers who had arrived in France and were going by train to the front.

And the little piles of woodbines, and the sticky soda bottles,
And the crushes in the 'Parlour', and the letters coming in?

Quiet night-time over Rouen, and the station full of soldiers,
All the youth and pride of England from the ends of all the
    earth;
And the rifles piled together, and the creaking of the
    sword-belts,
And the faces bent above them, and the gay, heart-breaking
    mirth.

Can I forget the passage from the cool white-bedded Aid
    Post
Past the long sun-blistered coaches of the khaki Red Cross
    train
To the truck train full of wounded, and the weariness and
    laughter,
And 'Good-bye, and thank you, Sister', and the empty yards
    again?

Can you recall the parcels that we made them for the
    railroad,
Crammed and bulging parcels held together by their string,
And the voices of the sergeants who called the Drafts
    together,
And the agony and splendour when they stood to save the
    King?

Can you forget their passing, the cheering and the waving,
The little group of people at the doorway of the shed,
The sudden awful silence when the last train swung to
    darkness,
And the lonely desolation, and the mocking stars o'erhead?

Can you recall the midnights, and the footsteps of night
    watchers,
Men who came from darkness and went back to dark again,
And the shadows on the rail-lines and the all inglorious
    labour,
And the promise of the daylight firing blue the
    window-pane?

Can you recall the passing through the kitchen door to
    morning,
Morning very still and solemn breaking slowly on the town,
And the early coastways engines that had met the ships at
    daybreak,
And the Drafts just out from England, and the day shift
    coming down?

Can you forget returning slowly, stumbling on the cobbles,
And the white-decked Red Cross barges dropping seawards
    for the tide,
And the search for English papers, and the blessed cool of
    water,
And the peace of half-closed shutters that shut out the world
    outside?

Can I forget the evenings and the sunsets on the island,
And the tall black ships at anchor far below our balcony,
And the distant call of bugles, and the white wine in the glasses,
And the long line of the street lamps, stretching Eastwards
    to the sea?

. . . When the world slips slow to darkness, when the office
    fire burns lower,
My heart goes out to Rouen, Rouen all the world away;

When other men remember I remember our Adventure
And the trains that go from Rouen at the ending of the day.

Anthem for Doomed Youth
by Wilfred Owen
(1893–1918)

What passing-bells for these who die as cattle?
    Only the monstrous anger of the guns.
    Only the stuttering rifles' rapid rattle
Can patter out their hasty orisons.
No mockeries now for them; no prayers nor bells,
    Nor any voice of mourning save the choirs, –
The shrill, demented choirs of wailing shells;
    And bugles calling for them from sad shires.

What candles may be held to speed them all?
    Not in the hands of boys, but in their eyes
Shall shine the holy glimmers of good-byes.
    The pallor of girls' brows shall be their pall;
Their flowers the tenderness of patient minds,
And each slow dusk a drawing-down of blinds.

The Soldier
by Rupert Brooke
(1887–1915)

If I should die, think only this of me:
   That there's some corner of a foreign field
That is for ever England. There shall be
   In that rich earth a richer dust concealed;
A dust whom England bore, shaped, made aware,
   Gave, once, her flowers to love, her ways to roam,
A body of England's, breathing English air,
   Washed by the rivers, blest by suns of home.

And think, this heart, all evil shed away,
   A pulse in the eternal mind, no less
      Gives somewhere back the thoughts by England given;
Her sights and sounds; dreams happy as her day;
   And laughter, learnt of friends; and gentleness,
      In hearts at peace, under an English heaven.

5. 'And then the justice'

Shakespeare's 'fifth age' brings us to middle age with the just-ice of the peace: 'In fair round belly, with good capon lined, With eyes severe and beard of formal cut, Full of wise saws and modern instances.' The middle-aged spread has set in; we are taking ourselves more seriously, indulging in deliver-ing nuggets of wisdom (the 'wise saws') and settling into our cliché-riven anecdotage (the 'modern instances').

To learn by heart, I have chosen three very different poems that should resonate with those who are familiar with the harsh realities of middle age. The first is a poem about being a poet in a world where real adults do real work. It is by the British 'modernist' poet, Basil Bunting: Quaker, pacifist, imprisoned as a conscientious objector at the end of the First World War, but serving with distinction in British Military Intelligence during the Second World War, journalist, music critic, diplomat, eccentric and firm believer in the importance of speaking poetry out loud. Late in life he published 'Advice to Young Poets', which begins:

I SUGGEST
1. Compose aloud; poetry is a sound.

The second poem is by Robert Hayden, who in the 1970s became the first African-American to serve as Consultant in Poetry to the Library of Congress, a role known today as US Poet Laureate. In the poem Hayden reflects on the reality of his father's working life.

The third poem is by the British journalist and humorist, Paul Jennings. It's a poem in which a middle-aged man (Jennings was coming up to forty when he wrote it) takes delight in wearing galoshes, hopelessly unfashionable but wonderfully useful waterproof overshoes, typically made of rubber.

What the Chairman Told Tom
by Basil Bunting
(1900–85)

Poetry? It's a hobby.
I run model trains.
Mr Shaw there breeds pigeons.

It's not work. You don't sweat.
Nobody pays for it.
You *could* advertise soap.

Art, that's opera; or repertory –
The Desert Song.
Nancy was in the chorus.

But to ask for twelve pounds a week –
married, aren't you? –
you've got a nerve.

How could I look a bus conductor
in the face
if I paid you twelve pounds?

Who says it's poetry, anyhow?
My ten year old
can do it *and* rhyme.

I get three thousand and expenses,
a car, vouchers,
but I'm an accountant.

They do what I tell them,
my company.
What do *you* do?

Nasty little words, nasty long words,
it's unhealthy.
I want to wash when I meet a poet.

They're Reds, addicts,
all delinquents.
What you write is rot.

Mr Hines says so, and he's a schoolteacher,
he ought to know.
Go and find *work*.

Those Winter Sundays
by Robert Hayden
(1913–80)

Sundays too my father got up early
and put his clothes on in the blueblack cold,
then with cracked hands that ached

from labor in the weekday weather made
banked fires blaze. No one ever thanked him.

I'd wake and hear the cold splintering, breaking.
When the rooms were warm, he'd call,
and slowly I would rise and dress,
fearing the chronic angers of that house,

Speaking indifferently to him,
who had driven out the cold
and polished my good shoes as well.
What did I know, what did I know
of love's austere and lonely offices?

Galoshes
by Paul Jennings
(1918–89)

I am having a rapprochement with galoshes
And some would say this heralds middle age;
Yes, sneering they would say
'Does he always wear *pince-nez*?
Old jossers wore galoshes when the ladies' hats were cloches,
Ha! Woollen combinations are this dodderer's next stage!'
Well, let the people snigger
Just because my feet look bigger,
For, colossal in galoshes, they are dry among the sploshes;
A story that won't wash is this story that galoshes,

So snug at slushy crossings, make a man a sloppy figure.
Oh, crossly, and still crosslier,
I have bought shoes even costlier,
Which, still quite new, let water through before I've crossed
    the street:
There's nothing manly, I repeat,
In always having cold wet feet;
Galoshlessness is foolishness when sharply slants the sleet –
And I utterly refuse
The expression 'overshoes',
To make galoshes posher I would scorn this feeble ruse.
The word 'galosh' is not strong, not weak,
It comes from *kalopous*, the Greek
For 'cobbler's last', and thus it's classed with hero times
    antique.
Come, Muse, through slush and sleet dry-footed with me trip so
That I may praise galoshes in a *kalopous* calypso.
Oh, when swishing buses splash,
And the rush-hour masses clash,
When it's marshy as molasses, how galoshes cut a dash!
It makes me quite impassioned
When they're dubbed unsmart, old-fashioned –
(For such, by gosh, the bosh is that's talked about galoshes)
Since the very finest leather
Is outsmarted altogether
By the classy, glossy polish of galoshes in such weather.

Come, galoshers, be assertive,
Drop that air discreet and furtive!
Let galosh shops' stocks be lavish
With designs and hues that ravish –
Men's galoshes black and British, but for ladies colours
    skittish

(And galoshes could make rings
Round those silly plastic things
Which tie up with clumsy strings)
Let us all have this *rapprochement* with galoshes
And see what health and happiness it brings!

6. 'The sixth age shifts into the lean and slippered pantaloon'

When You are Old
by W. B. Yeats
(1865–1939)

When you are old and grey and full of sleep,
And nodding by the fire, take down this book,
And slowly read, and dream of the soft look
Your eyes had once, and of their shadows deep;

How many loved your moments of glad grace,
And loved your beauty with love false or true,
But one man loved the pilgrim soul in you,
And loved the sorrows of your changing face;

And bending down beside the glowing bars,
Murmur, a little sadly, how Love fled
And paced upon the mountains overhead
And hid his face amid a crowd of stars.

The Last Laugh
by John Betjeman
(1906–84)

I made hay while the sun shone.
  My work sold.
Now, if the harvest is over
  And the world cold,
Give me the bonus of laughter
  As I lose hold.

A Poem Just For Me
by Roger McGough
(born 1937)

Where am I now when I need me
Suddenly where have I gone
I'm so alone here without me
Tell me please, what have I done?

Once I did most things together
I went for walks hand in hand
I shared myself so completely
I met my every demand.

Tell me I'll come back tomorrow
I'll keep my arms open wide
Tell me that I'll never leave me
My place is here at my side.

Maybe I've simply mislaid me
Like an umbrella or key
So until the day that I come my way
Here is a poem just for me.

7. 'Last scene of all . . . second childishness and mere oblivion'

Professor Goswami and her colleagues at the Memory Laboratory at Cambridge University tell me that the poetry you will remember when you reach the end of the road is probably the poetry you learnt when you were very young. 'First in, last out' is the essence of it. I was very *very* young when I first learnt this:

Buckingham Palace
by A. A. Milne
(1882–1956)

They're changing guard at Buckingham Palace –
Christopher Robin went down with Alice.
Alice is marrying one of the guard.
'A soldier's life is terrible hard,'
Says Alice.

They're changing guard at Buckingham Palace –
Christopher Robin went down with Alice.
We saw a guard in a sentry-box.
'One of the sergeants looks after their socks,'
                    Says Alice.

They're changing guard at Buckingham Palace –
Christopher Robin went down with Alice.
We looked for the King, but he never came.
'Well, God take care of him, all the same,'
                    Says Alice.

They're changing guard at Buckingham Palace –
Christopher Robin went down with Alice.
They've great big parties inside the grounds.
'I wouldn't be King for a hundred pounds,'
                    Says Alice.

They're changing guard at Buckingham Palace –
Christopher Robin went down with Alice.
A face looked out, but it wasn't the King's.
'He's much too busy a-signing things,'
                    Says Alice.

They're changing guard at Buckingham Palace –
Christopher Robin went down with Alice.
'Do you think the King knows all about *me*?'
'Sure to, dear, but it's time for tea,'
                    Says Alice.

What we were given as children is what we keep the long-est: our childhood is our friend to the end.

Reading the Classics
by Brian Patten
(born 1946)

The Secret Garden will never age;
The tangled undergrowth remains as fresh
As when the author put down her pen.
Its mysteries are as poignant now as then.

Though Time's a thief it cannot thieve
One page from the world of make-believe.

On the track the Railway Children wait;
Alice still goes back and forth through the glass;
In Tom's Midnight Garden Time unfurls,
And children still discover secret worlds.

At the Gates of Dawn Pan plays his pipes;
Mole and Ratty still float in awe downstream.
The weasels watch, hidden in the grass.
None cares how quickly human years pass.

Though Time's a thief it cannot thieve
One page from the world of make-believe.

Chapter Ten

Year In, Year Out
Poetry for all seasons

Are you sitting comfortably?

Well, you shouldn't be. Sitting, it seems, is the new smoking. According to researchers at Queen's University, Belfast, being seated for more than six hours a day is responsible for 70,000 deaths a year in the UK.

That's the bad news.

The good news is that a brisk walk even once a week is enough to reduce significantly your chances of early death. According to another study, this one published in the *British Journal of Sports Medicine* in 2019, gentle weekly exercise, such as walking, can cut the risk of premature mortality by almost 20 per cent.

What is true for the body is true for the mind. If you want to keep those synapses snappy – and keep that hippocampus happy – you need mental exercise alongside physical exercise. Learning poetry by heart, on the move and round the year, allows you to maintain body, mind and soul to maximum effect.

This is how you do it:

1. Choose your poem.
2. Pop the poem into your pocket (or your knapsack or your bumbag) so you can consult it as you walk.
3. Work on a line or two lines at a time and keep repeating them until they've stuck.
4. Try to walk in step with the rhythm of the words: make the pace of your strides match the beat of the poem.
5. Try not to cross a road or change direction or make a sharp turn *except* at the end of a line or a stanza.
6. Walk where you can talk: learning a poem out loud will help you remember it much more quickly.
7. Walk week in, week out, throughout the year, regardless of weather – and make the poem you are learning appropriate to the season.

Ecclesiastes, Chapter 3, Verses 1 to 8, in the King James Version of the Bible

To every thing there is a season, and a time to every purpose under the heaven:

A time to be born, and a time to die; a time to plant, and a time to pluck up that which is planted;

A time to kill, and a time to heal; a time to break down, and a time to build up;

A time to weep, and a time to laugh; a time to mourn, and a time to dance;

A time to cast away stones, and a time to gather stones together; a time to embrace, and a time to refrain from embracing;

A time to get, and a time to lose; a time to keep, and a
time to cast away;

A time to rend, and a time to sew; a time to keep silence,
and a time to speak;

A time to love, and a time to hate; a time of war, and a
time of peace.

New Year

Robert Burns, undisputed premier bard of Scotland, wrote
'Auld Lang Syne' in the Scots language in 1788. He based the
poem on an old Scottish folk song and, over the years and
around the world, it has become a tradition for it to be sung
at midnight on New Year's Eve. I give you Burns's original,
followed by an English translation. Then I give you a short
poem by Jackie Kay, a contemporary poet and novelist, the
third modern 'Makar', or Scottish poet laureate. Jackie was
born in Edinburgh to a Scottish mother and a Nigerian father.
She was adopted by a white couple at birth and brought up in
Glasgow, studying at the Royal Scottish Academy of Music
and Drama and at Stirling University, where she read Eng-
lish. She says: 'A poem is a little moment of belief.'

Auld Lang Syne
by Robert Burns
(1759–96)

Should auld acquaintance be forgot
   And never brought to mind?
Should auld acquaintance be forgot,
   And auld lang syne!

   For auld lang syne my jo,
     For auld lang syne,
   We'll tak a cup o' kindness yet,
     For auld lang syne.

And surely ye'll be your pint stowp!
   And surely I'll be mine!
And we'll take a cup o' kindness yet,
   For auld lang syne.
       For auld &c.

We twa hae run about the braes,
   And pou'd the gowans fine;
But we've wander'd mony a weary fitt,
Sin auld lang syne.
       For auld &c.

We twa hae paidl'd in the burn,
　Frae morning sun till dine;
But seas between us braid hae roar'd
　Sin auld lang syne.
　　　For auld &c.

And there's a hand, my trusty fiere!
　And gie's a hand o' thine!
And we'll tak a right gude-willie-waught,
　For auld lang syne.
　　　For auld &c.

*

Should old acquaintance be forgot
　And never brought to mind?
Should old acquaintance be forgot,
　And old lang syne?

　　For auld lang syne my dear,
　　　For auld lang syne,
　　We'll take a cup of kindness yet,
　　　For auld lang syne.

And surely you'll buy your pint cup!
　And surely I'll buy mine!
And we'll take a cup o' kindness yet,
　For auld lang syne.
　　　For auld etc.

We two have run about the slopes,
　And picked the daisies fine;
But we've wandered many a weary foot,
　Since auld lang syne.
　　　For auld etc.

We two have paddled in the stream,
 From morning sun till dine;
But seas between us broad have roared
 Since auld lang syne.
                For auld etc.

And there's a hand my trusty friend!
 And give me a hand o' thine!
And we'll take a right good-will draught,
 For auld lang syne.
                For auld etc.

Promise
by Jackie Kay
(born 1961)

Remember, the time of year
when the future appears
like a blank sheet of paper
clean calendar, a new chance.
On thick white snow

you vow fresh footprints
then watch them go
with the wind's hearty gust.
Fill your glass. Here's tae us. Promises
made to be broken, made to last.

Spring

Home-Thoughts, from Abroad
by Robert Browning
(1812–89)

I

Oh, to be in England,
Now that April's there,
And whoever wakes in England
Sees, some morning, unaware,
That the lowest boughs and the brushwood sheaf
Round the elm-tree bole are in tiny leaf,
While the chaffinch sings on the orchard bough
In England – now!

II

And after April, when May follows,
And the whitethroat builds, and all the swallows!
Hark, where my blossomed pear-tree in the hedge
Leans to the field and scatters on the clover
Blossoms and dewdrops – at the bent spray's edge –
That's the wise thrush; he sings each song twice over,
Lest you should think he never could recapture
The first fine careless rapture!
And though the fields look rough with hoary dew
All will be gay when noontide wakes anew
The buttercups, the little children's dower
– Far brighter than this gaudy melon-flower!

From *A Shropshire Lad* (Poem II)
by A. E. Housman
(1859–1936)

Loveliest of trees, the cherry now
Is hung with bloom along the bough,
And stands about the woodland ride
Wearing white for Eastertide.

Now, of my threescore years and ten,
Twenty will not come again,
And take from seventy springs a score,
It only leaves me fifty more.

And since to look at things in bloom
Fifty springs are little room,
About the woodlands I will go
To see the cherry hung with snow.

Summer

An August Midnight
by Thomas Hardy
(1840–1928)

I

A shaded lamp and a waving blind,
And the beat of a clock from a distant floor:
On this scene enter – winged, horned, and spined –
A longlegs, a moth, and a dumbledore;
While 'mid my page there idly stands
A sleepy fly, that rubs its hands . . .

II

Thus meet we five, in this still place,
At this point of time, at this point in space.
– My guests besmear my new-penned line,
Or bang at the lamp and fall supine.
'God's humblest, they!' I muse. Yet why?
They know Earth-secrets that know not I.

Settling
by Denise Levertov
(1923–97)

I was welcomed here – clear gold
of late summer, of opening autumn,
the dawn eagle sunning himself on the highest tree,

the mountain revealing herself unclouded, her snow
tinted apricot as she looked west,
Tolerant, in her steadfastness, of the restless sun
forever rising and setting.
                              Now I am given
a taste of the grey foretold by all and sundry,
a grey both heavy and chill. I've boasted I would not care,
I'm London-born. And I won't. I'll dig in,
into my days, having come here to live, not to visit.
Grey is the price
of neighboring with eagles, of knowing
a mountain's vast presence, seen or unseen.

Blackberry-Picking
by Seamus Heaney
(1939–2013)
for Philip Hobsbaum

Late August, given heavy rain and sun
For a full week, the blackberries would ripen.
At first, just one, a glossy purple clot
Among others, red, green, hard as a knot.
You ate that first one and its flesh was sweet
Like thickened wine: summer's blood was in it
Leaving stains upon the tongue and lust for
Picking. Then red ones inked up, and that hunger
Sent us out with milk-cans, pea-tins, jam-pots
Where briars scratched and wet grass bleached our boots.

Round hayfields, cornfields and potato-drills,
We trekked and picked until the cans were full,
Until the tinkling bottom had been covered
With green ones, and on top big dark blobs burned
Like a plate of eyes. Our hands were peppered
With thorn pricks, our palms sticky as Bluebeard's.

We hoarded the fresh berries in the byre.
But when the bath was filled we found a fur,
A rat-grey fungus, glutting on our cache.
The juice was stinking too. Once off the bush,
The fruit fermented, the sweet flesh would turn sour.
I always felt like crying. It wasn't fair
That all the lovely canfuls smelt of rot.
Each year I hoped they'd keep, knew they would not.

Autumn

To Autumn
by John Keats
(1795–1821)

Season of mists and mellow fruitfulness,
    Close bosom-friend of the maturing sun;
Conspiring with him how to load and bless
    With fruit the vines that round the thatch-eves run;
To bend with apples the moss'd cottage-trees,
    And fill all fruit with ripeness to the core;

To swell the gourd, and plump the hazel shells
With a sweet kernel; to set budding more,
And still more, later flowers for the bees,
Until they think warm days will never cease,
For Summer has o'erbrimm'd their clammy cells.

Who hath not seen thee oft amid thy store?
Sometimes whoever seeks abroad may find
Thee sitting careless on a granary floor,
Thy hair soft-lifted by the winnowing wind;
Or on a half-reap'd furrow sound asleep,
Drows'd with the fume of poppies, while thy hook
Spares the next swath and all its twinèd flowers;
And sometimes like a gleaner thou dost keep
Steady thy laden head across a brook;
Or by a cyder-press, with patient look,
Thou watchest the last oozings, hours by hours.

Where are the songs of Spring? Aye, where are they?
Think not of them, thou hast thy music too, –
While barrèd clouds bloom the soft-dying day,
And touch the stubble-plains with rosy hue;
Then in a wailful choir the small gnats mourn
Among the river sallows, borne aloft
Or sinking as the light wind lives or dies;
And full-grown lambs loud bleat from hilly bourn;
Hedge-crickets sing; and now with treble soft
The redbreast whistles from a garden-croft;
And gathering swallows twitter in the skies.

Winter

The Darkling Thrush
by Thomas Hardy
(1840–1928)

I leant upon a coppice gate
    When Frost was spectre-gray,
And Winter's dregs made desolate
    The weakening eye of day.
The tangled bine-stems scored the sky
    Like strings of broken lyres,
And all mankind that haunted nigh
    Had sought their household fires.

The land's sharp features seemed to be
    The Century's corpse outleant,
His crypt the cloudy canopy,
    The wind his death-lament.
The ancient pulse of germ and birth
    Was shrunken hard and dry,
And every spirit upon earth
    Seemed fervourless as I.

At once a voice arose among
    The bleak twigs overhead
In a full-hearted evensong
    Of joy illimited;
An aged thrush, frail, gaunt, and small,
    In blast-beruffled plume,

Had chosen thus to fling his soul
    Upon the growing gloom.

So little cause for carolings
    Of such ecstatic sound
Was written on terrestrial things
    Afar or nigh around,
That I could think there trembled through
    His happy good-night air
Some blessed Hope, whereof he knew
    And I was unaware.

Stopping by Woods on a Snowy Evening
by Robert Frost
(1874–1963)

Whose woods these are I think I know.
His house is in the village though;
He will not see me stopping here
To watch his woods fill up with snow.

My little horse must think it queer
To stop without a farmhouse near
Between the woods and frozen lake
The darkest evening of the year.

He gives his harness bells a shake
To ask if there is some mistake.

The only other sound's the sweep
Of easy wind and downy flake.

The woods are lovely, dark and deep,
But I have promises to keep,
And miles to go before I sleep,
And miles to go before I sleep.

Christmas

little tree
by E. E. Cummings
*(1894–1962)**

little tree
little silent Christmas tree
you are so little
you are more like a flower

---

* After Robert Frost, Edward Estlin Cummings was the most-read poet in
America in the twentieth century. He wrote some 2,900 poems, four plays,
two autobiographical novels, and much besides. Many of his poems feature
idiosyncratic presentation and syntax and required lower-case spellings, but
it is a myth that he insisted on avoiding capital letters at all times. Sometimes
he signed his name 'e e cummings'; sometimes he signed it 'E. E. Cummings'.
The challenge with his poetry is to speak it as he wrote it: as you learn it and
recite it, visualize how he has presented it on the page and speak it exactly as
you see it. 'see   i will comfort you' does sound different from 'See, I will
comfort you'.

who found you in the green forest
and were you very sorry to come away?
see   i will comfort you
because you smell so sweetly

i will kiss your cool bark
and hug you safe and tight
just as your mother would,
only don't be afraid

look   the spangles
that sleep all the year in a dark box
dreaming of being taken out and allowed to shine,
the balls the chains red and gold the fluffy threads,

put up your little arms
and i'll give them all to you to hold
every finger shall have its ring
and there won't be a single place dark or unhappy

then when you're quite dressed
you'll stand in the window for everyone to see
and how they'll stare!
oh but you'll be very proud

and my little sister and i will take hands
and looking up at our beautiful tree
we'll dance and sing
'Noel Noel'

Another Christmas Poem
by *Wendy Cope*
(born 1945)

Bloody Christmas, here again.
Let us raise a loving cup:
Peace on earth, goodwill to men,
And make them do the washing-up.

Talking Turkeys!!
by *Benjamin Zephaniah*
*(born 1958)**

Be nice to yu turkeys dis christmas
Cos turkeys just wanna hav fun
Turkeys are cool, turkeys are wicked
An every turkey has a Mum.
Be nice to yu turkeys dis christmas,
Don't eat it, keep it alive,

---

* Benjamin Zephaniah, the son of a Barbadian postman and a Jamaican nurse, was born and brought up in the Handsworth area of Birmingham, which he once called the 'Jamaican capital of Europe'. He is a Rastafari and dyslexic, but you don't need to be either to learn and speak this poem. Just memorize and speak what you see on the page.

It could be yu mate, an not on yu plate
Say, Yo! Turkey I'm on your side.

I got lots of friends who are turkeys
An all of dem fear christmas time,
Dey wanna enjoy it, dey say humans destroyed it
An humans are out of dere mind,
Yeah, I got lots of friends who are turkeys
Dey all hav a right to a life,
Not to be caged up an genetically made up
By any farmer an his wife.

Turkeys just wanna play reggae
Turkeys just wanna hip-hop
Can yu imagine a nice young turkey saying,
'I cannot wait for de chop'?
Turkeys like getting presents, dey wanna watch christmas TV,
Turkeys hav brains an turkeys feel pain
In many ways like yu an me.

I once knew a turkey called Turkey
He said 'Benji explain to me please,
Who put de turkey in christmas
An what happens to christmas trees?'
I said, 'I am not too sure turkey
But it's nothing to do wid Christ Mass
Humans get greedy an waste more dan need be
An business men mek loadsa cash.'

Be nice to yu turkey dis christmas
Invite dem indoors fe sum greens
Let dem eat cake an let dem partake
In a plate of organic grown beans,

Be nice to yu turkey dis christmas
An spare dem de cut of de knife,
Join Turkeys United an dey'll be delighted
An yu will mek new friends 'for life'.

Christmas Day in the Workhouse
by Ronnie Barker
(1929–2005)
*Inspired by George R. Sims (1847–1922)**

It was Christmas Day in the workhouse,
The merriest day of the year,
The paupers and the prisoners
Were all assembled there.

---

* George R. Sims was a journalist, poet, playwright, novelist, social reformer, celebrity, and Victorian and Edwardian man-about-town. He was also my paternal grandmother's first cousin and, when I was growing up, the most famous member of our family. I still have a bottle of the patent hair restorer 'Tatcho' which he promoted in his heyday. (Sadly, it appears to have lost its efficacy.) For a while, around the turn of the twentieth century, the highest paid writer in the land, he is now remembered for the melodramatic ballads he wrote depicting the dark and tragic lives of the downtrodden and the poor – of which the most famous is the one that begins 'It is Christmas Day in the workhouse'. The ballad was performed in public music halls and private parlours for many years, and much parodied from the time of its publication in 1877 onwards. When I first met the actor, writer and entertainer, Ronnie Barker, in the 1970s, he was intrigued to discover that I was a kinsman of George R. Sims and presented me with these edited highlights of his hilarious parody of Sims's haunting ballad.

In came the Christmas pudding,
When a voice that shattered glass
Said, 'We don't want your Christmas pudding,
So stick it there with the rest of the unwanted presents.'

The workhouse master then arose
And prepared to carve the duck.
He said, 'Who wants the parson's nose?'
And the prisoners shouted, 'You have it yourself, sir!'

The vicar brought his bible
And read out little bits.
Said one old crone at the back of the hall,
'This man gets on very well with everybody.'

The master rose to make a speech,
But just before he started,
The mistress, who was fifteen stone,
Gave three loud cheers and nearly choked herself.

And all the paupers then began
To pull their Christmas crackers.
One pauper held his too low down
And blew off both his paper hat and the man's next to him.

The mistress, dishing out the food,
Dropped custard down her front.
She cried, 'Aren't I a silly girl?'
And they answered 'You're a perfect picture as always ma'am!'

So then they all began to sing
Which shook the workhouse walls.
'Merry Christmas!' cried the master
And the inmates shouted: 'Best of luck to you as well sir!'

Chapter Eleven

Thirty Days Hath September
Useful poetry

Here are a few poems that are easy to learn – and *so* practical. Almost certainly, you will know a version of the first already.

The days in the month

Thirty days hath September,
April, June and November;
February has twenty-eight alone
All the rest have thirty-one
Except in Leap Year, that's the time
When February's Days are twenty-nine

The Kings and Queens of England

There have been quite a few English sovereigns since the overthrow of King Harold by William the Conqueror in 1066. Remembering them in the correct order isn't easy, unless you have mastered the verse that follows. It takes you from the Norman Conquest to the present day, but ignores Lady Jane

Grey, who was so briefly Queen of England and Ireland (from 10 to 19 July 1553) that she doesn't count, and Oliver Cromwell and his son, Richard, who ruled during the so-called 'Commonwealth' between 1653 and 1659, but whose ascendancy didn't last because they weren't the real thing.

To work out who is who, you must know that 'Willy' is a diminutive of 'William', 'Harry' a diminutive of 'Henry', 'Ste' is 'Stephen', 'Ned' is 'Edward', 'Dick' is 'Richard', and 'Bessie' and 'Lizzie' both diminutives of 'Elizabeth'. When a name is first mentioned that is the first monarch of that name.

> Willy, Willy, Harry, Ste,
> Harry, Dick, John, Harry three,
> One, two, three Neds, Richard two,
> Henries four, five, six – then who?
> Edwards four, five, Dick the bad,
> Harries twain and Ned the lad,
> Mary, Bessie, James the vain,
> Charlie, Charlie, James again,
> William & Mary, Anna Gloria,
> Four Georges, William and Victoria,
> Edward the Seventh next, and then
> George the Fifth in 1910.
> Edward the Eighth soon abdicated
> And so a George was reinstated.
> After Lizzie Two (who's still alive)
> Comes Charlie Three and Willie Five.
> And when they're all gone and up in heaven
> If it's still going it will be George Seven.
>
> That's the way our monarchs lie
> Since Harold got it in the eye!

Inspired by the poem that has helped British children remember the names and order of English kings and queens, Genevieve Madeline Ryan decided to do something similar for the presidents of the United States. She contacted Hugh Sidey, Presidential historian and White House correspondent, for help with historical accuracy, and composed a poem that has since been set to music. It is a long poem, but easily accessed online.

Professor Thomas Andrew Lehrer is a mathematician who taught at Harvard, the Massachusetts Institute of Technology and the University of California at Santa Cruz, and achieved international popularity in the 1950s and 1960s as Tom Lehrer, writer and performer of humorous songs. In this one, written in 1959, he set the names of the 102 chemical elements known at the time to the tune of the 'Major-General's Song' from the Gilbert and Sullivan operetta, *The Pirates of Penzance*.

The Elements
by Tom Lehrer
(born 1928)

There's antimony, arsenic, aluminum, selenium,
And hydrogen and oxygen and nitrogen and rhenium,
And nickel, neodymium, neptunium, germanium,
And iron, americium, ruthenium, uranium,

Europium, zirconium, lutetium, vanadium,
And lanthanum and osmium and astatine and radium,
And gold, protactinium and indium and gallium,
And iodine and thorium and thulium and thallium.

There's yttrium, ytterbium, actinium, rubidium,
And boron, gadolinium, niobium, iridium,
And strontium and silicon and silver and samarium,
And bismuth, bromine, lithium, beryllium, and barium.

There's holmium and helium and hafnium and erbium,
And phosphorus and francium and fluorine and terbium,
And manganese and mercury, molybdenum, magnesium,
Dysprosium and scandium and cerium and cesium.

And lead, praseodymium, and platinum, plutonium,
Palladium, promethium, potassium, polonium,
And tantalum, technetium, titanium, tellurium,
And cadmium and calcium and chromium and curium.

There's sulfur, californium, and fermium, berkelium,
And also mendelevium, einsteinium, nobelium,
And argon, krypton, neon, radon, xenon, zinc, and rhodium,
And chlorine, carbon, cobalt, copper, tungsten, tin and sodium.

These are the only ones of which the news has come to Harvard,
And there may be many others but they haven't been discavard.

How to Lose 2lbs a Week
by Gyles Brandreth
(born 1948)

To lose two pounds a week
To regain a figure slim and sleek
The rules are simple, if not nice:
No bread, potato, and no rice,
     And when it comes to pasta, *basta*!

Carbs are out, and booze is too.
It's tough, but do it and the news is you,
While inwardly resentful, bitter,
Outwardly are lither, fitter,
     Trimmer, slimmer – nippy, zippy!

     Yippee!

The diet works. It has my wife's blessing. She watches her weight, and to great effect. But not everyone approves.

Against Dieting
by Blake Morrison
(born 1950)

Please, darling, no more diets.
I've read the books on why it's
good for one's esteem.
I've watched you jogging lanes and pounding treadmills.
I've even shed some kilos of my own.
But enough. What are love handles
between friends? For half a stone
it isn't worth the sweat.
I've had it up to here with crispbread.
I doubt the premise, too.
Try to see it from my point of view.
I want not less but more of you.

If you are a married man, what follows could be the most useful poem in the book.

A Word to Husbands
by Ogden Nash
(1902–71)

To keep your marriage brimming
With love in the loving cup,
Whenever you're wrong, admit it;
Whenever you're right, shut up.

My favourite philosopher is probably Will Rogers (1879–1935), a Cherokee American showman, film star, humorist, columnist and social commentator from Oklahoma, who travelled the world, made seventy-one movies (fifty of them 'silents') and wrote more than four thousand newspaper columns featuring such nuggets of wisdom as these:

- Never let yesterday use up too much of today.
- Even if you're on the right track, you'll get run over if you just sit there.
- Good judgment comes from experience, and a lot of that comes from bad judgment.
- Everybody is ignorant, only on different subjects.
- Never miss a good chance to shut up.
- Too many people spend money they haven't earned to buy things they don't want to impress people they don't like.
- Everything is changing. People are taking their comedians seriously and the politicians as a joke.

I don't know whether Will Rogers came up with his line
'The best way out of a difficulty is through it' before or after
Robert Frost wrote 'The best way out is always through', but,
either way, it's good advice. The variation of the line I like is
the one that says, 'The best way out is through the door' – and
that's why I think this poem by the Czech immunologist and
poet, Miroslav Holub, is one of the most useful and inspiring
that I know. As you read it, and then as you learn it by heart,
be aware of the punctuation and the line-breaks.

The door
by Miroslav Holub
(1923–98)

Go and open the door.
Maybe outside there's
a tree, or a wood,
a garden,
or a magic city.

Go and open the door.
Maybe a dog's rummaging.
Maybe you'll see a face,
or an eye,
or the picture
of a picture.

Go and open the door.
If there's a fog
it will clear.

Go and open the door.
Even if there's only
the darkness ticking,
even if there's only
the hollow wind,
even if
nothing
is there,
go and open the door.

At least
there'll be
a draught.

Chapter Twelve

Come Live with Me, and Be My Love
Romance guaranteed

Poetry can transform your love life. Learning a poem by heart can move your relationship to the next level. It really can.

Here's how:

1. First, find your object of desire.
2. At your second date (not your first: these things shouldn't be rushed), move the conversation on to favourite things: ask the object of desire about their favourite film, their favourite book, their favourite poem . . . Take the name of the poem on board, but don't make a meal of it.
3. Between that second date and the fourth or fifth date (again, don't rush it: slowly slowly catchy monkey), look up the poem and learn it by heart – secretly.
4. At that fourth or fifth date, or later, or sooner, or whenever the moment feels just right, simply say: 'I have a present for you' – and then recite your beloved's favourite poem to them off by heart.

As a seduction technique, it's unbeatable. It's free, it's easy, and it never fails. It doesn't matter what the poem is: what matters is that you remembered what it was and then took the time and trouble to learn it off by heart so that, at an appropriate but unexpected moment, you could present it as a gift to the object of your desire.

If your gift is well received (and it will be), and it turns out your intended enjoys poetry as you do (if they don't, I'm not sure they are worth pursuing), you can then try doing something very intimate together: you can both learn the same poem by heart – perhaps one of these.

You can learn your jointly chosen poem separately or together, but once you have learnt it you must speak it to one another face to face. Until you have tried it, you won't believe how sexy the experience can be.

The Passionate Shepherd to His Love
by Christopher Marlowe
(1564–93)

Come live with me, and be my love,
And we will all the pleasures prove,
That valleys, groves, hills and fields,
Woods, or steepy mountain yields.

And we will sit upon the rocks,
Seeing the shepherds feed their flocks
By shallow rivers, to whose falls
Melodious birds sing madrigals.

And I will make thee beds of roses,
And a thousand fragrant posies,
A cap of flowers and a kirtle
Embroidered all with leaves of myrtle;

A gown made of the finest wool
Which from our pretty lambs we pull,
Fair lined slippers for the cold,
With buckles of the purest gold;

A belt of straw and ivy-buds,
With coral clasps and amber studs:
And if these pleasures may thee move,
Come live with me, and be my love.

The shepherd swains shall dance and sing
For thy delight each May-morning:
If these delights thy mind may move,
Then live with me, and be my love.

To His Coy Mistress
by Andrew Marvell
(1621–78)

Had we but world enough, and time,
This coyness, Lady, were no crime.
We would sit down, and think which way
To walk, and pass our long love's day.

Thou by the Indian Ganges' side
Shouldst rubies find: I by the tide
Of Humber would complain. I would
Love you ten years before the Flood:
And you should, if you please, refuse
Till the conversion of the Jews.
My vegetable love should grow
Vaster than empires, and more slow.
An hundred years should go to praise
Thine eyes, and on thy forehead gaze.
Two hundred to adore each breast;
But thirty thousand to the rest.
An age at least to every part,
And the last age should show your heart:
For, Lady, you deserve this state;
Nor would I love at lower rate.

But at my back I always hear
Time's wingèd chariot hurrying near;
And yonder all before us lie
Deserts of vast eternity.
Thy beauty shall no more be found;
Nor, in thy marble vault, shall sound
My echoing song: then worms shall try
That long-preserved virginity:
And your quaint honour turn to dust;
And into ashes all my lust.
The grave's a fine and private place,
But none, I think, do there embrace.

Now therefore, while the youthful hue
Sits on thy skin like morning dew,
And while thy willing soul transpires
At every pore with instant fires,
Now let us sport us while we may;

And now, like amorous birds of prey,
Rather at once our time devour,
Than languish in his slow-chapped power.
Let us roll all our strength and all
Our sweetness up into one ball:
And tear our pleasures with rough strife
Through the iron gates of life:
Thus, though we cannot make our sun
Stand still, yet we will make him run.

A Red, Red Rose
by Robert Burns
(1759–96)

My luve is like a red, red rose,
   That's newly sprung in June;
My luve is like the melodie,
   That's sweetly play'd in tune.
As fair art thou, my bonnie lass,
   So deep in luve am I,
And I will luve thee still, my dear,
   Till a' the seas gang dry.

Till a' the seas gang dry, my dear,
   And the rocks melt wi' the sun!
I will luve thee still, my dear,
   While the sands o' life shall run.

And fare-thee-weel, my only luve,
　And fare-thee-weel a while!
And I will come again, my luve,
　Tho' it were ten-thousand mile!

Meeting at Night
by Robert Browning
(1812–89)

The grey sea and the long black land;
And the yellow half-moon large and low;
And the startled little waves that leap
In fiery ringlets from their sleep,
As I gain the cove with pushing prow,
And quench its speed i' the slushy sand.

Then a mile of warm sea-scented beach;
Three fields to cross till a farm appears;
A tap at the pane, the quick sharp scratch
And blue spurt of a lighted match,
And a voice less loud, through its joys and fears,
Than the two hearts beating each to each!

Wild Nights
by Emily Dickinson
(1830–86)

Wild nights! Wild nights!
Were I with thee,
Wild nights should be
Our luxury!

Futile the winds
To a heart in port, –
Done with the compass,
Done with the chart.

Rowing in Eden!
Ah! the sea!
Might I but moor
To-night in thee!

I've Got You under My Skin
by Cole Porter
(1891–1964)*

I've got you under my skin,
I've got you deep in the heart of me,
So deep in my heart, you're really a part of me,
I've got you under my skin.

I tried so not to give in,
I said to myself, 'This affair it never will go so well.'
But why should I try to resist when, darling, I know so well
I've got you under my skin.

I'd sacrifice anything, come what might,
For the sake of having you near,
In spite of a warning voice that comes in the night,
And repeats and repeats in my ear,

'Don't you know, little fool, you never can win,
Use your mentality,
Wake up to reality.'
But each time I do, just the thought of you
Makes me stop, before I begin,
'Cause I've got you under my skin.

---

* Cole Porter's song was first performed in the 1936 musical movie, *Born to Dance*. Just occasionally, the lyrics of a song work wonderfully when spoken rather than sung. Give this a go and you will see what I mean.

Strawberries
by Edwin Morgan
(1920–2010)

There were never strawberries
like the ones we had
that sultry afternoon
sitting on the step
of the open french window
facing each other
your knees held in mine
the blue plates in our laps
the strawberries glistening
in the hot sunlight
we dipped them in sugar
looking at each other
not hurrying the feast
for one to come
the empty plates
laid on the stone together
with the two forks crossed
and I bent towards you
sweet in that air
in my arms
abandoned like a child
from your eager mouth
the taste of strawberries
in my memory
lean back again
let me love you

let the sun beat
on our forgetfulness
one hour of all
the heat intense
and summer lightning
on the Kilpatrick hills

let the storm wash the plates

Atlas

by U. A. Fanthorpe
(1929–2009)

There is a kind of love called maintenance,
Which stores the WD40 and knows when to use it;

Which checks the insurance, and doesn't forget
The milkman; which remembers to plant bulbs;

Which answers letters; which knows the way
The money goes; which deals with dentists

And Road Fund Tax and meeting trains,
And postcards to the lonely; which upholds

The permanently ricketty elaborate
Structures of living; which is Atlas.

And maintenance is the sensible side of love,
Which knows what time and weather are doing
To my brickwork; insulates my faulty wiring;
Laughs at my dryrotten jokes; remembers
My need for gloss and grouting; which keeps
My suspect edifice upright in air,
As Atlas did the sky.

Not Only
by Brian Patten
(born 1946)

Not only the leaf shivering with delight
No,
Not only the morning grass shrugging off the weight of frost
No,
Not only the wings of the crane fly consumed by fire
No,
Not only steam rising from the horse's back
No,
Not only the sound of the sunflower roaring
No,
Not only the golden spider spinning
No,
Not only the cathedral window deep inside the raindrop
No,
Not only the door opening at the back of the clouds
No,

Not only flakes of light settling like snow
No,
Not only the sky as blue and smooth as an egg
No,
Not only these things
No,
But without you none of these things.

The Beauty of Union
by George the Poet
(born 1991)*

There's an indescribable beauty in union
In two beings forming one new being
Entering each other's world
Surrendering each other's selves
Accepting the invitation to be everything to someone else
There's an unparalleled bravery in union
In telling the one you love:
'The only way that we can truly win

* George Mpanga, known as 'George the Poet', performed 'The Beauty of Union' as part of the BBC's coverage of the wedding of Prince Harry and Meghan Markle in 2018 – a broadcast that attracted a worldwide audience approaching two billion. No other love poem in history has been heard by so many people simultaneously. George has an association with Prince Harry as an ambassador for Sentebale, one of the prince's charitable foundations, which supports the mental health and wellbeing of children and young people affected by HIV in Lesotho and Botswana.

Is if I think of you in everything I do
And honour every decision you faithfully include me in.'
Love gives union true meaning
It illuminates the path
It wants us to compromise, communicate and laugh
It wants us to elevate, appreciate without pride
Love is oblivious to the outside
Even with an audience of millions
Even when that love bears immortal significance
All of this is met with cordial indifference
By the two people at the heart of it
Two individuals when they started it
Becoming two halves of one partnership
Such is the beauty of union
Such is the beauty of union

PS

As Shakespeare reminds us in *A Midsummer Night's Dream*, 'The course of true love never did run smooth.' You may find at that third date that the object of your desire does not have a favourite poem, never did, and never will. Poetry may not be their thing. Love may not be their thing.

Or love may be their thing, but not for ever.

I asked the triple-Oscar-winning lyricist, Sir Tim Rice, to suggest one of his lyrics to include here as a poem to learn by heart. He sent me a couple of possibilities, 'Anthem' from *Chess* and 'High Flying Adored' from *Evita*, plus, as he put it, 'one of my own favourites, the almost totally unknown "You Have To Learn To Live Alone", from my English translation

of a French show, *Starmania*, recorded by Cyndi Lauper in
1991.' That's the one I have chosen.

You Have To Learn To Live Alone
by *Tim Rice*
(born 1944)

We sleep together, close and warm
We calm each other through the storm
We set up home, but in a while
We're tempted by another's smile
When it's all played out
If the truth were known
You have to learn to live alone

They dance around the fading light
He holds her closer every night
He fell in love but she did not
But in the end he's all she's got
When it's all played out
When the truth is known
You have to learn to live alone

We fly around the world too fast
We cannot make a moment last
We love the crowd, we sing and play
We do it all, we get our way
When it's all played out

When the birds have flown
You have to learn to live alone

When we're all played out
If the truth were known
You have to learn to live alone

Love may not be your thing. Romantic love, that is. It may
pass you by – or run away as you run towards it. That's life.
Or can be. And is for many. In which case, I have an alterna-
tive poem for you to learn. A friend gave it to me. It is one of
my favourites.

Friendship
by Elizabeth Jennings
(1926–2001)

Such love I cannot analyse;
It does not rest in lips or eyes,
Neither in kisses nor caress.
Partly, I know, it's gentleness

And understanding in one word
Or in brief letters. It's preserved
By trust and by respect and awe.
These are the words I'm feeling for.

Two people, yes, two lasting friends.
The giving comes, the taking ends.
There is no measure for such things.
For this all Nature slows and sings.

This feels the right place, too, for these four lines:

From Dedicatory Ode
by Hilaire Belloc
(1870–1953)

From quiet homes and first beginning,
   Out to the undiscovered ends,
There's nothing worth the wear of winning,
   But laughter and the love of friends.

Chapter Thirteen

The Boy Stood on the Burning Deck
Poetry in performance

> A flea and a fly in a flue
> Were imprisoned, so what could they do?
> Said the fly, 'let us flee!'
> 'Let us fly!' said the flea.
> So they flew through a flaw in the flue.
>
> Ogden Nash (1902–71)

Ogden Nash is fun to read and fun to learn and fun to perform. I particularly like his verse about the flea and the fly in the flue because it's a bit of a tongue-twister and I am partial to those.

> Once a fellow met a fellow
> In a field of beans.
> Said a fellow to a fellow,
> 'If a fellow asks a fellow,
> Can a fellow tell a fellow
> What a fellow means?'

Everything I know about diction I learnt from the late, great Sir Donald Sinden (1923–2014), a fabulous thespian of the old school who could do the lot and did – from Shakespearean tragedy to high farce, from TV sitcoms to wide-screen weepies. It was Sir Donald who explained to me that when it comes to speaking on stage 'it's the *vowels* that give you *volume* and the *consonants* that give you *clarity*'. He introduced me to a simple vocal warm-up exercise that gets the mouth moving and gives you an opportunity both to open your vowels at volume and to hit your consonants with clarity. Before any performance, Sir Donald would position himself in front of his dressing-room mirror and repeat the following mantra:

> Hip bath, hip bath,
> Lavatory, lavatory,
> Bidet, bidet,
> Douche!

When it comes to good diction, that's really all you need to know.

My father had excellent diction. He was a lawyer, not an actor, but loved learning poems by heart and performing them for family and friends. He was born a long time ago, on 11 July 1910, at the beginning of the reign of King George V. He was brought up, therefore, before the era of radio and television, iPhone, podcast and YouTube. He was seventeen before he saw his first 'talking picture'. As young people, he and his elder brother and sisters made their own entertainment, at home, in the parlour, where they gathered around the piano to sing songs, or in the drawing room, in front of the fireplace, where they took it in turns to recite poetry to one another.

When my father died he left me two of his favourite books, best-selling Victorian volumes that had been given to him by *his* father:

GARRY'S ELOCUTIONIST
Selections in prose and verse adapted for
recitation and reading
Edited with introduction, by
Rupert Garry
Author of the elocutionist's *vade mecum:*
ELOCUTION, VOICE AND GESTURE

And

SUCCESSFUL RECITATIONS
The Royal Reciter and The Imperial Reciter
in one volume
Edited by Alfred H Miles

Alfred Henry Miles (1848–1929) was responsible for scores of books on assorted themes, ranging from poetry (*The Poets and the Poetry of the Century*, in ten volumes) through warfare (*Wars of the Olden Times: Abraham to Cromwell*) to advice for the lovesick and the lovelorn (*Wooing: Stories of the Course that Never Did Run Smooth*). He wrote poetry himself, usually in a rumpety-tumpety patriotic vein –

There's a doughty little Island in the ocean,
The dainty little darling of the free;
That pulses with the patriots' emotion,
And the palpitating music of the sea . . .

– and took the view that the 'easiest, and therefore often
the most successful, recitations are those which recite them-
selves; that is, recitations so charged with the picturesque
and the dramatic elements that they command attention and
excite interest in spite of poor elocution and even bad deliv-
ery.' I hope you will find a few such in the pages that follow.

Rupert Garry reckoned he knew the secret of successful
recitation: 'After distinct articulation and correct pronun-
ciation comes Expression, which has been called the soul
of oratory; for without it all reading, speaking, or reciting
is soulless and unintelligent. Expression depends primarily
upon a due attention to four points – Inflection, Modulation,
Emphasis, Pause.'

Garry is also keen on 'Correct Breathing' (through both
mouth and nose: 'the secret of breathing properly is to
keep the bellows well filled'), 'Appropriate Gesture' (but no
'unmeaning gesticulation', please) and 'Proper Feeling' ('You
must try to imagine that the thoughts embodied in the words
you are uttering are your own').

When it comes to understanding and learning a poem, my
advice would be exactly what Garry's was in 1888: 'First, you
must read it carefully to see what it is about. Next, you must
read it over several times in order to get at the author's mean-
ing. Read slowly, and at the end of each sentence, ask yourself
what the author meant to convey to the minds of his hearers.'

Trust the author. Respect the author. Speak what you
see on the page, noticing how it is presented on the page.
Reflect what you find on the page. Don't pretend what you

are reading is prose for the sake of sounding 'natural' or more 'real'. Poems aren't prose. If there are rhymes at the ends of lines, don't apologize for them: relish them.

There are infinite ways to perform a poem in public. The one essential is that you should be heard, which is why my four fundamental rules are: stand up, speak up, look up, look out. Beyond that:

- Take your time.
- Don't rush. Don't mumble.
- Go for clarity and simplicity. Let the words do the work.
- Don't feel you have to infuse your performance with 'feeling'. Let the feeling emerge from the text.
- Keep your hands loosely at your side or lightly held together in front of you.
- Only use gesture as you would if you were telling a story to a friend. Remember T. S. Eliot's useful note: 'poetry remains one person talking to another'.

The poems in this chapter have very little in common with one another (some are funny, some are sad; some are obviously dramatic; some more subtly thought-provoking), except that each of them works brilliantly when performed. They all sound good out loud. As they say in poetry-slam circles: they deliver on the phonaesthetics front.* Somehow something gets added to them when you lift them off the page, because they all either make a definite point in a declamatory style (e.g. 'Pied Beauty' by Gerard Manley Hopkins and 'Television' by Roald Dahl) or they tell a specific story, sometimes

---

* 'Phonaesthetics': the study of the aesthetic properties of speech sound, in particular the study of sound sequences.

set out as a yarn, sometimes presented in the form of a letter, sometimes given as a first-hand account of a personal experience.

The first six are ones that my father learnt as a boy and could recite to his dying day. I learnt them from him. 'The Listeners' by Walter de la Mare, 'Welsh Incident' by Robert Graves and 'The Arrest of Oscar Wilde at the Cadogan Hotel' by John Betjeman are three that I learnt for myself when I was a boy.

When Oscar Wilde was seventeen, in 1871, he became a student at Trinity College, Dublin, where his classics tutor was the celebrated Professor J. P. Mahaffy, whom Wilde later described as 'my first and best teacher', 'the scholar who showed me how to love Greek things'. Mahaffy wrote a book called *The Principles of the Art of Conversation* (1887) and in it he declared: 'The presence of a strong local accent is usually a hindrance to conversation. It marks a man as provincial, and suggests that the speaker has not moved much about the world, or even in the best society of his native country, in which such provincialism is carefully avoided, and set down as an index of mind and manners below the highest level.'

We think differently nowadays. We celebrate local accents. 'Speak as you are' – that's the rule in 2020. RP is no longer PC. 'Received pronunciation' is not taught in our leading drama schools any more. Once young actors were encouraged to speak in what was essentially the accent of the educated metropolitan middle classes. It is probably still quite useful to be able to do that if you're hoping for a bit part in *The Crown*, but if you are going to perform a poem in public you can do it in whatever accent suits you – or suits the piece.

Political correctness is a tricky business. It is considered acceptable for the American character actor, John Lithgow, to play Winston Churchill with an English accent; but would it be a mistake to speak any of the poems by African-American writers that are here in an African-American accent if you come from a different heritage? Probably. Can you give a Welsh lilt to your reading of 'Welsh Incident' by Robert Graves if you don't have genuine Welsh blood coursing through your veins? Possibly not. There are poems here that could only have been written by women, like 'Phenomenal Woman' by Maya Angelou: is it acceptable for a man to perform them? You decide.

When my father performed some of these poems he gave full vent to his histrionic tendencies, and I think, when it's appropriate to the poem, it's fun to do the same. Happily, the poets help you out. Speak the words as you find them and you will find they sound much as the author intended:

> 'Mr. Woilde, we 'ave come for tew take yew
> Where felons and criminals dwell:
> We must ask yew tew leave with us quoietly
> For this *is* the Cadogan Hotel.'

Speak the words as you find them; speak one line at a time, enjoying the rhyme; pay attention to the punctuation; tell the story; take your time; do it your way. On YouTube you can find performance poets and rappers speaking their stuff their way. Check out John Cooper Clarke and Kate Tempest doing their thing: they're mesmerizing. You can try imitating them – or not. Via YouTube listen to T. S. Eliot, Sir John Gielgud, Sir Alec Guinness and Edward Petherbridge each reading Eliot's great poem, 'Journey of the Magi' (page 384). Each speaks it in a different way. Listening to them is a reminder that there is no 'definitive' reading to be had of any poem. The reading will reflect the reader. Let your readings reflect you.

And enjoy.

Casabianca
by *Felicia Hemans*
*(1793–1835)**

The boy stood on the burning deck,
　　Whence all but he had fled;
The flame that lit the battle's wreck,
　　Shone round him o'er the dead.

Yet beautiful and bright he stood,
　　As born to rule the storm;
A creature of heroic blood,
　　A proud, though child-like form.

The flames rolled on – he would not go,
　　Without his Father's word;
That Father, faint in death below,
　　His voice no longer heard.

He called aloud: – 'Say, father, say
　　If yet my task is done?'

---

* First published in August 1826, the poem tells the story of Captain Louis de Casabianca and his twelve-year-old son, Giocante, who both perished on board the ship *Orient* during the Battle of the Nile in 1798. The poem was hugely popular throughout the Victorian era and learnt by schoolchildren in their thousands. Hemans's first poems, dedicated to the Prince of Wales, were published in her home city of Liverpool in 1808, when she was only fourteen, and were admired by, among others, Percy Bysshe Shelley. When she died of the dropsy in her early forties, William Wordsworth composed a memorial poem in her honour. Although she is mostly forgotten now, in one of her poems she coined the phrase 'the stately homes of England' which has become part of the language.

He knew not that the chieftain lay
  Unconscious of his son.

'Speak, Father!' once again he cried,
  'If I may yet be gone!'
– And but the booming shots replied,
  And fast the flames rolled on.

Upon his brow he felt their breath,
  And in his waving hair,
And looked from that lone post of death,
  In still, yet brave despair.

And shouted but once more aloud,
  'My Father! must I stay?'
While o'er him fast, through sail and shroud,
  The wreathing fires made way.

They wrapt the ship in splendour wild,
  They caught the flag on high,
And streamed above the gallant child,
  Like banners in the sky.

There came a burst of thunder sound –
  The boy – oh! where was he?
Ask of the winds that far around
  With fragments strewed the sea! –

With mast, and helm, and pennon fair,
  That well had borne their part –
But the noblest thing which perished there
  Was that young faithful heart!

The Siege of Belgrade
by *Alaric Alexander Watts*
*(1797–1864)**

An Austrian army, awfully arrayed,
Boldly by battery besieged Belgrade:
Cossack commanders cannonading come,
Dealing destruction's devastating doom.
Every endeavour engineers essay,
For fame, for fortune fighting – furious fray!
Generals 'gainst generals grapple, – gracious G–d!
How honours Heaven heroic hardihood!
Infuriate – indiscriminate in ill –
Kinsmen kill kindred, kindred kinsmen kill:
Labour low levels loftiest, longest lines,
Men march 'mid mounds, 'mid moles, 'mid murderous mines!
Now noisy noxious numbers notice nought
Of outward obstacles, opposing ought.
Poor patriots! – partly purchased, partly pressed, –
Quite quaking, quickly 'Quarter! Quarter!' 'quest,
Reason returns, religious right redounds,
Suwarrow stops such sanguinary sounds.

---

* Watts was a prolific British poet and journalist whose *oeuvre* is almost entirely forgotten, apart from this alliterative epic that tells the story of the siege of Belgrade of 1789 in twenty-six lines running from A to Z to A again. Google the history of the siege if you are intrigued. It was a complicated business in which a Habsburg Austrian army besieged an Ottoman Turkish force at the fortress of Belgrade and the Cossacks under the great Russia general, Alexander Suvorov (referred to in the poem as 'Suwarrow'), got involved. Never mind the military detail: enjoy the ingenuity of the alliteration.

Truce to thee, Turkey! – Triumph to thy train,
Unwise, unjust, unmerciful Ukraine!
Vanish vain victory! Vanish, victory vain!
Why wish we warfare? Wherefore welcome were
Xerxes, Ximenes, Xanthus, Xaviere?
Yield, yield, ye youths! ye yeomen, yield your yell;
Zeno's, Zampater's, Zoroaster's zeal,
Attracting all, arms against acts appeal!

Beat! Beat! Drums!
by Walt Whitman
(1819–1892)*

Beat! beat! drums! – Blow! bugles! blow!
Through the windows – through doors – burst like a force
   of ruthless men,
Into the solemn church, and scatter the congregation;
Into the school where the scholar is studying:
Leave not the bridegroom quiet – no happiness must he have
   now with his bride;
Nor the peaceful farmer any peace, plowing his field or
   gathering his grain;

---

* The great American poet, Walt Whitman, wrote this in the summer of 1861,
shortly after the Battle of Bull Run, during the American Civil War, at a time
when the start of every battle was marked with the beating of drums and the
blowing of bugles.

So fierce you whirr and pound, you drums – so shrill you
    bugles blow.

Beat! beat! drums! – Blow! bugles! blow!
Over the traffic of cities – over the rumble of wheels in the
    streets:
Are beds prepared for sleepers at night in the houses? No
    sleepers must sleep in those beds;
No bargainers' bargains by day – no brokers or speculators.
    Would they continue?
Would the talkers be talking? would the singer attempt to
    sing?
Would the lawyer rise in the court to state his case before the
    judge?
Then rattle quicker, heavier drums – you bugles wilder blow.

Beat! beat! drums! – Blow! bugles! blow!
Make no parley – stop for no expostulation;
Mind not the timid – mind not the weeper or prayer;
Mind not the old man beseeching the young man;
Let not the child's voice be heard, nor the mother's
    entreaties;
Make even the trestles to shake the dead, where they lie
    awaiting the hearses,
So strong you thump, O terrible drums – so loud you bugles
    blow.

The Walrus and the Carpenter
by Lewis Carroll
(1832–98)

The sun was shining on the sea,
    Shining with all his might:
He did his very best to make
    The billows smooth and bright –
And this was odd, because it was
    The middle of the night.

The moon was shining sulkily,
    Because she thought the sun
Had got no business to be there
    After the day was done –
'It's very rude of him,' she said,
    'To come and spoil the fun!'

The sea was wet as wet could be,
    The sands were dry as dry.
You could not see a cloud, because
    No cloud was in the sky:
No birds were flying overhead –
    There were no birds to fly.

The Walrus and the Carpenter
    Were walking close at hand;
They wept like anything to see
    Such quantities of sand:

'If this were only cleared away,'
    They said, 'it *would* be grand!'

'If seven maids with seven mops
    Swept it for half a year,
Do you suppose,' the Walrus said,
    'That they could get it clear?'
'I doubt it,' said the Carpenter,
    And shed a bitter tear.

'O Oysters, come and walk with us!'
    The Walrus did beseech.
'A pleasant walk, a pleasant talk,
    Along the briny beach:
We cannot do with more than four,
    To give a hand to each.'

The eldest Oyster looked at him,
    But never a word he said:
The eldest Oyster winked his eye,
    And shook his heavy head –
Meaning to say he did not choose
    To leave the oyster-bed.

But four young Oysters hurried up,
    All eager for the treat:
Their coats were brushed, their faces washed,
    Their shoes were clean and neat –
And this was odd, because, you know,
    They hadn't any feet.

Four other Oysters followed them,
    And yet another four;

And thick and fast they came at last,
    And more, and more, and more –
All hopping through the frothy waves,
    And scrambling to the shore.

The Walrus and the Carpenter
    Walked on a mile or so,
And then they rested on a rock
    Conveniently low:
And all the little Oysters stood
    And waited in a row.

'The time has come,' the Walrus said,
    'To talk of many things:
Of shoes – and ships – and sealing-wax –
    Of cabbages – and kings –
And why the sea is boiling hot –
    And whether pigs have wings.'

'But wait a bit,' the Oysters cried,
    'Before we have our chat;
For some of us are out of breath,
    And all of us are fat!'
'No hurry!' said the Carpenter.
    They thanked him much for that.

'A loaf of bread,' the Walrus said,
    'Is what we chiefly need:
Pepper and vinegar besides
    Are very good indeed –
Now if you're ready, Oysters dear,
    We can begin to feed.'

'But not on us!' the Oysters cried,
    Turning a little blue.
'After such kindness, that would be
    A dismal thing to do!'
'The night is fine,' the Walrus said.
    'Do you admire the view?

'It was so kind of you to come!
    And you are very nice!'
The Carpenter said nothing but
    'Cut us another slice:
I wish you were not quite so deaf –
    I've had to ask you twice!'

'It seems a shame,' the Walrus said,
    'To play them such a trick,
After we've brought them out so far,
    And made them trot so quick!'
The Carpenter said nothing but
    'The butter's spread too thick!'

'I weep for you,' the Walrus said:
    'I deeply sympathise.'
With sobs and tears he sorted out
    Those of the largest size,
Holding his pocket-handkerchief
    Before his streaming eyes.

'O Oysters,' said the Carpenter,
'You've had a pleasant run!
Shall we be trotting home again?'
But answer came there none –
And this was scarcely odd, because
They'd eaten every one.

The Yarn of the 'Nancy Bell'
by W. S. Gilbert
(1836–1911)*

'Twas on the shores that round our coast
From Deal to Ramsgate span,
That I found alone on a piece of stone
An elderly naval man.

His hair was weedy, his beard was long,
And weedy and long was he,
And I heard this wight on the shore recite,
In a singular minor key:

---

* William Schwenck Gilbert was a British playwright, poet and illustrator, who first found fame in the 1860s with his comic 'Bab Ballads', originally written for the popular magazine, *Fun*. 'The Yarn of the "Nancy Bell"' was one of the most popular. Between 1871 and 1896, he collaborated with the composer Arthur Sullivan (1842–1900) on fourteen hugely successful light operas. The seventh of these, *Iolanthe* (1882), features one of his most celebrated 'patter songs', in which the character of the Lord Chancellor reveals how 'love unrequited' has robbed him of his rest. Learning these lyrics will test your memory: performing them will test your diction. Good luck.

'Oh, I am a cook and a captain bold,
    And the mate of the *Nancy* brig,
And a bo'sun tight, and a midshipmite,
    And the crew of the captain's gig.'

And he shook his fists and he tore his hair,
    Till I really felt afraid,
For I couldn't help thinking the man had been drinking,
    And so I simply said:

'Oh, elderly man, it's little I know
    Of the duties of men of the sea,
And I'll eat my hand if I understand
    How you can possibly be

'At once a cook, and a captain bold,
    And the mate of the *Nancy* brig,
And a bo'sun tight, and a midshipmite,
    And the crew of the captain's gig.'

Then he gave a hitch to his trousers, which
    Is a trick all seamen larn,
And having got rid of a thumping quid,
    He spun this painful yarn:

'"Twas in the good ship *Nancy Bell*
    That we sailed to the Indian sea,
And there on a reef we come to grief,
    Which has often occurred to me.

'And pretty nigh all o' the crew was drowned
    (There was seventy-seven o' soul)
And only ten of the *Nancy*'s men
    Said "Here!" to the muster roll.

'There was me and the cook and the captain bold,
    And the mate of the *Nancy* brig,
And the bo'sun tight, and a midshipmite,
    And the crew of the captain's gig.

'For a month we'd neither wittles nor drink,
    Till a-hungry we did feel,
So, we drawed a lot, and, accordin' shot
    The captain for our meal.

'The next lot fell to the *Nancy*'s mate,
    And a delicate dish he made;
Then our appetite with the midshipmite
    We seven survivors stayed.

'And then we murdered the bo'sun tight,
    And he much resembled pig;
Then we wittled free, did the cook and me,
    On the crew of the captain's gig.

'Then only the cook and me was left,
    And the delicate question, "Which
Of us two goes to the kettle?" arose,
    And we argued it out as sich.

'For I loved that cook as a brother, I did,
    And the cook he worshipped me;
But we'd both be blowed if we'd either be stowed
    In the other chap's hold, you see.

'"I'll be eat if you dines off me," says Tom,
    "Yes, that," says I, "you'll be," –
"I'm boiled if I die, my friend," quoth I,
    And "Exactly so," quoth he.

'Says he, "Dear James, to murder me
    Were a foolish thing to do,
For don't you see that you can't cook *me*,
    While I can – and will – cook *you*!"

'So he boils the water, and takes the salt
    And the pepper in portions true
(Which he never forgot), and some chopped shallot,
    And some sage and parsley too.

'"Come here," says he, with a proper pride,
    Which his smiling features tell,
"'T will soothing be if I let you see
    How extremely nice you'll smell."

'And he stirred it round and round and round,
    And he sniffed at the foaming froth;
When I ups with his heels, and smothers his squeals
    In the scum of the boiling broth.

'And I eat that cook in a week or less,
   And – as I eating be
The last of his chops, why, I almost drops,
   For a wessel in sight I see.

    *   *   *   *   *   *

'And I never grieve, and I never smile,
   And I never larf nor play,
But I sit and croak, and a single joke
   I have – which is to say:

'Oh, I am a cook and a captain bold,
   And the mate of the *Nancy* brig,
And a bo'sun tight, and a midshipmite,
And the crew of the captain's gig!'

'The Lord Chancellor's Song' from *Iolanthe*
by *W. S. Gilbert*

Love, unrequited, robs me of my rest:
   Love, hopeless love, my ardent soul encumbers:
Love, nightmare like, lies heavy on my chest,
   And weaves itself into my midnight slumbers!

When you're lying awake with a dismal headache, and repose
   is taboo'd by anxiety,
I conceive you may use any language you choose to indulge
   in, without impropriety;

For your brain is on fire – the bedclothes conspire of usual
    slumber to plunder you:
First your counterpane goes, and uncovers your toes, and
    your sheet slips demurely from under you;
Then the blanketing tickles – you feel like mixed pickles – so
    terribly sharp is the pricking,
And you're hot, and you're cross, and you tumble and toss till
    there's nothing 'twixt you and the ticking.
Then the bedclothes all creep to the ground in a heap, and
    you pick 'em all up in a tangle;
Next your pillow resigns and politely declines to remain at its
    usual angle!
Well, you get some repose in the form of a doze, with hot
    eye-balls and head ever aching,
But your slumbering teems with such horrible dreams that
    you'd very much better be waking;
For you dream you are crossing the Channel, and tossing
    about in a steamer from Harwich –
Which is something between a large bathing machine and a
    very small second-class carriage –
And you're giving a treat (penny ice and cold meat) to a party
    of friends and relations –
They're a ravenous horde – and they all came on board at
    Sloane Square and South Kensington Stations.
And bound on that journey you find your attorney (who
    started that morning from Devon);
He's a bit undersized, and you don't feel surprised when he
    tells you he's only eleven.
Well, you're driving like mad with this singular lad (by-the-
    bye, the ship's now a four-wheeler),
And you're playing round games, and he calls you bad names
    when you tell him that 'ties pay the dealer';

But this you can't stand, so you throw up your hand, and you
    find you're as cold as an icicle,
In your shirt and your socks (the black silk with gold clocks),
    crossing Salisbury Plain on a bicycle:
And he and the crew are on bicycles too – which they've
    somehow or other invested in –
And he's telling the tars all the particu*lars* of a company he's
    interested in –
It's a scheme of devices, to get at low prices all goods from
    cough mixtures to cables
(Which tickled the sailors) by treating retailers as though
    they were all ve*get*ables –
You get a good spadesman to plant a small tradesman
    (first take off his boots with a boot-tree),
And his legs will take root, and his fingers will shoot, and
    they'll blossom and bud like a fruit-tree –
From the greengrocer tree you get grapes and green pea,
    cauliflower, pineapple and cranberries,
While the pastry-cook plant cherry brandy will grant, apple
    puffs, and three-corners, and Banburys –
The shares are a penny, and ever so many are taken by
    Rothschild and Baring,
And just as a few are allotted to you, you awake with a
    shudder despairing –
You're a regular wreck, with a crick in your neck, and no
    wonder you snore, for your head's on the floor, and
    you've needles and pins from your soles to your shins,
    and your flesh is a-creep, for your left leg's asleep, and
    you've cramp in your toes, and a fly on your nose, and
    some fluff in your lung, and a feverish tongue, and a thirst
    that's intense, and a general sense that you haven't been
    sleeping in clover;

But the darkness has passed, and it's daylight at last, and the
  night has been long – ditto ditto my song – and thank
  goodness they're both of them over!

Pied Beauty
by Gerard Manley Hopkins
(1844–89)*

Glory be to God for dappled things –
  For skies of couple-colour as a brinded cow;
    For rose-moles all in stipple upon trout that swim;
Fresh-firecoal chestnut-falls; finches' wings;
  Landscape plotted and pieced – fold, fallow, and plough;
    And áll trádes, their gear and tackle and trim.

All things counter, original, spare, strange;
  Whatever is fickle, freckled (who knows how?)
    With swift, slow; sweet, sour; adazzle, dim;
He fathers-forth whose beauty is past change:
                    Praise him.

---

* This is what is known as a 'curtal sonnet', a shortened sonnet of eleven
lines, and Hopkins's extraordinary way with words makes this a beautiful
piece of poetry to perform. Hopkins converted to Catholicism in 1866 and
went on to become a Jesuit priest and teacher. He wrote poems as a young
man, but burnt most of them when his calling came. It was only in 1875 that
he returned to verse. 'Pied Beauty' was written in the summer of 1877 and
inspired by the Welsh countryside – and God.

The Song of the Smoke
by W. E. B. Du Bois
*(1868–1963)**

I am the Smoke King
I am black!
I am swinging in the sky,
I am wringing worlds awry;
I am the thought of the throbbing mills,
I am the soul of the soul-toil kills,
Wraith of the ripple of trading rills;
Up I'm curling from the sod,
I am whirling home to God;
    I am the Smoke King
    I am black.

    I am the Smoke King,
    I am black!
I am wreathing broken hearts,
I am sheathing love's light darts;
    Inspiration of iron times
    Wedding the toil of toiling climes,
    Shedding the blood of bloodless crimes –
Lurid lowering 'mid the blue,

* In 1895, William Edward Burghardt Du Bois became the first African-American to receive a PhD from Harvard University. A sociologist, historian, poet and civil rights pioneer, he published the ground-breaking black anthem, 'The Song of the Smoke' in 1907, using rhyme, rhythm, assonance and alliteration to powerful effect. In 1909, he became one of the founders of the NAACP: the National Association for the Advancement of Colored People.

Torrid towering toward the true,
    I am the Smoke King,
    I am black.

    I am the Smoke King,
    I am black!
I am darkening with song,
I am hearkening to wrong!
    I will be black as blackness can –
    The blacker the mantle, the mightier the man!
    For blackness was ancient ere whiteness began.
I am daubing God in night,
I am swabbing Hell in white:
    I am the Smoke King
    I am black.

    I am the Smoke King
    I am black!
I am cursing ruddy morn,
I am hearsing hearts unborn:
    Souls unto me are as stars in a night,
    I whiten my black men – I blacken my white!
    What's the hue of a hide to a man in his might?
Hail! great, gritty, grimy hands –
Sweet Christ, pity toiling lands!
    I am the Smoke King
    I am black.

The Listeners
by Walter de la Mare
(1873–1956)

'Is there anybody there?' said the Traveller,
   Knocking on the moonlit door;
And his horse in the silence champed the grasses
   Of the forest's ferny floor:
And a bird flew up out of the turret,
   Above the Traveller's head:
And he smote upon the door again a second time;
   'Is there anybody there?' he said.
But no one descended to the Traveller;
   No head from the leaf-fringed sill
Leaned over and looked into his grey eyes,
   Where he stood perplexed and still.
But only a host of phantom listeners
   That dwelt in the lone house then
Stood listening in the quiet of the moonlight
   To that voice from the world of men:
Stood thronging the faint moonbeams on the dark stair,
   That goes down to the empty hall,
Hearkening in an air stirred and shaken
   By the lonely Traveller's call.
And he felt in his heart their strangeness,
   Their stillness answering his cry,
While his horse moved, cropping the dark turf,
   'Neath the starred and leafy sky;
For he suddenly smote on the door, even
   Louder, and lifted his head: –

'Tell them I came, and no one answered,
    That I kept my word,' he said.
Never the least stir made the listeners,
    Though every word he spake
Fell echoing through the shadowiness of the still house
    From the one man left awake:
Ay, they heard his foot upon the stirrup,
    And the sound of iron on stone,
And how the silence surged softly backward,
    When the plunging hoofs were gone.

Welsh Incident
by Robert Graves
(1895–1985)

'But that was nothing to what things came out
From the sea-caves of Criccieth yonder.'
'What were they? Mermaids? dragons? ghosts?'
'Nothing at all of any things like that.'
'What were they, then?'
                        'All sorts of queer things,
Things never seen or heard or written about,
Very strange, un-Welsh, utterly peculiar
Things. Oh, solid enough they seemed to touch,
Had anyone dared it. Marvellous creation,
All various shapes and sizes, and no sizes,
All new, each perfectly unlike his neighbour,
Though all came moving slowly out together.'

'Describe just one of them.'

       'I am unable.'

'What were their colours?'

        'Mostly nameless colours,
Colours you'd like to see; but one was puce
Or perhaps more like crimson, but not purplish.
Some had no colour.'

      'Tell me, had they legs?'

'Not a leg or foot among them that I saw.'
'But did these things come out in any order?
What o'clock was it? What was the day of the week?
Who else was present? How was the weather?'
'I was coming to that. It was half-past three
On Easter Tuesday last. The sun was shining.
The Harlech Silver Band played *Marchog Jesu*
On thirty-seven shimmering instruments,
Collecting for Caernarvon's (Fever) Hospital Fund.
The populations of Pwllheli, Criccieth,
Portmadoc, Borth, Tremadoc, Penrhyndeudraeth,
Were all assembled. Criccieth's mayor addressed them
First in good Welsh and then in fluent English,
Twisting his fingers in his chain of office,
Welcoming the things. They came out on the sand,
Not keeping time to the band, moving seaward
Silently at a snail's pace. But at last
The most odd, indescribable thing of all,
Which hardly one man there could see for wonder
Did something recognizably a something.'
'Well, what?'

     'It made a noise.'

        'A frightening noise?'

'No, no.'

    'A musical noise? A noise of scuffling?'

'No, but a very loud, respectable noise –
Like groaning to oneself on Sunday morning
In Chapel, close before the second psalm.'
'What did the mayor do?'
                              'I was coming to that.'

Minstrel Man
by Langston Hughes
(1901–67)

Because my mouth
Is wide with laughter
And my throat
Is deep with song,
You do not think
I suffer after
I have held my pain
So long?

Because my mouth
Is wide with laughter,
You do not hear
My inner cry?
Because my feet
Are gay with dancing,
You do not know
I die?

The Arrest of Oscar Wilde at
the Cadogan Hotel
by John Betjeman
(1906–84)*

He sipped at a weak hock and seltzer
    As he gazed at the London skies
Through the Nottingham lace of the curtains
    Or was it his bees-winged eyes?

To the right and before him Pont Street
    Did tower in her new built red,
As hard as the morning gaslight
    That shone on his unmade bed,

'I want some more hock in my seltzer,
    And Robbie, please give me your hand –
Is this the end or beginning?
    How can I understand?

---

* In 1895, Oscar Wilde was arrested, charged with indecent behaviour, tried twice and eventually imprisoned for two years. The arrest took place at the Cadogan Hotel in Pont Street, Chelsea. 'Robbie' is Wilde's friend, Robbie Ross. *The Yellow Book* was a literary quarterly enjoyed by Wilde and his circle. 'Buchan' is John Buchan, the novelist, who was just twenty at the time. Willis's was one of Wilde's favourite restaurants and the Savoy one of his favourite hotels. A 'hansom' was a horse-drawn carriage used as a cab and designed and patented in 1834 by Joseph Hansom.

'So you've brought me the latest *Yellow Book*:
    And Buchan has got in it now:
Approval of what is approved of
    Is as false as a well-kept vow.

'More hock, Robbie – where is the seltzer?
    Dear boy, pull again at the bell!
They are all little better than *cretins*,
    Though this *is* the Cadogan Hotel.

'One astrakhan coat is at Willis's –
    Another one's at the Savoy:
Do fetch my morocco portmanteau,
    And bring them on later, dear boy.'

A thump, and a murmur of voices –
    ('Oh why must they make such a din?')
As the door of the bedroom swung open
    And TWO PLAIN CLOTHES POLICEMEN came in:

'Mr. Woilde, we 'ave come for tew take yew
    Where felons and criminals dwell:
We must ask yew tew leave with us quoietly
    For this *is* the Cadogan Hotel.'

He rose, and he put down *The Yellow Book*.
    He staggered – and, terrible-eyed,
He brushed past the palms on the staircase
    And was helped to a hansom outside.

How to Get On in Society
by John Betjeman*

Phone for the fish-knives, Norman
  As Cook is a little unnerved;
You kiddies have crumpled the serviettes
  And I must have things daintily served.

Are the requisites all in the toilet?
  The frills round the cutlets can wait
Till the girl has replenished the cruets
  And switched on the logs in the grate.

It's ever so close in the lounge dear,
  But the vestibule's comfy for tea
And Howard is riding on horseback
  So do come and take some with me.

Now here is a fork for your pastries
  And do use the couch for your feet;

---

* In 1954 a British professor of linguistics, Alan Ross, triggered a national debate when he coined the terms 'U' and 'Non-U' English in an article exploring how language reflected social class. The 'U' (representing the upper classes) would speak of 'napkins', 'the lavatory', 'the drawing room', 'the hallway' and 'the sofa', while the aspiring middle class (the 'Non-U' folk) would speak of 'serviettes', 'the toilet', 'the lounge', 'the vestibule' and 'the couch'. Lots of people contributed to the debate – and still do. Should 'scone' rhyme with 'gone' or with 'bone'? Do you go 'riding' or 'horse-riding'? Do you say 'Pardon?' or 'What?' or 'Excuse me?' In England in the mid-1950s, John Betjeman (later Poet Laureate) joined in the fun. This is an easy one to learn – and a fun one to perform.

I know what I wanted to ask you –
    Is trifle sufficient for sweet?

Milk and then just as it comes dear?
    I'm afraid the preserve's full of stones;
Beg pardon, I'm soiling the doileys
    With afternoon tea-cakes and scones.

Television
by Roald Dahl
(1916–90)

The most important thing we've learned,
So far as children are concerned,
Is never, *never*, NEVER let
Them near your television set –
Or better still, just don't install
The idiotic thing at all.
In almost every house we've been,
We've watched them gaping at the screen.
They loll and slop and lounge about,
And stare until their eyes pop out.
(Last week in someone's place we saw
A dozen eyeballs on the floor.)
They sit and stare and stare and sit
Until they're hypnotised by it,
Until they're absolutely drunk
With all that shocking ghastly junk.

Oh yes, we know it keeps them still,
They don't climb out the window sill,
They never fight or kick or punch,
They leave you free to cook the lunch
And wash the dishes in the sink –
But did you ever stop to think,
To wonder just exactly what
This does to your beloved tot?
IT ROTS THE SENSES IN THE HEAD!
IT KILLS IMAGINATION DEAD!
IT CLOGS AND CLUTTERS UP THE MIND!
IT MAKES A CHILD SO DULL AND BLIND
HE CAN NO LONGER UNDERSTAND
A FANTASY, A FAIRYLAND!
HIS BRAIN BECOMES AS SOFT AS CHEESE!
HIS POWERS OF THINKING RUST AND FREEZE!
HE *CANNOT* THINK – HE ONLY SEES!
'All right!' you'll cry. 'All right!' you'll say,
'But if we take the set away,
What shall we do to entertain
Our darling children? Please explain!'
We'll answer this by asking you,
'What used the darling ones to do?
'How *used* they keep themselves contented
Before this monster was invented?'
Have you forgotten? Don't you know?
We'll say it very loud and slow:
THEY . . . USED . . . TO . . . READ! They'd READ and READ,
AND READ and READ, and then proceed
TO READ some more. Great Scott! Gadzooks!
One half their lives was reading books!
The nursery shelves held books galore!
Books cluttered up the nursery floor!

And in the bedroom, by the bed,
More books were waiting to be read!
Such wondrous, fine, fantastic tales
Of dragons, gypsies, queens, and whales
And treasure isles, and distant shores
Where smugglers rowed with muffled oars,
And pirates wearing purple pants,
And sailing ships and elephants,
And cannibals crouching round the pot,
Stirring away at something hot.
(It smells so good, what can it be?
Good gracious, it's Penelope.)
The younger ones had Beatrix Potter
With Mr. Tod, the dirty rotter,
And Squirrel Nutkin, Pigling Bland,
And Mrs. Tiggy-Winkle and –
Just How The Camel Got His Hump,
And How the Monkey Lost His Rump,
And Mr. Toad, and bless my soul,
There's Mr. Rat and Mr. Mole –
Oh, books, what books they used to know,
Those children living long ago!
So please, oh *please*, we beg, we pray,
Go throw your TV set away,
And in its place you can install
A lovely bookshelf on the wall.
Then fill the shelves with lots of books,
Ignoring all the dirty looks,
The screams and yells, the bites and kicks,
And children hitting you with sticks –
Fear not, because we promise you
That, in about a week or two
Of having nothing else to do,

They'll now begin to feel the need
Of having something to read.
And once they start – oh boy, oh boy!
You watch the slowly growing joy
That fills their hearts. They'll grow so keen
They'll wonder what they'd ever seen
In that ridiculous machine,
That nauseating, foul, unclean,
Repulsive television screen!
And later, each and every kid
Will love you more for what you did.

Thoughts after Ruskin
by Elma Mitchell
(1919–2000)*

Women reminded him of lilies and roses.
Me they remind rather of blood and soap,
Armed with a warm rag, assaulting noses,
Ears, neck, mouth and all the secret places:

---

* John Ruskin (1819–1900) was the most celebrated art critic of his day, known for his romanticized view of women and for the problems he faced in forming relations with them. Elma Mitchell was a formidable British poet, translator and librarian, whose dazzling way with words makes this a wonderfully powerful poem to perform.

Armed with a sharp knife, cutting up liver,
Holding hearts to bleed under a running tap,
Gutting and stuffing, pickling and preserving,
Scalding, blanching, broiling, pulverizing,
– All the terrible chemistry of their kitchens.

Their distant husbands lean across mahogany
And delicately manipulate the market,
While safe at home, the tender and the gentle
Are killing tiny mice, dead snap by the neck,
Asphyxiating flies, evicting spiders,
Scrubbing, scouring aloud, disturbing cupboards,
Committing things to dustbins, twisting, wringing,
Wrists red and knuckles white and fingers puckered,
Pulpy, tepid. Steering screaming cleaners
Around the snags of furniture, they straighten
And haul out sheets from under the incontinent
And heavy old, stoop to importunate young,
Tugging, folding, tucking, zipping, buttoning,
Spooning in food, encouraging excretion,
Mopping up vomit, stabbing cloth with needles,
Contorting wool around their knitting needles,
Creating snug and comfy on their needles.

Their huge hands! their everywhere eyes! their voices
Raised to convey across the hullabaloo,
Their massive thighs and breasts dispensing comfort,
Their bloody passages and hairy crannies,
Their wombs that pocket a man upside down!

And when all's over, off with overalls,
Quick consulting clocks, they go upstairs,
Sit and sigh a little, brushing hair,

And somehow find, in mirrors, colours, odours,
Their essences of lilies and of roses.

poetry readings
by Charles Bukowski
(1920–94)*

poetry readings have to be some of the saddest
damned things ever,
the gathering of the clansmen and clanladies,
week after week, month after month, year
after year,
getting old together,
reading on to tiny gatherings,
still hoping their genius will be
discovered,
making tapes together, discs together,
sweating for applause
they read basically to and for
each other,
they can't find a New York publisher
or one
within miles,
but they read on and on

---

* Bukowski was a German-born American poet and novelist – described by *Time* magazine as the 'laureate of American lowlife' – who sometimes ended his own poetry readings with this.

in the poetry holes of America,
never daunted,
never considering the possibility that
their talent might be
thin, almost invisible,
they read on and on
before their mothers, their sisters, their husbands,
their wives, their friends, the other poets
and the handful of idiots who have wandered
in
from nowhere.

I am ashamed for them,
I am ashamed that they have to bolster each other,
I am ashamed for their lisping egos,
their lack of guts.

if these are our creators,
please, please give me something else:

a drunken plumber at a bowling alley,
a prelim boy in a four rounder,
a jock guiding his horse through along the
rail,
a bartender on last call,
a waitress pouring me a coffee,
a drunk sleeping in a deserted doorway,
a dog munching a dry bone,
an elephant's fart in a circus tent,
a 6 p.m. freeway crush,
the mailman telling a dirty joke

anything
anything
but
these.

Homework
by Allen Ginsberg
(1926–97)*
Homage Kenneth Koch

If I were doing my Laundry I'd wash my dirty Iran
I'd throw in my United States, and pour on the Ivory Soap,
    scrub up Africa, put all the birds and elephants back in the
    jungle,
I'd wash the Amazon river and clean the oily Carib & Gulf
    of Mexico,
Rub that smog off the North Pole, wipe up all the pipelines
    in Alaska,
Rub a dub dub for Rocky Flats and Los Alamos, Flush that
    sparkly Cesium out of Love Canal

---

* This is America's great Beat poet, Allen Ginsberg, in 1980, running his coun-
try's and the world's social, economic, political and environmental problems
through a metaphorical washing machine. From the loss of jungle habitats in
Africa to the use of Agent Orange (a chemical defoliant sprayed by the US mili-
tary on jungles during the Vietnam War), it's a virtuoso riff that's a challenging
learn, but a rewarding one. The lesson is that not everything comes clean in the
wash. (It was written as a homage to Ginsberg's fellow poet, Kenneth Koch.)

Rinse down the Acid Rain over the Parthenon & Sphinx,
Drain the Sludge out of the Mediterranean basin & make
it azure again,
Put some blueing back into the sky over the Rhine, bleach
the little Clouds so snow return white as snow,
Cleanse the Hudson Thames & Neckar, Drain the Suds out
of Lake Erie
Then I'd throw big Asia in one giant Load & wash out the
blood & Agent Orange,
Dump the whole mess of Russia and China in the wringer,
squeeze out the tattletail Gray of U.S. Central American
police state,
& put the planet in the drier & let it sit 20 minutes or an
Aeon till it came out clean.

Phenomenal Woman
by Maya Angelou
*(1928–2014)**

Pretty women wonder where my secret lies.
I'm not cute or built to suit a fashion model's size
But when I start to tell them,
They think I'm telling lies.
I say,
It's in the reach of my arms,
The span of my hips,
The stride of my step,
The curl of my lips.
I'm a woman
Phenomenally.
Phenomenal woman,
That's me.

I walk into a room
Just as cool as you please,
And to a man,
The fellows stand or
Fall down on their knees.
Then they swarm around me,
A hive of honey bees.

---

* Maya Angelou was an American poet, singer, civil rights activist and phe-
nomenon, who published seven volumes of memoirs, the first of which, *I
Know Why the Caged Bird Sings* (1969), brought her international acclaim and
fame. Geri Halliwell told me this is the Spice Girls' favourite poem.

I say,
It's the fire in my eyes,
And the flash of my teeth,
The swing in my waist,
And the joy in my feet.
I'm a woman
Phenomenally.
Phenomenal woman,
That's me.

Men themselves have wondered
What they see in me.
They try so much
But they can't touch
My inner mystery.
When I try to show them
They say they still can't see.
I say,
It's in the arch of my back,
The sun of my smile,
The ride of my breasts,
The grace of my style.
I'm a woman

Phenomenally.
Phenomenal woman,
That's me.

Now you understand
Just why my head's not bowed.
I don't shout or jump about
Or have to talk real loud.
When you see me passing,

It ought to make you proud.
I say,
It's in the click of my heels,
The bend of my hair,
the palm of my hand,
The need of my care.
'Cause I'm a woman
Phenomenally.
Phenomenal woman,
That's me.

The Poetry Grand National
by Roger Stevens
(born 1948)*

The horses line up
They're under starter's orders
They're off
Adverb leaps gracefully over the first fence
Followed by Adjective
A sleek, Palomino poem
Simile is overtaking on the outside
Like a pebble skimming the water
Half-way round the course

---

* We are reaching the home straight with a verse that benefits greatly from being performed in the manner of the late, great racing commentator, Sir Peter O'Sullevan.

And Hyperbole is gaining on the leaders
Travelling at a million miles an hour
Adverb strides smoothly into first place
Haiku had good odds
But is far behind – and falls
At the last sylla-
ble
And as they flash past the winning post
The crowd is cheering
The winner is
Metaphor
Who quietly takes a bow

God, A Poem
by *James Fenton*
(born 1949)

A nasty surprise in a sandwich,
A drawing-pin caught in your sock,
The limpest of shakes from a hand which
You'd thought would be firm as a rock,

A serious mistake in a nightie,
A grave disappointment all round
Is all that you'll get from th'Almighty,
Is all that you'll get underground.

Oh he *said*: 'If you lay off the crumpet
I'll see you alright in the end.
Just hang on until the last trumpet.
Have faith in me, chum – I'm your friend.'

But if you remind him, he'll tell you:
'I'm sorry, I must have been pissed –
Though your name rings a sort of a bell. You
Should have guessed that I do not exist.

'I didn't exist at Creation,
I didn't exist at the Flood,
And I won't be around for Salvation
To sort out the sheep from the cud –

'Or whatever the phrase is. The fact is
In soteriological terms
I'm a crude existential malpractice
And you are a diet of worms.

'You're a nasty surprise in a sandwich.
You're a drawing-pin caught in my sock.
You're the limpest of shakes from a hand which
I'd have thought would be firm as a rock,

'You're a serious mistake in a nightie,
You're a grave disappointment all round –
That's all you are,' says th'Almighty,
'And that's all that you'll be underground.'

What the Teacher Said When Asked:
What Er We Avin for Geography, Miss?

by John Agard
(born 1949)

This morning I've got too much energy
much too much for geography

I'm in a high mood
so class don't think me crude
but you can stuff latitude and longitude

I've had enough of the earth's crust
today I want to touch the clouds

Today I want to sing out loud
and tear all maps to shreds

I'm not settling for riverbeds
I want the sky and nothing less

Today I couldn't care if east turns west
Today I've got so much energy
I could do press-ups on the desk
but that won't take much out of me

Today I'll dance on the globe
In a rainbow robe

while you class remain seated
on your natural zone
with your pens and things
watching my contours grow wings

All right, class, see you later.
If the headmaster asks for me
say I'm a million dreaming degrees
beyond the equator

a million dreaming degrees
beyond the equator

Shopping Trolleys
by Jenny Boult
(1951–2005)

notice how they have perfect steering
until you put something in them

their automatic response is to apply the brakes.
however they can be goaded forward

by the application of a foot sharply placed
on the rear bottom bar.   surprise is essential.

you can make them move their wheels
but there is no guarantee that they will all move

in the same direction.   the poor things
are terrified & only want to escape.   an average

family shopping turns them into nervous
wrecks for weeks.   you might think that those

trolleys you see out in carparks & under
sapling trees are sight-seeing.   they aren't.

they're trying to avoid having things put in them.
it's hopeless.   there's always someone who wants

to use them as garbage bins laundry baskets
billy carts or flower pots.   or bassinettes.

they are prolific breeders in the wild
& run in enormous herds

they rust in captivity & frequently collapse
during use.   recovery is unusual

i mustn't go down to the sea again
by John Cooper Clarke
(born 1949)

sunken yachtsmen
sinking yards
drunken Scotsmen

drinking hard
every lunatic and his friend
i mustn't go down to the sea again

the ocean drags
its drowning men
emotions flag
me down again
tell tracy babs and gwen
i mustn't go down to the sea again

the rain whips
the promenade
it drips on chips
they turn to lard
i'd send a card if i had a pen
i mustn't go down to the sea again

a string of pearls
from the bingo bar
for a girl
who looks like ringo starr
she's mad about married men
i mustn't go down to the sea again

the clumsy kiss
that ends in tears
how i wish
i wasn't here
tell tony mike and len
i mustn't go down to the sea again

Sonny's Lettah
(Anti-Sus Poem)
by Linton Kwesi Johnson
(born 1952)

Brixtan Prison
Jebb Avenue
Landan south-west two
Inglan

Dear Mama,
Good Day.
I hope dat wen
deze few lines reach yu,
they may find yu in di bes af helt.

Mama,
I really don't know how fi tell yu dis,
cause I did mek a salim pramis
fi tek care a likkle Jim
an try mi bes fi look out fi him.

Mama,
I really did try mi bes,
but nondiles
mi sarry fi tell you seh
poor likkle Jim get arres.

It woz di miggle a di rush howah
wen evrybady jus a hosel an a bosel
fi goh home fi dem evenin showah;
mi an Jim stan-up
waitin pan a bus,
nat cauzin no fus,
wen all af a sudden
a police van pull-up.

Out jump tree policeman,
di hole a dem carryin batan.
Dem waak straight up to mi an Jim.

One a dem hol awn to Jim
seh him tekin him in;
Jim tell him fi let goh a him
far him noh dhu notn
an him naw teef,
nat even a butn.
Jim start to wriggle
di police start to giggle.

Mama,
mek I tell yu whe dem dhu to Jim
Mama,
mek I tell yu whe dem dhu to him:

dem tump him in him belly
an it turn to jelly
dem lick him pan him back
and him rib get pap

dem lick him pan him hed
but it tuff like led
dem kick him in him seed
an it started to bleed

Mama,
I jus coudn stan-up deh
and noh dhu notn:

soh me jook one in him eye
an him started to cry
mi tump one in him mout
an him started to shout
mi kick one pan him shin
an him started to spin
mi tump him pan him chin
an him drap pan a bin

an crash
an ded.

Mama,
more policeman come dung
an beat mi to di grung;
dem charge Jim fi sus,
dem charge me fi murdah.

Mama,
don fret,
dont get depres
an doun-hearted.
Be af good courage
till I hear fram you.

I remain
your son,
Sonny.

Gran Can You Rap?
by Jack Ousbey

Gran was in her chair she was taking a nap
When I tapped her on the shoulder to see if she could rap.
Gran can you rap? Can you rap? Can you, Gran?
And she opened one eye and said to me, man,
   I'm the best rapping Gran this world's ever seen
   I'm a tip-top, slip-slap, rap-rap queen.

And she rose from the chair in the corner of the room
And she started to rap with a bim-bam-boom,
And she rolled up her eyes and she rolled round her head
And as she rolled by this is what she said,
   I'm the best rapping gran this world's ever seen
   I'm a nip-nap, yip-yap, rap-rap queen.

Then she rapped past my Dad and she rapped past my mother,
She rapped past me and my little baby brother.
She rapped her arms narrow she rapped her arms wide,
She rapped through the door and she rapped outside.
   She's the best rapping Gran this world's ever seen
   She's a drip-drop, trip-trap, rap-rap queen.

She rapped down the garden she rapped down the street,
The neighbours all cheered and they tapped their feet.
She rapped through the traffic lights as they turned red
As she rapped round the corner this is what she said,
    I'm the best rapping Gran this world's ever seen
    I'm a flip-flop, hip-hop, rap-rap queen.

    She rapped down the lane she rapped up the hill,
    And as she disappeared she was rapping still.
    I could hear Gran's voice saying, Listen, man,
    Listen to the rapping of the rap-rap Gran.
      I'm the best rapping Gran this world's ever seen
      I'm a –
        tip-top, slip-slap,
          nip-nap, yip-yap,
            hip-hop, trip-trap,
              touch yer cap,
            take a nap,
                happy, happy, happy, happy,
                  rap – rap – queen.

Love from a Foreign City
by *Lavinia Greenlaw*
(born 1962)

Dearest, the cockroaches are having babies.
One fell from the ceiling into my gin
with no ill effects. Mother has been.

I showed her the bite marks on the cot
And she gave me the name of her rat-catcher.
He was so impressed by the hole in her u-bend,
he took it home for his personal museum.
I cannot sleep. They are digging up children
on Hackney Marshes. The papers say
when that girl tried to scream for help,
the man cut her tongue out. Not far from here.
There have been more firebombs,
but only at dawn and out in the suburbs.
And a mortar attack. We heard it from the flat,
A thud like someone dropping a table.
They say the pond life coming out of the taps
is completely harmless. A law has been passed
on dangerous dogs: muzzles, tattoos, castration.
When the Labrador over the road jumped up
to say hello to Billie, he wet himself.
The shops in North End Road are all closing.
You can't get your shoes mended anywhere.
The one-way system keeps changing direction,
I get lost a hundred yards from home.
There are parts of the new *A to Z* marked simply
'under development'. Even street names
have been demolished. There is typhoid in Finchley.
Mother has bought me a lavender tree.

My First Day at School
by *Michaela Morgan*

14 November 1960. New Orleans, USA. Ruby Bridges, aged six, is the first black child to enter an all-white elementary school. She was escorted in by armed guards as protesters shout abuse at her.

I remember . . .
Momma scrubbed my face, hard.
Plaited my hair, tight.
Perched a hopeful white bow on my head,
Like a butterfly hoping for flight.

She shone my shoes, black, shiny, neat.
Another hopeful bow, on each toe,
To give wings to my feet.

My dress was standing to attention, stiff with starch.
My little battledress.
And now, my march.

Two marshals march in front of me.
Two marshals march behind of me.
The people scream and jeer at me.
Their faces are red, not white.

The marshals tower above me, a grey-legged wall.
Broad of back, white of face and tall, tall, tall.
I only see their legs and shoes, as black and shiny as mine.
They march along, stern and strong. I try to march in time.

One hisses to another, 'Slow down it ain't a race.
She only take little bitty girlie steps.'
I quicken my pace.

Head up.
Eyes straight.
I march into school.
To learn like any other kid can.

And maybe to teach a lesson too.

From *Brand New Ancients*
by Kate Tempest
(born 1985)*

Polish the silverware, dust off the telly screen,
it's holy hour on Saturday evening,

---

* Kate Tempest is a performance poet, playwright and novelist, who won the
Ted Hughes Award for *Brand New Ancients* in 2013, when, in the UK, Simon
Cowell and his *X Factor* series were dominating Saturday night TV. At the time,
I made a film for *The One Show* in which I interviewed primary schoolchildren
about their heroes and who they would most like to be. One child chose Win-
ston Churchill; another chose David Beckham; eighteen chose Simon Cowell.

the new Dionysus is in his dressing room preening,
the make-up girls hold their breath as they dream him
into a perfect bronze and then leave him
to his pre-show routine of stretching and breathing.
He winks in the mirror as he flosses his teeth,
pulls his trousers up to his nipples and strides out to the
    stage.
The permatanned God of our age.
We kneel down before him, we beg him for pardon,
mothers feast on the raw flesh of their children struck by the
    madness that floods the whole country, this provocation
    to savagery.
Let's all get famous. I need to be more than just this.
Give me my glory. A double page spread.
Let people weep when they hear that I'm dead.
Let people sleep in the street for a glimpse of my head
as I walk the red carpet into the den of the blessed.
Why celebrate this? Why not denigrate this?
I don't know the names of my neighbours,
but I know the names of the rich and the famous.
And the names of their ex-girlfriends
and their ex-girlfriends' new boyfriends.

Now, watch him shaking his head, he is furious:
how dare this contestant have thought for a second
that this godhead, this champion of unnatural selection,
should be subjected to another version
of a bridge over fucking troubled water.
I stare at the screen and I hear the troubadours sing
the Deeds of Simon. He took the eyes from our heads
and blamed us for our blindness.
Why is this interesting? Why are we watching?

Chapter Fourteen

Nowt So Queer as Folk
From Kubla Khan to Vincent Malloy

Here are seventeen poems about people – from the mighty
Kubla Khan, grandson of Genghis Khan and, from 1260
to 1294, fifth Khagan of the Mongol Empire, to the seven-
year-old Vincent Malloy, whose ambition in life was to grow
up to be like his hero, the star of the best Hammer Horror
films, Vincent Price. In between you will find an assort-
ment of arresting characters, some real, most imaginary, but
all brought to life in verses that are easy to learn by heart
because of the strength of their rhythm and the power of
their rhymes.

It's well known that singing in a choir makes people happy:
there is the camaraderie of being part of a group, there is the
enjoyment of rehearsal, there is the sense of satisfaction in
the performance and the applause that follows it. Speaking
a poem with a group is equally rewarding – and the poems
in the last chapter and this are particularly suited to the
purpose. That said, in my book, almost every poem gains
something by being spoken out loud, and gains something
extra by being spoken by a variety of voices.

Working on this book is what inspired me to team up with

Aatif Hassan and the team at Dukes Education in Britain to launch the 'Poetry Together' project. The idea is a simple one:

- to get young people to learn a poem by heart, a poem of their choosing;
- to get old people to learn a poem by heart, the same poem;
- and then to get them together to perform the poem together – and have tea.

And that's it. Different generations – old and young – meeting up, having tea, and speaking a poem, all together.*

'Words mean more than what is set down on paper,' according to Maya Angelou. 'It takes the human voice to imbue them with the shades of deeper meaning.'

---

* If you know a school or a care home that you think might like to take part, get them to explore the Poetry Together website and find out more: www. poetrytogether.com. It's open to all. It's free. It's fun.

Kubla Khan
Or, A Vision in a Dream. A Fragment.
by Samuel Taylor Coleridge
*(1772–1834)**

In Xanadu did Kubla Khan
A stately pleasure-dome decree:
Where Alph, the sacred river, ran
Through caverns measureless to man
   Down to a sunless sea.
So twice five miles of fertile ground
With walls and towers were girdled round:
And there were gardens bright with sinuous rills,
Where blossomed many an incense-bearing tree;
And here were forests ancient as the hills,
Enfolding sunny spots of greenery.

But oh! that deep romantic chasm which slanted
Down the green hill athwart a cedarn cover!
A savage place! as holy and enchanted
As e'er beneath a waning moon was haunted
By woman wailing for her demon-lover!

---

* Famously, Coleridge claimed to have composed this poem in 1797, having taken opium after reading a work describing Xanadu, the summer palace of the Mongol ruler and Emperor of China, Kubla Khan. Waking from his drug-infused sleep, Coleridge set about writing the lines that came to him from his dream until he was interrupted by 'a person from Porlock' – a nearby village. The poem could not be completed according to his original plan because the interruption caused Coleridge to forget the rest of the lines. He kept the 'fragment' for private readings until 1816 when, encouraged by Lord Byron, he had it published.

And from this chasm, with ceaseless turmoil seething,
As if this earth in fast thick pants were breathing,
A mighty fountain momently was forced:
Amid whose swift half-intermitted burst
Huge fragments vaulted like rebounding hail,
Or chaffy grain beneath the thresher's flail:
And 'mid these dancing rocks at once and ever
It flung up momently the sacred river.
Five miles meandering with a mazy motion
Through wood and dale the sacred river ran,
Then reached the caverns measureless to man,
And sank in tumult to a lifeless ocean:
And 'mid this tumult Kubla heard from far
Ancestral voices prophesying war!

   The shadow of the dome of pleasure
   Floated midway on the waves;
   Where was heard the mingled measure
   From the fountain and the caves.
It was a miracle of rare device,
A sunny pleasure-dome with caves of ice!

   A damsel with a dulcimer
   In a vision once I saw:
   It was an Abyssinian maid
   And on her dulcimer she played,
   Singing of Mount Abora.
   Could I revive within me
   Her symphony and song,
   To such a deep delight 'twould win me,
That with music loud and long,
I would build that dome in air,
That sunny dome! those caves of ice!

And all who heard should see them there,
And all should cry, Beware! Beware!
His flashing eyes, his floating hair!
Weave a circle round him thrice,
And close your eyes with holy dread,
For he on honey-dew hath fed,
And drunk the milk of Paradise.

Abou Ben Adhem
by Leigh Hunt
(1784–1859)*

Abou Ben Adhem (may his tribe increase!)
Awoke one night from a deep dream of peace,
And saw, within the moonlight in his room,
Making it rich, and like a lily in bloom,
An angel writing in a book of gold: –
Exceeding peace had made Ben Adhem bold,
And to the presence in the room he said,
'What writest thou?' – The vision raised its head,
And with a look made of all sweet accord,
Answered, 'The names of those who love the Lord.'
'And is mine one?' said Abou. 'Nay, not so,'

---

* 'Abou Ben Adhem' recounts a story about Ibrahim ibn Adham, one of the
most prominent of the early Sufi saints, who lived in the eighth century and,
according to legend, had been a prince until he renounced his throne in favour
of a life of asceticism and devotion to God and his fellow men.

Replied the angel. Abou spoke more low,
But cheerly still; and said, 'I pray thee then,
Write me as one that loves his fellow-men.'

The angel wrote, and vanished. The next night
It came again with a great wakening light,
And showed the names whom love of God had blessed,
And lo! Ben Adhem's name led all the rest.

Gunga Din
by Rudyard Kipling
*(1865–1936)**

You may talk o' gin and beer
When you're quartered safe out 'ere,
An' you're sent to penny-fights an' Aldershot it;
But when it comes to slaughter
You will do your work on water,
An' you'll lick the bloomin' boots of 'im that's got it.
Now in Injia's sunny clime,
Where I used to spend my time

---

* Kipling's poem, written in 1890, is set in British India and written from the point of view of an English soldier. It tells the story of an Indian water-bearer – a 'bhisti' – who, while bullied and badly treated by the British, proves himself a hero when he is shot and killed while saving the soldier's life. The soldier regrets the abuse dealt to Din and, in a line that has become famous, recognizes that the bhisti is the better man of the two. ('Din', incidentally, while often pronounced to rhyme with 'pin' should really be pronounced to rhyme with 'green'.)

A-servin' of 'Er Majesty the Queen,
Of all them blackfaced crew
The finest man I knew
Was our regimental bhisti, Gunga Din.
     He was 'Din! Din! Din!
  'You limpin' lump o' brick-dust, Gunga Din!
     'Hi! Slippy *hitherao*!
     'Water, get it! *Panee lao!*
  'You squidgy-nosed old idol, Gunga Din.'

The uniform 'e wore
Was nothin' much before,
An' rather less than 'arf o' that be'ind,
For a piece o' twisty rag
An' a goatskin water-bag
Was all the field-equipment 'e could find.
When the sweatin' troop-train lay
In a sidin' through the day,
Where the 'eat would make your bloomin' eyebrows crawl,
We shouted 'Harry By!'
Till our throats were bricky-dry,
Then we wopped 'im 'cause 'e couldn't serve us all.
     It was 'Din! Din! Din!
  'You 'eathen, where the mischief 'ave you been?
     'You put some *juldee* in it
     'Or I'll *marrow* you this minute
  'If you don't fill up my helmet, Gunga Din!'

'E would dot an' carry one
Till the longest day was done;
An' 'e didn't seem to know the use o' fear.
If we charged or broke or cut,
You could bet your bloomin' nut,

'E'd be waitin' fifty paces right flank rear.
With 'is mussick on 'is back,
'E would skip with our attack,
An' watch us till the bugles made 'Retire,'
An' for all 'is dirty 'ide
'E was white, clear white, inside
When 'e went to tend the wounded under fire!
      It was 'Din! Din! Din!'
  With the bullets kickin' dust-spots on the green.
      When the cartridges ran out,
      You could hear the front-ranks shout,
  'Hi! ammunition-mules an' Gunga Din!'

I sha'n't forgit the night
When I dropped be'ind the fight
With a bullet where my belt-plate should 'a' been.
I was chokin' mad with thirst,
An' the man that spied me first
Was our good old grinnin', gruntin' Gunga Din.
'E lifted up my 'ead,
An' he plugged me where I bled,
An' 'e guv me 'arf-a-pint o' water green:
It was crawlin' and it stunk,
But of all the drinks I've drunk,
I'm gratefullest to one from Gunga Din.
      It was 'Din! Din! Din!
  ''Ere's a beggar with a bullet through 'is spleen;
      ''E's chawin' up the ground,
      'An' 'e's kickin' all around:
  'For Gawd's sake git the water, Gunga Din!'

'E carried me away
To where a dooli lay,

An' a bullet come an' drilled the beggar clean.
'E put me safe inside,
An' just before 'e died,
'I 'ope you liked your drink,' sez Gunga Din.
So I'll meet 'im later on
At the place where 'e is gone –
Where it's always double drill and no canteen;
'E'll be squattin' on the coals
Givin' drink to poor damned souls,
An' I'll get a swig in hell from Gunga Din!
      Yes, Din! Din! Din!
  You Lazarushian-leather Gunga Din!
      Though I've belted you and flayed you,
      By the livin' Gawd that made you,
You're a better man than I am, Gunga Din!

Richard Cory
by Edwin Arlington Robinson
(1869–1935)*

Whenever Richard Cory went down town,
We people on the pavement looked at him:
He was a gentleman from sole to crown,
Clean favored, and imperially slim.

---

* This is a powerful poem with a shocking pay-off written by a remarkable American poet, four times nominated for the Nobel Prize for Literature and best known for short, dramatic poems like this that tell the stories of people from small East Coast towns.

And he was always quietly arrayed,
And he was always human when he talked;
But still he fluttered pulses when he said,
'Good-morning,' and he glittered when he walked.

And he was rich – yes, richer than a king –
And admirably schooled in every grace:
In fine, we thought that he was everything
To make us wish that we were in his place.

So on we worked, and waited for the light,
And went without the meat, and cursed the bread;
And Richard Cory, one calm summer night,
Went home and put a bullet through his head.

Lord Lundy
*Who Was Too Freely Moved to Tears, and
Thereby Ruined His Political Career*
by Hilaire Belloc
(1870–1953)

Lord Lundy from his earliest years
Was far too freely moved to Tears.
For instance if his Mother said,
'Lundy! It's time to go to Bed!'
He bellowed like a Little Turk.
Or if his father, Lord Dunquerque,
Said, 'Hi!' in a Commanding Tone,

'Hi, Lundy! Leave the Cat alone!'
Lord Lundy, letting go its tail,
Would raise so terrible a wail
As moved his Grandpapa the Duke
To utter the severe rebuke:
'When I, Sir! was a little Boy,
An Animal was not a Toy!'

His father's Elder Sister, who
Was married to a Parvenoo,
Confided to Her Husband, 'Drat!
The Miserable, Peevish Brat!
Why don't they drown the Little Beast?'
Suggestions which, to say the least,
Are not what we expect to hear
From Daughters of an English Peer.
His grandmamma, His Mother's Mother,
Who had some dignity or other,
The Garter, or no matter what,
I can't remember all the Lot!
Said, 'Oh! That I were Brisk and Spry
To give him that for which to cry!'
(An empty wish, alas! for she
Was Blind and nearly ninety-three).

The Dear Old Butler thought – but there!
I really neither know nor care
For what the Dear Old Butler thought!
In my opinion, Butlers ought
To know their place, and not to play
The Old Retainer night and day.
I'm getting tired and so are you,
Let's cut the poem into two!

It happened to Lord Lundy then,
As happens to so many men:
Towards the age of twenty-six,
They shoved him into politics;
In which profession he commanded
The income that his rank demanded
In turn as Secretary for
India, the Colonies, and War.
But very soon his friends began
To doubt if he were quite the man:
Thus if a member rose to say
(As members do from day to day),
'Arising out of that reply . . . !'
Lord Lundy would begin to cry.
A Hint at harmless little jobs
Would shake him with convulsive sobs.

While as for Revelations, these
Would simply bring him to his knees,
And leave him whimpering like a child.
It drove his Colleagues raving wild!
They let him sink from Post to Post,
From fifteen hundred at the most
To eight, and barely six – and then
To be Curator of Big Ben! . . .
And finally there came a Threat
To oust him from the Cabinet!

The Duke – his aged grand-sire – bore
The shame till he could bear no more.
He rallied his declining powers,

Summoned the youth to Brackley Towers,
And bitterly addressed him thus –
'Sir! you have disappointed us!
We had intended you to be
The next Prime Minister but three:
The stocks were sold; the Press was squared:
The Middle Class was quite prepared.
But as it is! . . . My language fails!
Go out and govern New South Wales!'

The Aged Patriot groaned and died:
And gracious! how Lord Lundy cried!

Matilda
Who Told Lies and Was Burned to Death
by Hilaire Belloc

Matilda told such Dreadful Lies,
It made one Gasp and Stretch one's Eyes;
Her Aunt, who, from her Earliest Youth,
Had kept a Strict Regard for Truth,
Attempted to Believe Matilda:
The effort very nearly killed her,
And would have done so, had not She
Discovered this Infirmity.
For once, towards the Close of Day,
Matilda, growing tired of play,
And finding she was left alone,

Went tiptoe to the Telephone
And summoned the Immediate Aid
Of London's Noble Fire-Brigade.
Within an hour the Gallant Band
Were pouring in on every hand,
From Putney, Hackney Downs, and Bow
With Courage high and Hearts a-glow
They galloped, roaring though the Town,
'Matilda's House is Burning Down!'
Inspired by British Cheers and Loud
Proceeding from the Frenzied Crowd,
They ran their ladders through a score
Of windows on the Ball Room Floor;
And took Peculiar Pains to Souse
The Pictures up and down the House,
Until Matilda's Aunt succeeded
In showing them they were not needed;
And even then she had to pay
To get the Men to go away!

. . . . .

It happened that a few Weeks later
Her Aunt was off to the Theatre
To see that Interesting Play
The Second Mrs Tanqueray.
She had refused to take her Niece
To hear this Entertaining Piece:
A Deprivation Just and Wise
To Punish her for Telling Lies.
That Night a Fire *did* break out –
You should have heard Matilda Shout!
You should have heard her Scream and Bawl,
And throw the window up and call

To People passing in the Street –
(The rapidly increasing Heat
Encouraging her to obtain
Their confidence) – but it was all in vain!
For every time She shouted 'Fire!'
They only answered 'Little Liar'!
And therefore when her Aunt returned,
Matilda, and the House, were burned.

The Lion and Albert
by Marriott Edgar
*(1880–1951)**

There's a famous seaside place called Blackpool,
    That's noted for fresh air and fun,
And Mr and Mrs Ramsbottom
    Went there with young Albert, their son.

A grand little lad was young Albert,
    All dressed in his best; quite a swell
With a stick with an 'orse's 'ead 'andle,
    The finest that Woolworth's could sell.

---

* This is perhaps the best-known of the verses made famous by the actor, entertainer and singer, Stanley Holloway (1890–1982), noted at the end of his life for playing Alfred P. Doolittle in the musical *My Fair Lady* on stage and screen, but celebrated in his heyday for performing versified monologues like this. You can hear how he did it on YouTube, but once you have heard the master, feel free to do it your way.

They didn't think much to the Ocean;:
　　The waves, they were fiddlin' and small,
There was no wrecks and nobody drownded,
　　Fact, nothing to laugh at at all.

So, seeking for further amusement,
　　They paid and went into the Zoo,
Where they'd Lions and Tigers and Camels
　　And old ale and sandwiches, too.

There was one great big Lion called Wallace;
　　His nose were all covered with scars –
He lay in a somnolent posture
　　With the side of his face on the bars.

Now Albert had heard about Lions,
　　How they was ferocious and wild –
To see Wallace lying so peaceful,
　　Well, it didn't seem right to the child.

So straightway the brave little feller,
　　Not showing a morsel of fear,
Took his stick with its 'orse's 'ead 'andle
　　And pushed it in Wallace's ear.

You could see that the Lion didn't like it,
　　For giving a kind of a roll,
He pulled Albert inside the cage with 'im,
　　And swallowed the little lad 'ole.

Then Pa, who had seen the occurrence,
    And didn't know what to do next,
Said 'Mother! Yon lion's 'et Albert,'
    And Mother said 'Well, I am vexed!'

Then Mr and Mrs Ramsbottom –
    Quite rightly, when all's said and done –
Complained to the Animal Keeper
    That the Lion had eaten their son.

The keeper was quite nice about it;
    He said 'What a nasty mishap.
Are you sure that it's your boy he's eaten?'
    Pa said 'Am I sure? There's his cap!'

The manager had to be sent for.
    He came and he said 'What's to do?'
Pa said 'Yon Lion's 'et Albert,
    And 'im in his Sunday clothes, too.'

Then Mother said, 'Right's right, young feller;
    I think it's a shame and a sin
For a lion to go and eat Albert,
    And after we've paid to come in.'

The manager wanted no trouble,;
    He took out his purse right away,
Saying 'How much to settle the matter?'
    And Pa said 'What do you usually pay?'

But Mother had turned a bit awkward
    When she saw where her Albert had gone.
She said 'No! someone's got to be summonsed' –
    So that was decided upon.

Then off they all went to the P'lice Station,
    In front of the Magistrate chap;
They told 'im what happened to Albert,
    And proved it by showing his cap.

The Magistrate gave his opinion
    That no one was really to blame
And he said that he hoped the Ramsbottoms
    Would have further sons to their name.

At that Mother got proper blazing,
    'And thank you, sir, kindly,' said she.
'What, waste all our lives raising children
    To feed ruddy lions? Not me!'

Miranda

by Reginald Arkell
(1881–1959)*

Miranda was the nicest child,
Perhaps at times a little wild;
She loved the parents she had got,
And liked 'Old Grumpy' quite a lot.
She only had one tiny vice –
She thought an earwig wasn't nice.
Now earwigs are the <u>nicest</u> things;
They have no bites, they have no stings.
That nipper at the other end
Is never used to nip a friend.
I keep an earwig for a pet,
And he has never nipped me yet.
And so, Miranda, when you meet
An earwig walking down the street,
Don't start to scream and run away –

---

* My friend and neighbour, Miranda Corben, introduced me to this poem. It was written for her by Reginald Arkell, scriptwriter and comic novelist, who was a friend of her maternal grandfather, A. G. Street, farmer, writer and broadcaster. Miranda explains how the poem came to be written: 'As a little girl I was terrified of earwigs, because my parents had put up a wooden swing for me in the garden, suspended from ropes tied round a large branch on the tree outside our front door. Earwigs loved to nest in between the ropes and the branch, and therefore often fell on my head when I used the swing! One day Reginald Arkell came with my grandfather Street ('Old Grumpy' in the poem) to tea with us, and witnessed one of my tantrums . . .' Miranda suggests that, in an ideal world, a poem should be specially written for every child to encourage him/her to learn it – and then others – by heart.

Just stop and pass the time of day.
And he will smile and raise his hat;
His nippers are just right for that!

Disobedience

by A. A. Milne

(1882–1956)

James James
Morrison Morrison
Weatherby George Dupree
Took great
Care of his Mother,
Though he was only three.
James James
Said to his Mother,
'Mother,' he said, said he;
'You must never go down to the end of the town, if you don't
   go down with me.'

James James
Morrison's Mother
Put on a golden gown.
James James
Morrison's Mother
Drove to the end of the town.
James James
Morrison's Mother

Said to herself, said she:
'I can get right down to the end of the town and be back in
time for tea.'

King John
Put up a notice,
'LOST or STOLEN or STRAYED!
JAMES JAMES
MORRISON'S MOTHER
SEEMS TO HAVE BEEN MISLAID.
LAST SEEN
WANDERING VAGUELY:
QUITE OF HER OWN ACCORD,
SHE TRIED TO GET DOWN TO THE END OF THE TOWN —
FORTY SHILLINGS REWARD!'

James James
Morrison Morrison
(Commonly known as Jim)
Told his
Other relations
Not to go blaming *him*.
James James
Said to his Mother,
'Mother,' he said, said he:
'You must *never* go down to the end of the town without
consulting me.'

James James
Morrison's mother
Hasn't been heard of since.
King John said he was sorry,
So did the Queen and Prince.

King John
(Somebody told me)
Said to a man he knew:
'If people go down to the end of the town, well, what can
anyone do?'

(*Now then, very softly*)
J. J.
M. M.
W. G. Du P.
Took great
C/o his M*****
Though he was only 3.
J. J. said to his M*****
'M*****,' he said, said he:
'You-must-never-go-down-to-the-end-of-the-town-if-you-
don't-go-down-with-ME!'

The Tale of Custard the Dragon
by Ogden Nash
(1902–71)

Belinda lived in a little white house,
With a little black kitten and a little gray mouse,
And a little yellow dog and a little red wagon,
And a realio, trulio, little pet dragon.

Now the name of the little black kitten was Ink,
And the little gray mouse, she called her Blink,
And the little yellow dog was sharp as Mustard,
But the dragon was a coward, and she called him
    Custard.

Custard the dragon had big sharp teeth,
And spikes on top of him and scales underneath,
Mouth like a fireplace, chimney for a nose,
And realio, trulio daggers on his toes.

Belinda was as brave as a barrelful of bears,
And Ink and Blink chased lions down the stairs,
Mustard was as brave as a tiger in a rage,
But Custard cried for a nice safe cage.

Belinda tickled him, she tickled him unmerciful,
Ink, Blink and Mustard, they rudely called him Percival,
They all sat laughing in the little red wagon
At the realio, trulio, cowardly dragon.

Belinda giggled till she shook the house,
And Blink said 'Weeck!' which is giggling for a mouse,
Ink and Mustard rudely asked his age,
When Custard cried for a nice safe cage.

Suddenly, suddenly they heard a nasty sound,
And Mustard growled, and they all looked around.
'Meowch!' cried Ink, and 'Ooh!' cried Belinda,
For there was a pirate, climbing in the winda.

Pistol in his left hand, pistol in his right,
And he held in his teeth a cutlass bright,

His beard was black, one leg was wood;
It was clear that the pirate meant no good.

Belinda paled, and she cried, 'Help! Help!'
But Mustard fled with a terrified yelp,
Ink trickled down to the bottom of the household,
And little mouse Blink strategically mouseholed.

But up jumped Custard, snorting like an engine,
Clashed his tail like irons in a dungeon,
With a clatter and a clank and a jangling squirm
He went at the pirate like a robin at a worm.

The pirate gaped at Belinda's dragon,
And gulped some grog from his pocket flagon,
He fired two bullets, but they didn't hit,
And Custard gobbled him, every bit.

Belinda embraced him, Mustard licked him,
No one mourned for his pirate victim.
Ink and Blink in glee did gyrate
Around the dragon that ate the pyrate.

But presently up spoke little dog Mustard,
'I'd have been twice as brave if I hadn't been
    flustered.'
And up spoke Ink and up spoke Blink,
'We'd have been three times as brave, we think.'
And Custard said, 'I quite agree
That everybody is braver than me.'

Belinda still lives in her little white house,
With her little black kitten and her little gray mouse,

And her little yellow dog and her little red wagon,
And her realio, trulio, little pet dragon.

Belinda is as brave as a barrelful of bears,
And Ink and Blink chase lions down the stairs,
Mustard is as brave as a tiger in a rage,
But Custard keeps crying for a nice safe cage.

Earl's Court Road Pub
by *Diana Morgan*
*(1908–96)**

She's here at Opening Time each day
On the dot. Her name is Gray;
She's quite the lady, forty-something, fair,
Must have been pretty once – nice reddish hair;
She lives in Colehern Court across the way.
Well, as I said, she comes in every day.
Sits in her corner with a gin and ton.
Each time I look – 'I'll have another, Ron.'
By three she's pretty tight, the last to go.
I see her 'cross the street – you never know.
At half past five as I unlock the door
She's on the step. So it begins once more.

---

* This was one of a series of poems by Diana Morgan – Welsh-born, London-based actress, revue writer, film scriptwriter and poet – written about characters she had observed in different pubs in and around London.

She's very chatty with the wife and I;
She's keen on racing; even when she's high
She's never awkward, just gets white and sad.
We often wonder of the life she's had.
She never mentions husband, kiddies, friends.
She must have pots of money, for she spends
At least two quid a session here each day.
She never ever seems to go away –
Even in summer when the sun is high
And London dead and dusty. One night I
Said, 'Why don't you take a trip to Gay Paree?'
She only smiled and said, 'This one's on me.'

She's very generous we have always found –
Standing drinks and paying round on round.
The regulars like her: 'Morning, Mrs Gray!'
'Good morning, Frank – what's it to be today?'
The lads all know that she's an easy touch.
But she don't take 'em back with – not much:
Say once or twice a year. We always know,
'Cos she don't make the morning session. Oh
It's not she minds us knowing she's been stung,
It's just the fact the bastards are so young!
But she'll be back at night: 'Good evening, Ron!'
'Evening, Madam' – 'The usual – gin and ton.'

Sonia Snell

by Cyril Fletcher
(1913–2005)*

This is the tale of Sonia Snell,
To whom an accident befell.
An accident which may well seem
Embarrassing in the extreme.
It happened, as it does to many,
That Sonia had to spend a penny.
She entered in with modest grace
The properly appointed place
Provided at the railway station,
And there she sat in meditation,
Unfortunately unacquainted
The woodwork had been newly painted
Which made poor Sonia realise
Her inability to rise.
And though she struggled, pulled and yelled
She found that she was firmly held.
She raised her voice in mournful shout
'Please someone come and help me out.'
Her cries for help then quickly brought

---

* Cyril Fletcher was a comedian, pantomime dame and radio and television star, who made his name in the 1930s performing comic and sentimental poems that he called 'Odd Odes'. He befriended me when I was in my early twenties and made me the youngest speaker on the 'public speaking circuit' when he recruited me to his speakers' agency, Associated Speakers, in 1971. Soon afterwards I created a one-man show for him in which he played Lewis Carroll and recited a number of Carroll's best-known verses.

A crowd of every kind and sort.
They stood around and feebly sniggered
And all they said was 'I'll be jiggered.'
'Gor blimey' said the ancient porter
'We ought to soak her off with water.'
The Station Master and the staff
Were most perverse and did not laugh
But lugged at Sonia's hands and feet
But could not get her off the seat.
The carpenter arrived at last
And, finding Sonia still stuck fast
Remarked, 'I know what I can do',
And neatly sawed the seat right through.
Sonia arose, only to find
A wooden halo on behind.
An ambulance came down the street
And bore her off, complete with seat
To take the wooden bustled gal
Off quickly to the hospital.
They hurried Sonia off inside
After a short but painful ride
And seizing her by heels and head
Laid her face down on the bed.
The doctors all came on parade
To render her immediate aid.
A surgeon said, 'Upon my word
Could anything be more absurd,
Have any of you, I implore,
Seen anything like this before?'
'Yes' said a student, unashamed,
'Frequently . . . but never framed.'

A Hand in the Bird
by Roald Dahl
(1916–90)

I'm a maiden who is forty,
And a maiden I shall stay.
There are some who call me haughty,
But I care not what they say.

I was running the tombola
At our church bazaar today,
And doing it with gusto
In my usual jolly way . . .

When suddenly, I knew not why,
There came a funny feeling
Of something *crawling up my thigh*!
I nearly hit the ceiling!

A mouse! I thought. How foul! How mean!
How exquisitely tickly!
Quite soon I know I'm going to scream.
I've got to catch it quickly.

I made a grab. I caught the mouse,
Now right inside my knickers.
A mouse my foot! It was a HAND!
Great Scott! It was the vicar's!

Timothy Winters
by Charles Causley
(1917–2003)*

Timothy Winters comes to school
With eyes as wide as a football-pool,
Ears like bombs and teeth like splinters:
A blitz of a boy is Timothy Winters.

His belly is white, his neck is dark,
And his hair is an exclamation-mark.
His clothes are enough to scare a crow
And through his britches the blue winds blow.

When teacher talks he won't hear a word
And he shoots down dead the arithmetic-bird,
He licks the pattern off his plate
And he's not even heard of the Welfare State.

Timothy Winters has bloody feet
And he lives in a house on Suez Street,
He sleeps in a sack on the kitchen floor
And they say there aren't boys like him anymore.

---

* Charles Causley was a Cornish writer, poet and schoolmaster. Of Timothy Winters he said: 'People always ask me whether this was a real boy. My God, he certainly was. Poor old boy. I don't know where he is now. I was thunderstruck when people thought I had made it up! He was a real bloke. Poor little devil.'

Old Man Winters likes his beer
And his missus ran off with a bombardier,
Grandma sits in the grate with a gin
And Timothy's dosed with an aspirin.

The Welfare Worker lies awake
But the law's as tricky as a ten-foot snake,
So Timothy Winters drinks his cup
And slowly goes on growing up.

At Morning Prayers the Master helves
for children less fortunate than ourselves,
And the loudest response in the room is when
Timothy Winters roars 'Amen!'

So come one angel, come on ten:
Timothy Winters says 'Amen
Amen amen amen amen.'
Timothy Winters, Lord.

                        Amen.

Poem

by Frank O'Hara
(1926–66)*

Lana Turner has collapsed!
I was trotting along and suddenly
it started raining and snowing
and you said it was hailing
but hailing hits you on the head
hard so it was really snowing and
raining and I was in such a hurry
to meet you but the traffic
was acting exactly like the sky
and suddenly I see a headline
LANA TURNER HAS COLLAPSED!
there is no snow in Hollywood
there is no rain in California
I have been to lots of parties
and acted perfectly disgraceful
but I never actually collapsed
oh Lana Turner we love you get up

---

* Lana Turner (1921–95) was a hugely famous American beauty and film star.
Frank O'Hara was a writer, poet, art critic and curator of the Museum of Modern Art in New York.

The Phantom Lollipop Lady
by Adrian Henri
(1932–2000)*

The phantom lollipop lady
haunts the crossroads
where the old school used to be;
they closed it down in 1973.

The old lollipop lady
loved her job, and stood there
for seven years altogether,
no matter how bad the weather.

When they pulled the old school down
she still stood there every day:
a pocketful of sweets for the little ones,
smiles and a joke for the big ones.

One day the lollipop lady
was taken away to hospital.
Without her standing there
the corner looked, somehow, bare.

---

* Adrian Henri was a British poet and painter, remembered as the founder of poetry-rock group the Liverpool Scene and as one of three poets in the best-selling anthology *The Mersey Sound*.

After a month and two operations
the lollipop lady died;
the children felt something missing:
she had made her final crossing.

Now if you go down alone at dusk
just before the streetlights go on,
look closely at the corner over there:
in the shadows by the lamp-post you'll see her.

Helping phantom children across the street,
holding up the traffic with a ghostly hand;
at the twilight crossing where four roads meet
the phantom lollipop lady stands.

Vincent Malloy
by Tim Burton
(born 1958)*

Vincent Malloy is seven years old
He's always polite and does what he's told
For a boy his age, he's considerate and nice
But he wants to be just like Vincent Price

---

* Vincent Malloy is the hero of a short animation made by the film director
Tim Burton in 1982 and narrated by Burton's childhood hero, the actor Vin-
cent Price – best remembered by most as the star of assorted horror films, best
remembered by me as probably the most charming man I ever met.

He doesn't mind living with his sister, dog and cats
Though he'd rather share a home with spiders and bats
There he could reflect on the horrors he's invented
And wander dark hallways, alone and tormented

Vincent is nice when his aunt comes to see him
But imagines dipping her in wax for his wax museum

He likes to experiment on his dog Abercrombie
In the hopes of creating a horrible zombie
So he and his horrible zombie dog
Could go searching for victims in the London fog

His thoughts, though, aren't only of ghoulish crimes
He likes to paint and read to pass some of the times
While other kids read books like Go, Jane, Go!
Vincent's favourite author is Edgar Allan Poe

One night, while reading a gruesome tale
He read a passage that made him turn pale

Such horrible news he could not survive
For his beautiful wife had been buried alive!
He dug out her grave to make sure she was dead
Unaware that her grave was his mother's flower bed

His mother sent Vincent off to his room
He knew he'd been banished to the tower of doom
Where he was sentenced to spend the rest of his life
Alone with the portrait of his beautiful wife

While alone and insane encased in his tomb
Vincent's mother burst suddenly into the room
She said: 'If you want to, you can go out and play
It's sunny outside, and a beautiful day.'

Vincent tried to talk, but he just couldn't speak
The years of isolation had made him quite weak
So he took out some paper and scrawled with a pen:
'I am possessed by this house, and can never leave it again.'
His mother said: 'You're not possessed, and you're not almost
    dead
These games that you play are all in your head
You're not Vincent Price, you're Vincent Malloy
You're not tormented or insane, you're just a young boy
You're seven years old and you are my son
I want you to get outside and have some real fun.'

Her anger now spent, she walked out through the hall
And while Vincent backed slowly against the wall
The room started to swell, to shiver and creak
His horrid insanity had reached its peak

He saw Abercrombie, his zombie slave
And heard his wife call from beyond the grave
She spoke from her coffin and made ghoulish demands
While, through cracking walls, reached skeleton hands

Every horror in his life that had crept through his dreams
Swept his mad laughter to terrified screams!
To escape the madness, he reached for the door
But fell limp and lifeless down on the floor

His voice was soft and very slow
As he quoted 'The Raven' from Edgar Allan Poe:
'and my soul from out that shadow
that lies floating on the floor
shall be lifted?
Nevermore . . .'

Chapter Fifteen

Funeral Blues
Poems at the end of the road

'You live and learn,' said the playwright and poet, Noël Coward, before adding tartly, 'Then, of course, you die and forget it all.' Death is inevitable. The Grim Reaper is always waiting in the wings. Resistance is futile. As Shakespeare succinctly puts it in *Hamlet*: 'All that lives must die, Passing through nature to eternity.' 'It's not that I'm afraid to die,' said Woody Allen famously, 'I just don't want to be there when it happens.'

> For a thousand years in thy sight are but as yesterday when it is past, and as a watch in the night.
>
> Thou carriest them away as with a flood; they are as a sleep: in the morning they are like grass which groweth up.
>
> In the morning it flourisheth, and groweth up; in the evening it is cut down, and withereth.
>
> For we are consumed by thine anger, and by thy wrath are we troubled.
>
> Thou hast set our iniquities before thee, our secret sins in the light of thy countenance.

> For all our days are passed away in thy wrath: we spend our years as a tale that is told.
>
> The days of our years are threescore years and ten; and if by reason of strength they be fourscore years, yet is their strength labour and sorrow; for it is soon cut off, and we fly away.
>
> Psalm 90, verses 4–10

Now that I have achieved the three-score-years-and-ten promised in the Book of Psalms, I am taking a more personal interest in death. I have to: people keep reminding me how old I am. I have been asked to be the 'new face' of the Stannah Stairlift; I have been invited to sponsor home-delivered easy-to-digest ready-meals for 'senior seniors'; in a TV commercial I am now the voice of the Tena Flex-Plus Supersoft Incontinence Pad. (According to the advertising agency, my voice is exactly what the product requires: it is 'smooth, mature, absorbent'.)

I take a personal interest in death befitting someone of my age, and I take a professional interest, too. One of my forebears was a Kenyon and, in Britain and around the world, the Kenyons have been leaders in the undertaking business since the 1870s. For some years, I have been the proud host of the annual British Funeral Directors' Awards saluting the work of the best of the best in the dying trade. (The evening ends with the two big prizes: one is for the Crematorium of the Year – the 'Crème de la Crem' award – and the other is the Lifetime Achievement award for 'Thinking outside the Box'.) I go to a lot of funerals, too. And I have had to organize two or three, as well. It isn't easy.

Saying goodbye is never easy. A funeral is inevitably a sad event – even when the deceased has been blessed with a long and a good life. When it is the funeral of someone who has died young, it is simply heartbreaking. As we approach our own point of departure, here are some poems of consolation and condolence: poems to help you reflect on those you have liked and loved and lost, poems to learn by heart to speak at a funeral or a memorial gathering.

Death, be not proud
by John Donne
(1572–1631)

Death, be not proud, though some have called thee
Mighty and dreadful, for thou art not so;
For those whom thou thinkst thou dost overthrow
Die not, poor Death, nor yet canst thou kill me;
From rest and sleep, which but thy pictures be,
Much pleasure, then from thee, much more must flow,
And soonest our best men with thee do go,
Rest of their bones, and soul's delivery.
Thou art slave to fate, chance, kings, and desperate men,
And dost with poison, war, and sickness dwell;
And poppy or charms can make us sleep as well
And better than thy stroke; why swellst thou then?
One short sleep past, we wake eternally,
And death shall be no more: Death, thou shalt die.

Epitaph on a Friend
by Robert Burns
(1759–96)

An honest man here lies at rest,
As e'er God with his image blest:
The friend of man, the friend of truth,
The friend of age, and guide of youth:
Few hearts like his, with virtue warm'd,
Few heads with knowledge so inform'd:
If there's another world, he lives in bliss;
If there is none, he made the best of this.

Music, when soft voices die
by Percy Bysshe Shelley
(1792–1822)
To——

Music, when soft voices die,
Vibrates in the memory –
Odours, when sweet violets sicken,
Live within the sense they quicken.

Rose leaves, when the rose is dead,
Are heaped for the beloved's bed;
And so thy thoughts, when thou art gone,
Love itself shall slumber on.

Crossing the Bar
by Alfred, Lord Tennyson
(1809–92)

Sunset and evening star,
    And one clear call for me!
And may there be no moaning of the bar,
    When I put out to sea,

But such a tide as moving seems asleep,
    Too full for sound and foam,
When that which drew from out the boundless deep
    Turns again home.

Twilight and evening bell,
    And after that the dark!
And may there be no sadness of farewell,
    When I embark;

For tho' from out our bourne of Time and Place
    The flood may bear me far,
I hope to see my Pilot face to face
    When I have crost the bar.

From 'Song of Myself' in *Leaves of Grass*
by Walt Whitman
(1819–92)

I depart as air, I shake my white locks at the runaway sun,
I effuse my flesh in eddies, and drift it in lacy jags.

I bequeath myself to the dirt to grow from the grass I love,
If you want me again look for me under your boot-soles.

You will hardly know who I am or what I mean,
But I shall be good health to you nevertheless,
And filter and fibre your blood.

Failing to fetch me at first keep encouraged,
Missing me one place search another,
I stop somewhere waiting for you.

Everything passes and vanishes
by William Allingham
(1824–89)

Everything passes and vanishes;
Everything leaves its trace;
And often you see in a footstep
What you could not see in a face.

Song

by Christina Rossetti
(1830–94)

When I am dead, my dearest,
   Sing no sad songs for me;
Plant thou no roses at my head,
   Nor shady cypress tree:
Be the green grass above me
   With showers and dewdrops wet;
And if thou wilt, remember,
   And if thou wilt, forget.

I shall not see the shadows,
   I shall not fear the rain;
I shall not hear the nightingale
   Sing on, as if in pain:
And dreaming through the twilight
   That doth not rise nor set,
Haply I may remember,
   And haply may forget.

Death is nothing at all
by Henry Scott Holland
*(1847–1918)**

Death is nothing at all.
It does not count.
I have only slipped away into the next room.
Nothing has happened.

Everything remains exactly as it was.
I am I, and you are you,
and the old life that we lived so fondly together is untouched,
    unchanged.
Whatever we were to each other, that we are still.

Call me by the old familiar name.
Speak of me in the easy way which you always used.
Put no difference into your tone.
Wear no forced air of solemnity or sorrow.

Laugh as we always laughed at the little jokes that we enjoyed
    together.
Play, smile, think of me, pray for me.

---

* Henry Scott Holland was Regius Professor of Divinity at Oxford University and a canon of St Paul's Cathedral in London where, in May 1910, shortly after the death of Edward VII, he delivered a sermon known as 'The King of Terrors'. It was written as prose, but since Holland's death has come to be presented and read as if it was a piece of poetry.

Let my name be ever the household word that it always was.
Let it be spoken without an effort, without the ghost of a
 shadow upon it.

Life means all that it ever meant.
It is the same as it ever was.
There is absolute and unbroken continuity.
What is this death but a negligible accident?

Why should I be out of mind because I am out of sight?
I am but waiting for you, for an interval,
somewhere very near,
just round the corner.

All is well.
Nothing is hurt; nothing is lost.
One brief moment and all will be as it was before.
How we shall laugh at the trouble of parting when we meet
 again!

Now When the Number of My Years
by Robert Louis Stevenson
(1850–94)

Now when the number of my years
 Is all fulfilled, and I
 From sedentary life
 Shall rouse me up to die,

Bury me low and let me lie
Under the wide and starry sky.
Joying to live, I joyed to die,
Bury me low and let me lie.

Clear was my soul, my deeds were free,
Honour was called my name,
I fell not back from fear
Nor followed after fame.
Bury me low and let me lie
Under the wide and starry sky.
Joying to live, I joyed to die,
Bury me low and let me lie.

Bury me low in valleys green
And where the milder breeze
Blows fresh along the stream,
Sings roundly in the trees –
Bury me low and let me lie
Under the wide and starry sky.
Joying to live, I joyed to die,
Bury me low and let me lie.

Requiescat
by Oscar Wilde
*(1854–1900)**

Tread lightly, she is near
  Under the snow,
Speak gently, she can hear
  The daisies grow.

All her bright golden hair
  Tarnished with rust,
She that was young and fair
  Fallen to dust.

Lily-like, white as snow,
  She hardly knew
She was a woman, so
  Sweetly she grew.

Coffin-board, heavy stone,
  Lie on her breast,
I vex my heart alone,
  She is at rest.

---

* Oscar Wilde's younger sister died, not long before her tenth birthday, in 1867. According to her mother, Isola died of 'a sudden effusion on the brain'. Oscar was twelve at the time and inconsolable. As a child he frequently visited Isola's grave, and decorated an envelope to preserve a lock of her hair, which he kept all his life. He wrote this poem in her memory in 1881.

Peace, Peace, she cannot hear
Lyre or sonnet,
All my life's buried here,
Heap earth upon it.

Parta Quies
by A. E. Housman
(1859–1936)

Good-night; ensured release,
Imperishable peace,
Have these for yours,
While sea abides, and land,
And earth's foundations stand,
and heaven endures.

When earth's foundations flee,
nor sky nor land nor sea
At all is found
Content you, let them burn:
It is not your concern;
Sleep on, sleep sound.

Idyll
by Siegfried Sassoon
(1886–1967)

In the grey summer garden I shall find you
With day-break and the morning hills behind you.
There will be rain-wet roses; stir of wings;
And down the wood a thrush that wakes and sings.
Not from the past you'll come, but from that deep
Where beauty murmurs to the soul asleep:
And I shall know the sense of life re-born
From dreams into the mystery of morn
Where gloom and brightness meet. And standing there
Till that calm song is done, at last we'll share
The league-spread, quiring symphonies that are
Joy in the world, and peace, and dawn's one star.

'You'll Never Walk Alone' from *Carousel*
by Oscar Hammerstein II
(1895–1960)

When you walk through a storm
Hold your head up high
And don't be afraid of the dark
At the end of a storm

There's a golden sky
And the sweet silver song of a lark
Walk on through the wind
Walk on through the rain
Though your dreams be tossed and blown
Walk on, walk on
With hope in your heart
And you'll never walk alone
You'll never walk alone
Walk on, walk on
With hope in your heart
And you'll never walk alone
You'll never walk alone

When I Have Fears
by Noël Coward
(1899–1973)

When I have fears, as Keats had fears,
Of the moment I'll cease to be
I console myself with vanished years
Remembered laughter, remembered tears,
And the peace of the changing sea.

When I feel sad, as Keats felt sad,
That my life is so nearly done
It gives me comfort to dwell upon
Remembered friends who are dead and gone
And the jokes we had and the fun.

How happy they are I cannot know
But happy I am who loved them so.

Funeral Blues
by W. H. Auden
(1907–73)*

Stop all the clocks, cut off the telephone,
Prevent the dog from barking with a juicy bone,
Silence the pianos and with muffled drum
Bring out the coffin, let the mourners come.

Let aeroplanes circle moaning overhead
Scribbling on the sky the message He is Dead, Put crêpe
bows round the white necks of the public doves,
Let the traffic policemen wear black cotton gloves.

---

* This has become one of the most popular poems spoken at funerals since
it was featured in the 1994 film, Four Weddings and a Funeral.

He was my North, my South, my East and West,
My working week and my Sunday rest,
My noon, my midnight, my talk, my song;
I thought that love would last forever: I was wrong.

The stars are not wanted now: put out every one;
Pack up the moon and dismantle the sun;
Pour away the ocean and sweep up the wood.
For nothing now can ever come to any good.

If I Should Go Before the Rest of You
by Joyce Grenfell
(1910–79)

If I should go before the rest of you
Break not a flower nor inscribe a stone,
Nor when I'm gone speak in a Sunday voice
But be the usual selves that I have known.
Weep if you must, Parting is hell,
But Life goes on, So sing as well.

Do not go gentle into that good night
by Dylan Thomas
(1914–1953)

Do not go gentle into that good night,
Old age should burn and rave at close of day;
Rage, rage against the dying of the light.

Though wise men at their end know dark is right,
Because their words had forked no lightning they
Do not go gentle into that good night.

Good men, the last wave by, crying how bright
Their frail deeds might have danced in a green bay,
Rage, rage against the dying of the light.

Wild men who caught and sang the sun in flight,
And learn, too late, they grieved it on its way,
Do not go gentle into that good night.

Grave men, near death, who see with blinding sight
Blind eyes could blaze like meteors and be gay,
Rage, rage against the dying of the light.

And you, my father, there on the sad height,
Curse, bless, me now with your fierce tears, I pray.
Do not go gentle into that good night.
Rage, rage against the dying of the light.

On the Death of Harold Wilson
by Mary Wilson
(1916–2018)*

My love you have stumbled slowly
On the quiet way to death
And you lie where the wind blows strongly
With a salty spray on its breath
For this men of the island bore you
Down paths where the branches meet
And the only sounds were the crunching grind
Of the gravel beneath their feet
And the sighing slide of the ebbing tide
On the beach where the breakers meet

---

* Mary Wilson was a fine poet and a lovely lady, whose husband, Harold Wilson (1916–95), was twice British Prime Minister. In his final years he suffered from dementia, and is buried in St Mary's Old Churchyard in the Scilly Isles where the Wilsons had a much-loved holiday home.

The Good
by Brendan Kennelly
(born 1936)

The good are vulnerable
As any bird in flight.
They do not think of safety,
Are blind to possible extinction
And when most vulnerable
Are most themselves.
The good are real as the sun,
Are best perceived through clouds
Of casual corruption
That cannot kill the luminous sufficiency
That shines on city, sea and wilderness,
Fastidiously revealing
One man to another,
Who yet will not accept
Responsibilities of light.
The good incline to praise,
To have the knack of seeing that
The best is not destroyed
Although forever threatened.
The good go naked in all weathers,
And by their nakedness rebuke
The small protective sanities
That hide men from themselves.
The good are difficult to see
Though open, rare, destructible.
Always, they retain a kind of youth,

The vulnerable grace
Of any bird in flight,
Content to be itself,
Accomplished master and potential victim,
Accepting what the earth or sky intends.
I think that I know one or two
Among my friends.

Let me Die a Youngman's Death
by Roger McGough
(born 1937)

Let me die a youngman's death
not a clean & inbetween
the sheets holywater death
not a famous-last-words
peaceful out of breath death

When I'm 73
& in constant good tumour
may I be mown down at dawn
by a bright red sports car
on my way home
from an allnight party

Or when I'm 91
with silver hair
& sitting in a barber's chair
may rival gangsters
with hamfisted tommyguns burst in
& give me a short back & insides

Or when I'm 104
& banned from the Cavern
may my mistress
catching me in bed with her daughter
& fearing for her son
cut me up into little pieces
& throw away every piece but one

Let me die a youngman's death
not a free from sin tiptoe in
candle wax & waning death
not a curtains drawn by angels borne
'what a nice way to go' death

Chapter Sixteen

A to Z
An alphabet of poets

From Auden to Zephaniah, from Byron to Yeats, via Eliot and Frost, Kipling and Larkin, these are the 'classics', the pick of the pops, the best loved, the most frequently quoted, the most often learnt, the most easily remembered: twenty-six poems to learn by heart from twenty-six poets whose work has stood the test of time and, with good reason, lingers in the memory.

A

Night Mail
by W. H. Auden
(1907–73) *

I

This is the Night Mail crossing the Border,
Bringing the cheque and the postal order,

Letters for the rich, letters for the poor,
The shop at the corner, the girl next door.

Pulling up Beattock, a steady climb:
The gradient's against her, but she's on time.

Past cotton-grass and moorland boulder
Shovelling white steam over her shoulder,

Snorting noisily as she passes
Silent miles of wind-bent grasses.

Birds turn their heads as she approaches,
Stare from bushes at her blank-faced coaches.

---

* The poem was written in 1936 as a 'verse commentary' to accompany a
documentary film produced by the General Post Office Film Unit. *Night Mail*,
with music by Benjamin Britten, celebrated the nightly postal train operated by
the London, Midland and Scottish Railway (LMS) from London to Glasgow.

Sheep-dogs cannot turn her course;
They slumber on with paws across.

In the farm she passes no one wakes,
But a jug in a bedroom gently shakes.

II

Dawn freshens, Her climb is done.
Down towards Glasgow she descends,
Towards the steam tugs yelping down a glade of cranes,
Towards the fields of apparatus, the furnaces
Set on the dark plain like gigantic chessmen.
All Scotland waits for her:
In dark glens, beside pale-green lochs,
Men long for news.

III

Letters of thanks, letters from banks,
Letters of joy from girl and boy,
Receipted bills and invitations
To inspect new stock or to visit relations,
And applications for situations,
And timid lovers' declarations,
And gossip, gossip from all the nations,
News circumstantial, news financial,
Letters with holiday snaps to enlarge in,
Letters with faces scrawled on the margin,
Letters from uncles, cousins, and aunts,
Letters to Scotland from the South of France,
Letters of condolence to Highlands and Lowlands,
Written on paper of every hue,
The pink, the violet, the white and the blue,

The chatty, the catty, the boring, the adoring,
The cold and official and the heart's outpouring,
Clever, stupid, short and long,
The typed and the printed and the spelt all wrong.

IV
Thousands are still asleep,
Dreaming of terrifying monsters
Or of friendly tea beside the band in Cranston's or
Crawford's:

Asleep in working Glasgow, asleep in well-set Edinburgh,
Asleep in granite Aberdeen,
They continue their dreams,
But shall wake soon and hope for letters,
And none will hear the postman's knock
Without a quickening of the heart,
For who can bear to feel himself forgotten?

B

She Walks in Beauty
by George Gordon, Lord Byron
(1788–1824)

She walks in beauty, like the night
   Of cloudless climes and starry skies;
And all that's best of dark and bright
   Meet in her aspect and her eyes:
Thus mellow'd to that tender light
   Which heaven to gaudy day denies.

One shade the more, one ray the less,
   Had half impair'd the nameless grace
Which waves in every raven tress,
   Or softly lightens o'er her face;
Where thoughts serenely sweet express
   How pure, how dear their dwelling place.

And on that cheek, and o'er that brow,
   So soft, so calm, yet eloquent,
The smiles that win, the tints that glow,
   But tell of days in goodness spent,
A mind at peace with all below,
   A heart whose love is innocent!

C

The Rolling English Road
by G. K. Chesterton
(1874–1936)*

Before the Roman came to Rye or out to Severn strode,
The rolling English drunkard made the rolling English road.
A reeling road, a rolling road, that rambles round the shire,
And after him the parson ran, the sexton and the squire;
A merry road, a mazy road, and such as we did tread
The night we went to Birmingham by way of Beachy Head.

I knew no harm of Bonaparte and plenty of the Squire,
And for to fight the Frenchman I did not much desire;
But I did bash their baggonets because they came arrayed
To straighten out the crooked road an English drunkard made,
Where you and I went down the lane with ale-mugs in our
    hands,
The night we went to Glastonbury by way of Goodwin
    Sands.

---

* The poem, when it first appeared in 1913, was called 'A Song of Temperance
Reform' and was written to give voice to Chesterton's opposition to the grow-
ing campaign, on both sides of the Atlantic, for the prohibition of alcohol.
Beachy Head is a chalky headland in East Sussex, notorious as a place where
people have taken their own lives; Goodwin Sands is a treacherous sandbank
at the southern end of the North Sea that has claimed many sailors' lives;
Bannockburn was the site of a famous battle between the Scots and the Eng-
lish in 1314 in which many were slain; Kensal Green is the location of a large
London cemetery established in 1832.

His sins they were forgiven him; or why do flowers run
Behind him; and the hedges all strengthening in the sun?
The wild thing went from left to right and knew not which
    was which,
But the wild rose was above him when they found him in the
    ditch.
God pardon us, nor harden us; we did not see so clear
The night we went to Bannockburn by way of Brighton Pier.

My friends, we will not go again or ape an ancient rage,
Or stretch the folly of our youth to be the shame of age,
But walk with clearer eyes and ears this path that wandereth,
And see undrugged in evening light the decent inn of death;
For there is good news yet to hear and fine things to be seen,
Before we go to Paradise by way of Kensal Green.

D

Leisure
by *W. H. Davies*
*(1871–1940)**

What is this life if, full of care,
We have no time to stand and stare.

No time to stand beneath the boughs
And stare as long as sheep or cows.

No time to see, when woods we pass,
Where squirrels hide their nuts in grass.

No time to see, in broad daylight,
Streams full of stars, like skies at night.

No time to turn at Beauty's glance,
And watch her feet, how they can dance.

No time to wait till her mouth can
Enrich that smile her eyes began.

A poor life this is if, full of care,
We have no time to stand and stare.

---

* William Henry Davies was a Welsh-born poet who spent much of his early
life as a tramp, travelling on the open road in both the UK and the USA,
observing the passing scene.

E

Journey of the Magi
by T. S. Eliot
(1888–1965)

'A cold coming we had of it,
Just the worst time of the year
For a journey, and such a long journey:
The ways deep and the weather sharp,
The very dead of winter.'
And the camels galled, sore-footed, refractory,
Lying down in the melting snow.
There were times we regretted
The summer palaces on slopes, the terraces,
And the silken girls bringing sherbet.
Then the camel men cursing and grumbling
And running away, and wanting their liquor and women,
And the night-fires going out, and the lack of shelters,
And the cities hostile and the towns unfriendly
And the villages dirty and charging high prices:
A hard time we had of it.
At the end we preferred to travel all night,
Sleeping in snatches,
With the voices singing in our ears, saying
That this was all folly.

Then at dawn we came down to a temperate valley,
Wet, below the snow line, smelling of vegetation,
With a running stream and a water-mill beating the
    darkness,
And three trees on the low sky.
And an old white horse galloped away in the meadow.
Then we came to a tavern with vine-leaves over the lintel,
Six hands at an open door dicing for pieces of silver,
And feet kicking the empty wine-skins.
But there was no information, and so we continued
And arrived at evening, not a moment too soon
Finding the place; it was (you might say) satisfactory.

    All this was a long time ago, I remember,
And I would do it again, but set down
This set down
This: were we led all that way for
Birth or Death? There was a Birth, certainly,
We had evidence and no doubt. I had seen birth and death,
But had thought they were different; this Birth was
Hard and bitter agony for us, like Death, our death.
We returned to our places, these Kingdoms,
But no longer at ease here, in the old dispensation,
With an alien people clutching their gods.
I should be glad of another death.

F

The Road Not Taken
by Robert Frost
(1874–1963)

Two roads diverged in a yellow wood,
And sorry I could not travel both
And be one traveler, long I stood
And looked down one as far as I could
To where it bent in the undergrowth;

Then took the other, as just as fair,
And having perhaps the better claim,
Because it was grassy and wanted wear;
Though as for that the passing there
Had worn them really about the same,

And both that morning equally lay
In leaves no step had trodden black.
Oh, I kept the first for another day!
Yet knowing how way leads on to way,
I doubted if I should ever come back.

I shall be telling this with a sigh
Somewhere ages and ages hence:
Two roads diverged in a wood, and I –
I took the one less traveled by,
And that has made all the difference.

I'd Love to Be a Fairy's Child
by Robert Graves
(1895–1985)

Children born of fairy stock
Never need for shirt or frock,
Never want for food or fire,
Always get their heart's desire:
Jingle pockets full of gold,
Marry when they're seven years old.
Every fairy child may keep
Two strong ponies and ten sheep;
All have houses, each his own,
Built of brick or granite stone;
They live on cherries, they run wild –
I'd love to be a fairy's child.

H

Invictus
by *William Ernest Henley*
*(1849–1903)**

Out of the night that covers me,
  Black as the pit from pole to pole,
I thank whatever gods may be
  For my unconquerable soul.

In the fell clutch of circumstance
  I have not winced nor cried aloud.

---

* As a boy, Henley suffered from tuberculosis. As a consequence, aged sixteen, his left leg was amputated. In his early twenties, he was told that his right leg would need to be amputated, too. In August 1873 he travelled to Edinburgh where the eminent surgeon Joseph Lister treated him, successfully saving his leg. It was during his recovery that Henley began to write the poem that became 'Invictus'. It first appeared in 1888 without a title and, when reproduced in late-Victorian newspapers and journals, it was called, variously, 'Myself', 'Song of a Strong Soul', 'Clear Grit', 'Master of His Fate', 'Captain of My Soul', 'Urbs Fortitudinis' and 'De Profundis'. The title 'Invictus' – the Latin for 'Unconquered' – was given to the poem by Arthur Quiller-Couch when he included it in *The Oxford Book of English Verse* in 1900. In a speech to the House of Commons in September 1941, Winston Churchill paraphrased the last two lines of the poem, with his rallying cry: 'We still are master of our fate. We still are captain of our souls.' Later, while imprisoned on Robben Island in South Africa, Nelson Mandela, who knew the poem by heart, recited it to other prisoners. The Invictus Games, the international Paralympic-style multi-sport event created by Prince Harry, in which wounded and injured armed services personnel compete, is inspired by the poem.

Under the bludgeonings of chance
　　My head is bloody, but unbowed.

Beyond this place of wrath and tears
　　Looms but the Horror of the shade,
And yet the menace of the years
　　Finds and shall find me unafraid.

It matters not how strait the gate,
　　How charged with punishments the scroll,
I am the master of my fate:
　　I am the captain of my soul.

I

The Camp Fires of the Past
by Rex Ingamells
(1913–55)*

A thousand, thousand camp fires every night,
in ages gone, would twinkle to the dark
from crest and valley in the rolling bush,
from mulga scrub and mallee scrub, from dunes

---

* Rex Ingamells was an Australian poet and one of the pioneers of the Jindy-
worobak Movement which, in the 1930s and 1940s, saw white Australian
writers trying to contribute to a uniquely Australian culture by resisting the
influx of 'alien art' and showing what they hoped was a true 'understanding
of Australia's history and traditions, primeval, colonial and modern'.

of Central sand, from gaps in straggling ranges,
from gibber plains and plains of iron-wood,
through leaves and in the open, from the mangroves
by shore of Carpenteria, from rocks
and beaches of the Bight . . . . for countless aeons,
a thousand, thousand camp fires burned each night,
and, by the fires, the Old Men told their tales
which held their listeners spellbound . . . Every night
among the fires men chanted to the beat
of stick and boomerangs and clap of hands,
or drone-and-boom of didgeridoo, the songs
rising and falling, trailing, quickening,
while eyes gleamed bright, through smoke drift, bodies shone
and dusked in fitful glow amid the shadows . . . . . .

J

Warning
by Jenny Joseph
(1932–2018)*

When I am an old woman I shall wear purple
With a red hat which doesn't go, and doesn't suit me,
And I shall spend my pension on brandy and summer gloves
And satin sandals, and say we've no money for butter.

---

* According to more than one poll, 'Warning' by Jenny Joseph, first pub-
lished in 1961, is now, by a margin, Britain's 'most popular post-war poem'.

I shall sit down on the pavement when I'm tired
And gobble up samples in shops and press alarm bells
And run my stick along the public railings
And make up for the sobriety of my youth.
I shall go out in my slippers in the rain
And pick flowers in other people's gardens
And learn to spit.
You can wear terrible shirts and grow more fat
And eat three pounds of sausages at a go
Or only bread and pickle for a week
And hoard pens and pencils and beermats and things in
    boxes.

But now we must have clothes that keep us dry
And pay our rent and not swear in the street
And set a good example for the children.
We must have friends to dinner and read the papers.

But maybe I ought to practise a little now?
So people who know me are not too shocked and surprised
When suddenly I am old and start to wear purple.

K

If –
by Rudyard Kipling
(1865–1936)*

If you can keep your head when all about you
    Are losing theirs and blaming it on you;
If you can trust yourself when all men doubt you,
    But make allowance for their doubting too;
If you can wait and not be tired by waiting,
    Or being lied about, don't deal in lies,
Or being hated, don't give way to hating,
    And yet don't look too good, nor talk too wise;

If you can dream – and not make dreams your master;
    If you can think – and not make thoughts your aim,
If you can meet with Triumph and Disaster
    And treat those two impostors just the same;
If you can bear to hear the truth you've spoken
    Twisted by knaves to make a trap for fools,
Or watch the things you gave your life to, broken,
    And stoop and build 'em up with worn-out tools;

---

* 'If –' regularly tops the poll as Britain's 'best-loved poem'. First published in 1910, it was written in the 1890s in the form of advice to the poet's only son, John Kipling, who was born in 1897 and killed in September 1915, at the Battle of Loos during the First World War, just six weeks after his eighteenth birthday.

If you can make one heap of all your winnings
  And risk it on one turn of pitch-and-toss,
And lose, and start again at your beginnings
  And never breathe a word about your loss;
If you can force your heart and nerve and sinew
  To serve your turn long after they are gone,
And so hold on when there is nothing in you
  Except the Will which says to them: 'Hold on!'

If you can talk with crowds and keep your virtue,
  Or walk with Kings – nor lose the common touch,
If neither foes nor loving friends can hurt you,
  If all men count with you, but none too much;
If you can fill the unforgiving minute
  With sixty seconds' worth of distance run,
Yours is the Earth and everything that's in it,
  And – which is more – you'll be a Man, my son!

L

This Be The Verse
by Philip Larkin
(1922–85)

They fuck you up, your mum and dad.
  They may not mean to, but they do.
They fill you with the faults they had
  And add some extra, just for you.

But they were fucked up in their turn
    By fools in old-style hats and coats,
Who half the time were soppy-stern
    And half at one another's throats.

Man hands on misery to man.
    It deepens like a coastal shelf.
Get out as early as you can,
    And don't have any kids yourself.

M

Sea-Fever
by John Masefield
(1878–1967)*

I must go down to the seas again, to the lonely sea and the
    sky,
And all I ask is a tall ship and a star to steer her by,
And the wheel's kick and the wind's song and the white sail's
    shaking,
And a grey mist on the sea's face and a grey dawn breaking.

---

* John Masefield loomed large in my childhood because my father had met
him (and Mrs Masefield) in 1930 when the new Poet Laureate came to a stu-
dent production of Milton's *Samson Agonistes* at Exeter College in Oxford. In
the play, my father played the part of Manoa, Samson's father, and would
intone great speeches from the play until his dying day. Whenever anything
went awry at home, my father would immediately cry:

I must go down to the seas again, for the call of the
        running tide
Is a wild call and a clear call that may not be denied;
And all I ask is a windy day with the white clouds flying,
And the flung spray and the blown spume, and the sea-gulls
        crying.

I must go down to the seas again, to the vagrant gypsy
        life,
To the gull's way and the whale's way where the wind's like a
        whetted knife;
And all I ask is a merry yarn from a laughing fellow-rover,
And quiet sleep and a sweet dream when the long trick's
        over.

Come, come, no time for lamentation now,
    Nor yet much cause . . .
My father also introduced me to Masefield's long poem, 'Biography', which
ends with four lines that are among my favourites:
    Best trust the happy moments. What they gave
    Makes man less fearful of the certain grave,
    And gives his work compassion and new eyes.
    The days that make us happy make us wise.

N

Vitaï Lampada
by *Henry Newbolt*
*(1862–1938)**

There's a breathless hush in the Close to-night –
Ten to make and the match to win –
A bumping pitch and a blinding light,
An hour to play and the last man in.
And it's not for the sake of a ribboned coat,
Or the selfish hope of a season's fame,
But his captain's hand on his shoulder smote
'Play up! play up! and play the game!'

The sand of the desert is sodden red, –
Red with the wreck of a square that broke; –
The Gatling's jammed and the Colonel dead,
And the regiment blind with dust and smoke.
The river of death has brimmed his banks,

---

* Written in 1892, the poem takes its title from a quotation by the Roman poet, Lucretius, which means 'the torch of life'. It refers to how a schoolboy, a future soldier, learns selfless commitment to duty playing cricket in the Close at Clifton College, the public school to which Newbolt won a scholarship and where he became head boy in 1881. The engagement mentioned in verse two is the Battle of Abu Klea, which took place in the Sudan in January 1885 during the unsuccessful expedition to rescue General Gordon, the British Governor-General. Frederick Burnaby is the colonel referred to in the line 'The Gatling's jammed and the Colonel's dead', although it was a Gardner machine gun, not a Gatling, that jammed, and the square did not break up disastrously as the poem suggests.

And England's far, and Honour a name,
But the voice of a schoolboy rallies the ranks:
'Play up! play up! and play the game!'

This is the word that year by year,
While in her place the school is set,
Every one of her sons must hear,
And none that hears it dare forget.
This they all with a joyful mind
Bear through life like a torch in flame,
And falling fling to the host behind –
'Play up! play up! and play the game!'

O

Dulce et Decorum est
by Wilfred Owen
(1893–1918)*

Bent double, like old beggars under sacks,
Knock-kneed, coughing like hags, we cursed through sludge,
Till on the haunting flares we turned our backs,
And towards our distant rest began to trudge.

* Henry Newbolt's 'Vitaï Lampada' was a hugely popular poem in its day,
but resented – and satirized – by some of those who experienced the reality of
war on the front lines between 1914 and 1918. Of the First World War poets,
Wilfred Owen is reckoned the greatest by many, and 'Dulce et Decorum est'
his finest achievement. Like Newbolt's title, Owen's is taken from a quotation
by a Roman poet: the phrase 'Dulce et Decorum est pro patria mori' means

Men marched asleep. Many had lost their boots,
But limped on, blood-shod. All went lame; all blind;
Drunk with fatigue; deaf even to the hoots
Of gas-shells dropping softly behind.

Gas! GAS! Quick, boys! – An ecstasy of fumbling
Fitting the clumsy helmets just in time,
But someone still was yelling out and stumbling
And flound'ring like a man in fire or lime. –
Dim through the misty panes and thick green light,
As under a green sea, I saw him drowning.

In all my dreams before my helpless sight,
He plunges at me, guttering, choking, drowning.

If in some smothering dreams, you too could pace
Behind the wagon that we flung him in,
And watch the white eyes writhing in his face,
His hanging face, like a devil's sick of sin,
If you could hear, at every jolt, the blood
Come gargling from the froth-corrupted lungs
Bitten as the cud
Of vile, incurable sores on innocent tongues, –
My friend, you would not tell with such high zest
To children ardent for some desperate glory,
The old Lie: *Dulce et decorum est*
Pro patria mori.

'It is sweet and fitting to die for one's country' and comes from Horace. The
first draft of the poem was written in October 1917 and addressed to Owen's
mother, with the message: 'Here is a gas poem done yesterday (which is not pri-
vate, but not final).' In November 1918, Owen was killed in action at the age of
twenty-five, one week before the Armistice. Only five of his poems were pub-
lished during his lifetime. 'Dulce et decorum est' first appeared in print in 1920.

Annabel Lee
by Edgar Allan Poe
(1809–49)

It was many and many a year ago,
    In a kingdom by the sea,
That a maiden there lived whom you may know
    By the name of Annabel Lee; –
And this maiden she lived with no other thought
    Than to love and be loved by me.

She was a child and *I* was a child,
    In this kingdom by the sea,
But we loved with a love that was more than love –
    I and my Annabel Lee –
With a love that the wingèd seraphs of Heaven
    Coveted her and me.

And this was the reason that, long ago,
    In this kingdom by the sea,
A wind blew out of a cloud by night
    Chilling my Annabel Lee;
So that her high-born kinsmen came
    And bore her away from me,
To shut her up, in a sepulchre
    In this kingdom by the sea.

The angels, not half so happy in Heaven,
     Went envying her and me: —
Yes! that was the reason (as all men know,
     In this kingdom by the sea)
That the wind came out of the cloud, chilling
     And killing my Annabel Lee.

But our love it was stronger by far than the love
     Of those who were older than we —
     Of many far wiser than we —
And neither the angels in Heaven above
     Nor the demons down under the sea
Can ever dissever my soul from the soul
     Of the beautiful Annabel Lee: —

For the moon never beams without bringing me dreams
     Of the beautiful Annabel Lee;
And the stars never rise, but I see the bright eyes
     Of the beautiful Annabel Lee;
And so, all the night-tide, I lie down by the side
Of my darling, my darling, my life and my bride
     In her sepulchre there by the sea —
     In her tomb by the side of the sea.

Q

In youth I dreamed
by Arthur Quiller-Couch
(1863–1944)*

In youth I dreamed, as other youths have dreamt,
  Of love, and thrummed an amateur guitar
To verses of my own, – a stout attempt
  To hold communion with the Evening Star
I wrote a sonnet, rhymed it, made it scan.
Ah me! how trippingly those last lines ran. –

O Hesperus! O happy star! to bend
  O'er Helen's bosom in the trancèd west,
  To match the hours heave by upon her breast,
And at her parted lip for dreams attend –
  If dawn defraud thee, how shall I be deemed,
  Who house within that bosom, and am dreamed?

---

* Sir Arthur Quiller-Couch was an English poet and novelist whose work often appeared under the pseudonym 'Q' and whose major achievement was editing the first, and hugely popular, *Oxford Book of English Verse* in 1900. Among his many admirers was the author Kenneth Grahame, who said that the character of 'Ratty' in his book, *The Wind in the Willows*, was based on Quiller-Couch. The 'Moxon' mentioned in the poem was Edward Moxon (1801–58), like Quiller-Couch, another 'minor bard' best remembered for publishing other poets, such as Shelley and Browning.

For weeks I thought these lines remarkable;
    For weeks I put on airs and called myself
A bard: till on a day, as it befell,
    I took a small green Moxon from the shelf
At random, opened at a casual place,
And found my young illusions face to face

With this: — *'Still steadfast, still unchangeable,*
    Pillow'd upon my fair Love's ripening breast
To feel for ever its soft fall and swell,
    Awake for ever in a sweet unrest;
Still, still to hear her tender-taken breath,
And so live ever, — or else swoon to death.'

O gulf not to be crossed by taking thought!
    O heights by toil not to be overcome!
Great Keats, unto your altar straight I brought
    My speech, and from the shrine departed dumb.
— And yet sometimes I think you played it hard
Upon a rather hopeful minor bard.

How many seconds in a minute?
by Christina Rossetti
(1830–94)

How many seconds in a minute?
Sixty, and no more in it.

How many minutes in an hour?
Sixty for sun and shower.

How many hours in a day?
Twenty-four for work and play.

How many days in a week?
Seven both to hear and speak.

How many weeks in a month?
Four, as the swift moon runn'th.

How many months in a year?
Twelve the almanack makes clear.

How many years in an age?
One hundred says the sage.

How many ages in time?
No one knows the rhyme.

Not Waving but Drowning
by Stevie Smith
(1902–71)

Nobody heard him, the dead man,
But still he lay moaning:
I was much further out than you thought
And not waving but drowning.

Poor chap, he always loved larking
And now he's dead
It must have been too cold for him his heart gave way,
They said.

Oh, no no no, it was too cold always
(Still the dead one lay moaning)
I was much too far out all my life
And not waving but drowning.

T

Adlestrop
by Edward Thomas
(1878–1917)*

Yes. I remember Adlestrop –
The name, because one afternoon
Of heat the express-train drew up there
Unwontedly. It was late June.

The steam hissed. Someone cleared his throat.
No one left and no one came
On the bare platform. What I saw
Was Adlestrop – only the name

And willows, willow-herb, and grass,
And meadowsweet, and haycocks dry,
No whit less still and lonely fair
Than the high cloudlets in the sky.

And for that minute a blackbird sang
Close by, and round him, mistier,
Farther and farther, all the birds
Of Oxfordshire and Gloucestershire.

---

* The poem recalls an experience that took place a few weeks before the
outbreak of the First World War in 1914, and was published three weeks after
Thomas's death at the Battle of Arras in 1917.

U

January

by John Updike
(1932–2009)*

The days are short,
  The sun a spark
Hung thin between
  The dark and dark.

Fat snowy footsteps
  Track the floor.
Milk bottles burst
  Outside the door.

The river is
  A frozen place
Held still beneath
  The trees of lace.

The sky is low.
  The wind is gray.
The radiator
  Purrs all day.

---

* People think of Updike as a great American novelist: he was also a poet and
an advocate of learning poetry by heart. 'Any activity becomes creative when
the doer cares about doing it right, or better,' he said. Another of his lines
seems to me to be bang on the money when it comes to the value of simply
taking time out to learn a poem: 'What art offers is space – a certain breath-
ing room for the spirit.'

The Retreat
by Henry Vaughan
(1621–95)

Happy those early days! when I
Shined in my angel-infancy.
Before I understood this place
Appointed for my second race,
Or taught my soul to fancy aught
But a white, celestial thought;
When yet I had not walked above
A mile or two from my first love,
And looking back (at that short space)
Could see a glimpse of his bright face;
When on some gilded cloud or flower
My gazing soul would dwell an hour,
And in those weaker glories spy
Some shadows of eternity;
Before I taught my tongue to wound
My conscience with a sinful sound,
Or had the black art to dispense
A several sin to every sense,
But felt through all this fleshly dress
Bright shoots of everlastingness.
    Oh how I long to travel back,
And tread again that ancient track!
That I might once more reach that plain

Where first I left my glorious train,
From whence the enlightened spirit sees
That shady city of palm trees;
But (ah!) my soul with too much stay
Is drunk, and staggers in the way.
Some men a forward motion love,
But I by backward steps would move,
And when this dust falls to the urn
In that state I came return.

W

The Magic Box
by Kit Wright
(born 1944)

I will put in the box

the swish of a silk sari on a summer night,
fire from the nostrils of a Chinese dragon,
the tip of a tongue touching a tooth

I will put in the box

a snowman with a rumbling belly,
a sip of the bluest water from Lake Lucerne,
a leaping spark from an electric fish.

I will put in the box

three violet wishes spoken in Gujarati,
the last joke of an ancient uncle
and the first smile of a baby.

I will put in the box

a fifth season and a black sun,
a cowboy on a broomstick
and a witch on a white horse.

My box is fashioned from ice and gold and steel,
with stars on the lid and secrets in the corners.
Its hinges are the toe joints
of dinosaurs.

I shall surf in my box on the great
high-rolling breakers of the wild Atlantic,
then wash ashore on a yellow beach
the colour of the sun.

X

The Silver Swan
by Anon.*

The silver swan, who living had no note,
When death approached, unlocked her silent throat,
Leaning her breast upon the reedy shore,
Thus sang her first and last, and sang no more:
'Farewell, all joys! O death, come close mine eyes!
More geese than swans now live, more fools than wise.'

Y

The Lake Isle of Innisfree
by W. B. Yeats
(1865–1939)

I will arise and go now, and go to Innisfree,
And a small cabin build there, of clay and wattles made:
Nine bean-rows will I have there, a hive for the honey-bee,
And live alone in the bee-loud glade.

---

* This is one of the loveliest poems by one of the most prolific poets: Anon.
Orlando Gibbons (1583–1625) set the poem to music, first published in 1612 in
his *First Set of Madrigals and Motets in Five Parts*. The author of the words remains
anonymous.

And I shall have some peace there, for peace comes
    dropping slow,
Dropping from the veils of the morning to where the cricket
    sings;
There midnight's all a glimmer, and noon a purple glow,
And evening full of the linnet's wings.

I will arise and go now, for always night and day
I hear lake water lapping with low sounds by the shore;
While I stand on the roadway, or on the pavements grey,
I hear it in the deep heart's core.

Z

The British
by Benjamin Zephaniah
(born 1958)
Serves 60 million

Take some Picts, Celts and Silures
And let them settle,
Then overrun them with Roman conquerors.

Remove the Romans after approximately four hundred years
Add lots of Norman French to some
Angles, Saxons, Jutes and Vikings, then stir vigorously.

Mix some hot Chileans, cool Jamaicans, Dominicans,
Trinidadians and Bajans with some Ethiopians,
Chinese, Vietnamese and Sudanese.

Then take a blend of Somalians, Sri Lankans, Nigerians
And Pakistanis,
Combine with some Guyanese
And turn up the heat.

Sprinkle some fresh Indians, Malaysians, Bosnians,
Iraqis and Bangladeshis together with some
Afghans, Spanish, Turkish, Kurdish, Japanese
And Palestinians
Then add to the melting pot.
Leave the ingredients to simmer.

As they mix and blend allow their languages to flourish
Binding them together with English.
Allow time to be cool.

Add some unity, understanding, and respect for the future
Serve with justice
And enjoy.

*Note: All the ingredients are equally important. Treating one ingredient
better than another will leave a bitter unpleasant taste.*

*Warning: An unequal spread of justice will damage the people and
cause pain.*

Give justice and equality to all.

Epilogue

Everything Is Going to Be All Right

For me, poetry lifts the spirit, and learning poetry by heart sharpens the mind.

Poetry enhances life. Sharing it with babies (even before they are born), with infants and with children helps to empower them with the gift of language. Reading poetry at any age can be a recreation, a consolation, a diversion, a delight. Sometimes it can be a challenge, too. As E. B. White, the author of the children's classic, *Charlotte's Web*, explained: 'A poet dares be just so clear and no clearer . . . He unzips the veil from beauty, but does not remove it. A poet utterly clear is a trifle glaring.'

As anyone who has done it will tell you (as I hope you are telling yourself now), learning poetry by heart is profoundly satisfying. As I hope I have demonstrated, it is also good for you. It boosts your brainpower and, consequently, helps keep your mind alive – and ticking, thinking and feeling.

Poetry makes me happy and helps me cope with sadness and adversity when they come my way. If you have got this far in the book, I hope you have enjoyed the journey. I trust you have re-encountered some old friends in the course of it and made some intriguing new acquaintances, too.

To end with, here are some of my all-time favourites – poems that, in my book, exemplify the power of both poetry and positive thinking. I know the poems quite well, but not yet by heart. I thought I might try to learn one a month over the coming year.

Care to join me?

Happy the man
by John Dryden
(1631–1700)

Happy the man, and happy he alone,
    He who can call today his own;
    He who, secure within, can say:
'Tomorrow do thy worst, for I have lived today.
    Be fair or foul or rain or shine,
The joys I have possessed, in spite of fate, are mine.
    Not heav'n itself upon the past has pow'r;
But what has been, has been, and I have had my hour.'

Still-Life

by Elizabeth Daryush
(1887–1977)

Through the open French window the warm sun
lights up the polished breakfast-table, laid
round a bowl of crimson roses, for one –
a service of Worcester porcelain, arrayed
near it a melon, peaches, figs, small hot
rolls in a napkin, fairy rack of toast,
butter in ice, high silver coffee pot,
and, heaped on a salver, the morning's post.

She comes over the lawn, the young heiress,
from her early walk in her garden-wood
feeling that life's a table set to bless
her delicate desires with all that's good,

that even the unopened future lies
like a love-letter, full of sweet surprise.

i thank You God
by E. E. Cummings
(1894–1962)

i thank You God for most this amazing
day: for the leaping greenly spirits of trees
and a blue true dream of sky; and for everything
which is natural which is infinite which is yes

(i who have died am alive again today,
and this is the sun's birthday; this is the birth
day of life and love and wings and of the gay
great happening illimitably earth)

how should tasting touching hearing seeing
breathing any – lifted from the no
of all nothing – human merely being
doubt unimaginable You?

(now the ears of my ears awake and
now the eyes of my eyes are opened)

Days
by Philip Larkin
(1922–85)

What are days for?
Days are where we live.
They come, they wake us
Time and time over.
They are to be happy in:
Where can we live but days?

Ah, solving that question
Brings the priest and the doctor
In their long coats
Running over the fields.

The Good News
by Thich Nhat Hanh
(born 1926)

They don't publish
the good news.
The good news is published
by us.
We have a special edition every moment,

and we need you to read it.
The good news is that you are alive,
and the linden tree is still there,
standing firm in the harsh Winter.
The good news is that you have wonderful eyes
to touch the blue sky.
The good news is that your child is there before you,
and your arms are available:
hugging is possible.
They only print what is wrong.
Look at each of our special editions.
We always offer the things that are not wrong.
We want you to benefit from them
and help protect them.
The dandelion is there by the sidewalk,
smiling its wondrous smile,
singing the song of eternity.
Listen! You have ears that can hear it.
Bow your head.
Listen to it.
Leave behind the world of sorrow
and preoccupation
and get free.
The latest good news
is that you can do it.

Getting Older
by Elaine Feinstein
(born 1930)

The first surprise: I like it.
Whatever happens now, some things
that used to terrify have not:

I didn't die young, for instance. Or lose
my only love. My three children
never had to run away from anyone.

Don't tell me this gratitude is complacent.
We all approach the edge of the same blackness
which for me is silent.

Knowing as much sharpens
my delight in January freesia,
hot coffee, winter sunlight. So we say

as we lie close on some gentle occasion:
every day won from such
darkness is a celebration.

Everything is Going to be All Right
by Derek Mahon
(born 1941)

How should I not be glad to contemplate
the clouds clearing beyond the dormer window
and a high tide reflected on the ceiling?
There will be dying, there will be dying,
but there is no need to go into that.
The poems flow from the hand unbidden
and the hidden source is the watchful heart.
The sun rises in spite of everything
and the far cities are beautiful and bright.
I lie here in a riot of sunlight
watching the day break and the clouds flying.
Everything is going to be all right.

Epic!

Some longer poems to look out for now that you've mastered the craft and art of learning poetry by heart:

'Diary of a Church Mouse' by John Betjeman (1906–84)
'The Old Vicarage, Granchester' by Rupert Brooke (1887–1915)
'The Pied Piper of Hamelin' by Robert Browning (1812–89)
'The Secret People' by G. K. Chesterton (1874–1936)
'The Rime of the Ancient Mariner' by Samuel Taylor Coleridge (1772–1834)
'Jack and the Beanstalk' by Roald Dahl (1916–90)
'Lasca' by Frank Desprez (1853–1916)
'The Christmas Truce' by Carol Ann Duffy (born 1955)
'The Love Song of J. Alfred Prufrock' by T. S. Eliot (1888–1965)
'Elegy Written in a Country Churchyard' by Thomas Gray (1716–71)
'Ode to a Nightingale' by John Keats (1795–1821)
'The Whitsun Weddings' by Philip Larkin (1922–85)
'Hiawatha's Wooing' from *The Song of Hiawatha* by Henry Wadsworth Longfellow (1807–82)
'Right Royal' by John Masefield (1878–1967)
'The Tay Bridge Disaster' by William McGonagall (1825–1902)
'The Highwayman' by Alfred Noyes (1880–1958)
'The Raven' by Edgar Allan Poe (1809–49)
'The Song of Lunch' by Christopher Reid (born 1949)
'Chocolate Cake' by Michael Rosen (born 1946)
'How the Grinch Stole Christmas' by Dr Seuss (1904–91)
'In the Workhouse, Christmas Day' by George R. Sims (1847–1922)

'Ballad of a Hero' by Kate Tempest (born 1985)
'The Lady of Shalott' by Alfred, Lord Tennyson (1809–92)
'Fern Hill' by Dylan Thomas (1914–53)
'The Ballad of Reading Gaol' by Oscar Wilde (1854–1900)

Acknowledgements

'A poet can survive everything but a misprint,' said Oscar Wilde. I am very grateful to my publisher, Dan Bunyard, and the team at Michael Joseph Penguin, including Beatrix McIntyre, Alice Mottram, Kit Shepherd, Jill Cole, Beth Cockeram and Olivia Thomas, for ensuring that everything in the book is as misprint-free as I hope it is and that the publishing process has been a happy one. I am particularly grateful to Agatha Russell and Ruth Learner for securing all the permissions necessary to reproduce the poems that are in copyright. While every effort has been made to contact copyright holders, the publishers will be happy to correct any error of omission or commission at the earliest opportunity.

I am personally grateful, as ever, to my literary agent, Jonathan Lloyd of Curtis Brown, and to the many people who have helped with this project – not least my parents, Charles and Alice Brandreth, who introduced me to so many of the poems featured, and to two of my teachers, Rachel Field and Harold Gardiner, who, without knowing it, more than half a century ago set me on the path that has led to this book.

People who have kindly suggested poems for the book include Tom Alban, Sheri Bankes, Stefan Bednarczyk, Susan Bowles, Ruth Boyer, Michèle Brown, Leslie and Evie Bricusse, Dan Bunyard, Miranda Corben, Rebecca Croft, HRH The Duchess of Cornwall, Dame Judi Dench, the late Barbara Dorf, Sir Bob Geldof, Moya Gosiewski, Maxine Higgs, Anthony Holden, Roger McGough, Michael Rosen, Brian Sibley and Dorothy Wilbraham. I am very grateful to Sir Simon Russell Beale, Sir Ian McKellen, Sir Tim Rice, Sir Tom

Stoppard and Simon Williams for permission to reproduce their contributions, and to the families of Ronnie Barker, Cyril Fletcher, Paul Jennings, Celia Johnson and Mary Wilson for permission to reproduce theirs.

I am particularly grateful to Professor Usha Goswami of the University of Cambridge Department of Psychology for her guidance, and to Aatif Hassan and Olivia Haywood and the team at Dukes Education involved in the 'Poetry Together' project, as well as to Professor Brendan O'Sullivan and Caroline Ford from the University of Chester, where they are helping set up the University of Chester poetry portal on YouTube.

If anyone feels their contribution has not been properly acknowledged, or if you find any inadvertent errors or misattributions, please get in touch.

When in trouble, when in doubt,
Run in circles, scream and shout!

Anon.

Permissions

John Agard

'Toussaint L'Ouverture acknowledges Wordsworth's sonnet "To Toussaint L'Ouverture" by John Agard from *Alternative Anthem: Selected Poems* (2009), reprinted by permission Bloodaxe Books.

'What the teacher said when asked: What er we avin for geography, Miss?' By John Agard, from *A Caribbean Dozen: Poems from Caribbean Poets* (ed. John Agard and Grace Nichols, 1994), reprinted by permission Bloodaxe Books.

Allan Ahlberg

'Please Mrs Butler' by Allan Ahlberg from *Please Mrs Butler* (1983), reprinted by permission Puffin Books, an imprint and division of Penguin Random House LLC.

Simon Armitage

'The Catch' by Simon Armitage reproduced from 'Kid' copyright ©1992 by Simon Armitage. Reprinted by permission from Faber and Faber Limited.

Maya Angelou

'Phenomenal Woman' by Maya Angelou from *And Still I Rise: A Book of Poems*, copyright © 1978 by Maya Angelou. Used by permission of Random House, an imprint and division of Penguin Random House LLC. All rights reserved, and Little, Brown and Company, an imprint of Hachette Book Group.

W. H. Auden

'Funeral Blues' by W. H. Auden from *The Year's Poetry* (John Lane, Bodley Head, 1938), by permission Curtis Brown Limited, N.Y.

Clerihews by W. H. Auden from *Academic Graffiti* (1952, 1970), by permission Curtis Brown Limited, N.Y.

Night Mail by W. H. Auden ('verse commentary' for film, 1936), by permission Curtis Brown Limited, N.Y.

Ronnie Barker

'Christmas Day in the Workhouse' from *The Two Ronnies* copyright © 2005 BBC by Bill Cotton, performed by Ronnie Barker and Ronnie

425

Corbet, reprinted by permissions of Ronnie Barker's family and estate as agreed by Gyles Brandreth.

Hilaire Belloc

'Lord Lundy' by Hilaire Belloc, first published in *Cautionary Tales For Children*, Eveleigh Nash, 1907, reprinted by permission of Peters Fraser & Dunlop (www.petersfraserdunlop.com) on behalf of Hilaire Belloc.

'Matilda' by Hilaire Belloc, first published in *Cautionary Tales For Children*, Eveleigh Nash, 1907, reprinted by permission of Peters Fraser & Dunlop (www.petersfraserdunlop.com) on behalf of Hilaire Belloc.

'Tarantella' by Hilaire Belloc, 1929, reprinted by permission of Peters Fraser & Dunlop (www.petersfraserdunlop.com) on behalf of Hilaire Belloc.

'Dedicatory Ode' by Hilaire Belloc, 1910 reprinted by permission of Peters Fraser & Dunlop (www.petersfraserdunlop.com) on behalf of Hilaire Belloc.

Connie Bensley

'In the Palm of His Hand' by Connie Bensley, from *Finding a Leg to Stand On: New & Selected Poems* (2012), reprinted by permission Bloodaxe Books.

Edmund Clerihew Bentley

'Sir Humphrey Davy' by Edmund Clerihew Bentley, published in *1902,* reprinted with permission Curtis Brown Limited, UK.

John Betjeman

'The Arrest of Oscar Wilde in the Cadogan Hotel' by John Betjeman, reprinted by permission The Estate of John Betjeman and Hodder and Stoughton.

'A Subaltern's Love Song' by John Betjeman, reprinted by permission The Estate of John Betjeman and Hodder and Stoughton.

'How to Get On in Polite Society' by John Betjeman, reprinted by permission The Estate of John Betjeman and Hodder and Stoughton

'The Last Laugh' by John Betjeman, reprinted by permission The Estate of John Betjeman and Hodder and Stoughton.

Jenny Boult

'Shopping Trolleys' by Jenny Boult (aka Magenta Bliss) from *Flight 39*, Abalone Press, 1986, reprinted with permission Fiona McHugh and the estate of Jenny Boult.

Charles Bukowski

Poetry Readings by Charles Bukowski from *Poetry Readings*, Black Sparrow Press, reprinted by permission HarperCollins Publishers.

Basil Bunting

'What the Chairman Told Tom' by Basil Bunting, from *Complete Poems by Basil Bunting,* published by Bloodaxe Books (2000), reprinted by permission Bloodaxe Books.

Tim Burton

'Vincent Malloy' by Tim Burton from *Vincent* (film, 1982), reprinted by permission William Morris Agency, and Tim Burton.

May Wedderburn Cannan

'Rouen April 26-May 25, 1915' by May Wedderburn Cannan from *In War Time* by May Wedderburn Cannan in 1917, reprinted by permission Clara May Abrahams and the estate of May Wedderburn Cannan.

James Carter

'Take a Poem' by James Carter first published in *Zim Zam Zoom!* by Otter-Barry Books in 2016, reprinted by permission the author and Otter-Barry Books.

Charles Causley

'Timothy Winters' by Charles Causley from *Collected Poems 1951-2000*, reprinted by permission Macmillan Publishers Limited, and David Higham and the estate of Charles Causley.

John Cooper Clarke

'TO-CON-VEY ONE'S MOOD' by John Cooper Clarke from *The Luckiest Guy Alive* (2018), reprinted by permission Picador, an imprint of Pan Macmillan.

'I mustn't go down to the sea again' by John Cooper Clarke from *Ten Years in an Open Necked Shirt* (2012), reprinted by permission Vintage, an imprint of Random House UK.

Wendy Cope

'Another Christmas Poem' by Wendy Cope from *Christmas Poems* (2017), reprinted by permission Faber & Faber Limited, and United Agents LLP.

'Making Cocoa for Kingsley Amis' by Wendy Cope from *Making Cocoa for Kingsley Amis* (1986), reprinted by permission Faber & Faber Limited.

'Shakespeare at School' by Wendy Cope (uncollected), reprinted with permission United Agents LLP.

Noël Coward
'When I have fears' by Noël Coward, AND 'Any Part of Piggy' by Noël Coward, reprinted by permission from Alan Brodie Representation and the Noël Coward Trust.

Countee Cullen
'Yet Do I Marvel' by Countee Cullen from 'Color' (1925) reprinted by permission Amistad Research Center, New Orleans, LA.

E.E. Cummings
'i thank You God' by e.e. Cummings from Xaipe: Seventy-One Poems (Oxford University Press, 1950), reprinted by permission W.W. Norton & Company Limited and the estate of e.e. Cummings.

Roald Dahl
'Television' by Roald Dahl, from *CHARLIE AND THE CHOC-OLATE FACTORY* © The Roald Dahl Story Company Limited, 1964, reprinted by permission The Roald Dahl Story Company Limited and Penguin Books Limited and Used by permission of Viking Children's Books, an imprint of Penguin Young Readers Group, a division of Penguin Random House LLC. All rights reserved.

'A HAND IN THE BIRD' by Roald Dahl from *RHYME STEW* by Roald Dahl, illustrated by Quentin Blake, copyright © 1989 by Roald Dahl (Jonathan Cape Limited & Penguin Books Limited, 1989), reprinted by permission Jonathan Cape Limited & Penguin Books Limited and © Roald Dahl and The Roald Dahl Story Company Limited and Used by permission of Viking Children's Books, an imprint of Penguin Young Readers Group, a division of Penguin Random House LLC. All rights reserved.

'Hot and Cold' by Roald Dahl from *RHYME STEW* by Roald Dahl, illustrated by Quentin Blake, copyright © 1989 by Roald Dahl (Jonathan Cape Limited & Penguin Books Limited, 1989), reprinted by permission Jonathan Cape Limited & Penguin Books Limited and © Roald Dahl and The Roald Dahl Story Company Limited and Used by permission of Viking Children's Books, an imprint of Penguin Young Readers Group, a division of Penguin Random House LLC. All rights reserved.

'A Little Nonsense Now and Then by Roald Dahl from *Charlie and*

Eleanor Farjeon
'Cats Sleep, Anywhere' by Eleanor Farjeon from *Blackbird Has Spoken: Selected Poems for Children* (2000), reprinted by permission Macmillan Publishers Limited.

'I quarreled with my brother' by Eleanor Farjeon, from *Silver Sand and Snow* (1951), reprinted by permission Michael Joseph, Penguin Random House UK.

Elaine Feinstein
'Getting Older' by Elaine Feinstein from *Selected Poems* (1994), reprinted by permission Carcanet Press.

James Fenton
'God, a poem' by James Fenton from *The Memory of War and Children in Exile* (©James Fenton 1983) is reprinted by permission of United Agents LLP.

Flanders and Swann
'The Hippopotamus Song' by Flanders and Swann (first recording and first release Feb and May 1957), reproduced by permission Warner/ Chapell Music, UK.

Cyril Fletcher
'Sonia Snell' lyrics by Cyril Fletcher, reprinted by permission of Cyril Fletcher's family as agreed by the author of this book Gyles Brandreth.

Roy Fuller
'In the Bathroom' by Roy Fuller, reprinted by permission of John Fuller.

Allen Ginsberg
'Homework' by Allen Ginsberg, from *Collected poems, 1947–1997* Allen Ginsberg, HarperCollins Publishers ©2006, reprinted by permission HarperCollins Publishers and Wylie Literary Agency, UK.

Louise Gluck
'Horse' by Louise Gluck, from *The Triumph of Archilles*, Ecco Press, US, 1985, reprinted by permission The Wylie Agency AND Carcanet Press.

Robert Graves
'Welsh Incident' by Robert Graves from *The Complete Poems in One Volume* (1999), reprinted by permission Carcanet Press.

Lavinia Greenlaw
'Love from a foreign city' by Lavinia Greenlaw from *Night Photograph*

Roger McCough

'The Midnight Skaters from Pillow Talk' by Roger McCough, from *Pillow Talk,* Viking, 1990, Reprinted by permission Peter, Fraser & Dunlop, UK.

'Let Me Die a Youngman's Death' by Roger McCough, from *Sky in the Pie*, Puffin, 1985, Reprinted by permission Peter, Fraser & Dunlop, UK.

'A Poem Just for Me' by Roger McCough, from *Pillow Talk*, Viking, 1990. Reprinted by permission Peter, Fraser & Dunlop, UK.

Colin McNaughton

'Ode to the Invisible Man' by Colin McNaughton, published in *Making Friends with Frankenstein*, 1994, reprinted by permission of Walker Books and Colin McNaughton.

Hollie McNish

'Cocoon' by Hollie McNish, from *Plum* (Picador, 2017), by permission Johnson and Alcock and Holly McNish.

Spike Milligan

'Return to Sorrento (3rd Class)' from *Muses with Milligan* (Dekka, LP, 1965), by permission of Spike Milligan Productions and the Estate of Spike Milligan.

'The Herring is a Lucky Fish' from *Muses with Milligan* (Dekka, LP, 1965), by permission Spike Milligan Productions and the Estate of Spike Milligan.

'The Land of the Bumbley Boo' from *Muses with Milligan* (Dekka, LP, 1965), by permission Spike Milligan Productions and the Estate of Spike Milligan.

'Things that go Bump in the Night' from *Muses with Milligan* (Dekka, LP, 1965), by permission Spike Milligan Productions and the Estate of Spike Milligan.

A.A. Milne

'Buckingham Palace' by A.A. Milne from *The Sunny Side* (1921), reprinted by permission Curtis Brown Limited UK and the Estate of A.A. Milne.

'Sneezles' by A.A. Milne from *Now We Are Six* (1927), reprinted by permission Curtis Brown Limited UK and the Estate of A.A. Milne.

'The King's Breakfast' by A.A. Milne from *When We Were Very Young* (1924), reprinted by permission Curtis Brown Limited UK and the Estate of A.A. Milne.

'Disobedience' by A.A. Milne from *When We Were Very Young* (1924), reprinted by permission Curtis Brown Limited UK and the Estate of A.A. Milne.

Elma Mitchell
'Thoughts After Ruskin' by Elma Mitchell from *People Etcetera: New and Selected Poems* by Elma Mitchell (Peterloo Poets, 1987), reprinted by permission Peterloo Poets and the Estate of Elma Mitchell.

Diana Morgan
'Earl's Court Road Pub' by Diana Morgan, reprinted by very kind permission of Diana Morgan's family and estate as agreed with Gyles Brandreth.

Michaela Morgan
'My First Day At School' by Michaela Morgan, from *Reaching The Stars* (2017), Macmillan, reprinted by permission the author.

Edwin Morgan
'Strawberries' by Edwin Morgan from *Collected Poems* (1990), reproduced by permission Carcanet Press and the Estate of Edwin Morgan.

Blake Morrison
'Against Dieting' by Blake Morrison (uncollected), by permission of United Agents LLP on behalf of Blake Morrison.

Ogden Nash
'The Turkey' by Ogden Nash from *Selected Poetry of Ogden Nash* (Little, Brown Company, Inc, 1995) reprinted by permission Curtis Brown NY, Limited, the Ogden Nash Estate and Carlton Publishing Group Limited.

'A Word to Husbands' by Ogden Nash from *Selected Poetry of Ogden Nash* (Little, Brown Company, Inc, 1995), reprinted by permission Curtis Brown, Limited. And the Ogden Nash Estate and Carlton Publishing Group Limited.

'A Flea and a Fly in a Flue' reprinted by permission Curtis Brown, Limited. And the Ogden Nash Estate and Carlton Publishing Group Limited.

'The Tale of Custard the Dragon' by Ogden Nash from *The Tale of Custard the Dragon* (Little, Brown, 1936) reprinted by permission Curtis Brown, Limited. And the Ogden Nash Estate AND Carlton Publishing Group Limited.

436

Mary Wilson
'On the Death of Harold Wilson' by Mary Wilson, reprinted by permission the family and estate of Mary Wilson as agreed with Gyles Brandreth.

Kit Wright
'The Magic Box' by Kit Wright from *The Magic Box Poems for Children* (Pan Macmillan, 2013), reprinted by kind permission the author.

Richard Wright
'From across the lake' by Richard Wright, from *Haiku – This Other World* (Arcade Publishing, 1998), reprinted by permission of John Hawkins and Associates, and the Estate of Richard Wright.

Benjamin Zephaniah
'Be nice to your turkeys dis Christmas' and 'Who's Who' by Benjamin Zephaniah from *Talking Turkeys* (1995), reprinted by permission Puffin, Penguin Random House, UK.

'The British' by Benjamin Zephaniah from *Wicked World* (2000), reprinted by permission Puffin, Penguin Random House, UK.

Index of Poets and Poems

Index of First Lines

Tyger, Tyg

Come live with me and be my runcible spoon

I remember, I remember, the pobble who has no toes

I remember,

trunkless legs of stone?

Shall I compare thee to two vast and

Stop all the clocks, c